More Tales of the Defective Detective in the Pulps

More Tales of the Defective Detective in the Pulps

Gary Hoppenstand
Garyn G. Roberts
Ray B. Browne

Bowling Green State University Popular Press
Bowling Green, Ohio 43403

Note: The following stories are facsimile reprints from the original pulp magazines. Effort has been made to include the advertising of the time, as well as the fiction.

Copyright © 1985 Bowling Green State University Popular Press

Library of Congress Catalogue Card No: 85-073561

ISBN: 0-87972-335-1 Clothbound
      0-87972-336-X Paperback

To Pat Browne
aider & abettor
a second time around

Acknowledgements

The editors would like to thank Robert Weinberg and Blazing Publications, for permission to reprint the following stories, Pam Thompson, for her assistance in procuring the original copies of *Dime Mystery Magazine*, the folks at the Popular Press, for their faith in the project, and our family and friends, whose support knows no bounds.

Contents

Monstrous Crimes of Deformity:
The Defective Detective Carries On

Gary Hoppenstand, Garyn G. Roberts, Ray B. Browne

AS THE PULPS REACHED THEIR GOLDEN AGE in early and mid-Thirties America, a problem emerged. Robert Kenneth Jones, in *The Shudder Pulps*, claims that the heroes of those wonderful detective and horror stories were becoming overshadowed by their villainous counterparts.[1] Yellow menaces, mad doctors and crazed half human/half beasts perpetrated their deviltry in countless tales of terror, and stole the limelight. Some of these abominations—the Mysterious Wu Fang, Dr. Yen Sin and Dr. Death—became so popular that they were granted their own magazines. At the same time, the popular "weird menace" formula achieved new dimensions, as did public sentiment about these stories. In the late Thirties the weird menace saga, responding to criticism and outcry concerning its lurid nature, compromised its themes of hideous torture and voluptuous girls in peril. New York's mayor Fiorello La Guardia was one prominent figure who led the campaign against the "evils" of these "sadistic," "sexual" fantasies and their subsequent ill effects on the innocents of America. Working with parent-teacher organizations and the like, these campaigners posed a substantial threat to the pioneers of the weird menace formula. Publishers, always bending to changing social mores, were quick to change, and accommodate their essential mass market. Ironically, the sadism and sexuality against which the movement fought did not alter its intensity. Rather, it changed its focus. The emphasis turned to a different form of sensationalism—one which put the detective back in the lead. The defective detective was born.

But detectives had defects of one form or another long before the Depression. In fact the hero—represented in some societies by the detective—of all people and all ages is *different* from other people, either physically or mentally. Odysseus, in the works of Homer, is the wily hero; Achilles is the physical hero. In the world of detective fiction progenitors, Poe's investigators were not altogether normal, nor was Sherlock Holmes; and Mycroft, Sherlock's exaggerated brother, was, to say the least, somewhat bizarre. None was, however, as outlandish and pronounced as

1

those of the defective detective of the late Thirties. Though obviously the extremes of the genre came about because all writers were trying to outdo other writers, the degree of the difference from normality must be accounted for in other ways. In one way, the handicap of this hero was substituted for some of the traditional sadistic fun generally attributed to the weird menace story. Such was the case of Russell Gray's Ben Bryn, Edith and Ejler Jacobson's Nat Perry, John Kobler's Peter Quest and Leon Bryne's Dan Holden.

But on a deeper and more meaningful scale the defective detectives of the early war years were a form of representation of a defective American society. In 1939 America's role in World War II was that of a disgruntled observer. Since saleable popular fiction evidences a fine balance of convention and invention, as John G. Cawelti suggests in *Adventure, Mystery and Romance*, and further a balance of reality and fantasy, these stories of woe reflected social consciousness. And, they provided a satisfactory solution for the American public. The defective detective was the deformed hero who overcame his weaknesses and employed ingenuity and brute force to subdue the evils and injustices of the world, just as, by extension, a deformed society could overcome its deformities and return to normal.

Society, after all, had many models, of both the powerful deformed force for good and of the powerful deformed force for evil. Glyn A. Roberts has suggested the parallel between the political leaders and the images they projected. While Hitler, Mussolini and Churchill were dominating the headlines, another man severely crippled physically by polio yet a genius of intellect and a tower of brute force was capturing the attention of the American public—he was President of the United States, Franklin Delano Roosevelt. Besides a figure of numerous accomplishments in the face of the Great Depression and world conflict, Roosevelt was a symbol for America. He was a defective hero, and being such a profound, pervasive legend of the good times was quite possibly a real life model for the deformed crime fighters of the pulps.

But Roosevelt was not the only defective hero of the time. Fiorello La Guardia, mayor of New York City (a prominent figure, as mentioned earlier) was so physically and vocally ill-proportioned that in the eyes of the cartoonists he became grotesque—an object of laughter and ridicule. Eleanor Roosevelt, the First Lady, was generally derided by being not very handsome, a physical deformity which was emphasized by her high, squeaky voice.

But the forces of evil also were and had been very defective. The world of the late Thirties was the zoo of such gangsters as Al "Scarface" Capone, Baby Face Nelson, Pretty Boy Floyd, and dozens of others. In fact, the times were so out of joint, to use Hamlet's description of his era, that they demanded grotesque heroes to face them down. There is more than a suggestion that the defective detective hero served as a primitive force, a grotesque front—a mask—to frighten away the spirits of evil, as they have always done and still do in societies under great duress.

One of the latest manifestations of the "defective" detective, if "defective" means both incomplete and deliberately different, comes in the names given to the detectives, or lack of them given to their detectives by two recent authors. Thomas B. Dewey, for example, gives his thoroughly democratic detective the thoroughly democratic name of "Mac," nothing else—no surname—just "Mac." Bill Pronzini goes one step further in making his detective "nameless," that is he is so democratic and mythic that he has no name. This characteristic becomes a kind of secular religion, for in primitive religions the gods are given names that no one is allowed to pronounce; with Pronzini's detective no one can pronounce it—that is, no reader—because we don't know what it is. But Pronzini's use of the "nameless" detective brings detective fiction full circle as far as the defective detective is concerned. Some people suggest that the classical story of the Sphinx was the first detective tale. It was a primitive mythic tale of identification. Pronzini's development of a mythic nameless detective though the ultimate in democratic anonymity is also the original in mythic proportions.

Authors of the defective detective stories came from varied backgrounds. Russell Gray (the pseudonym for Bruno Fischer) was not the first newspaperman to turn to the more lucrative market of pulp fiction. Robert Kenneth Jones largely attributes Gray's phenomenal success as a pulpster to this journalistic background.[2] His argument is convincing. These magazines, with their columns and interspersed ads, were the fictional counterparts of the daily news tabloids. Pulp writers were reporters of a sort, relaying fantasy as if it were actual history. Probably the most polished of the terror writers, Russell Gray, wrote prose that was exceptionally clean, crisp, and marked by a straightforward, slam-bang style. His first story was "The Cat Woman" and was sold to Popular Publications in 1936.

Two of Gray's most significant characters were detectives Calvin Kane and Ben Bryn, and these helped launch the author into his new career.

He tried to put across a chracter named Calvin Kane, who was saddled with a deformed body, and siddled like a crab as he dragged his withered right leg along. One shoulder was six inches higher than the other. But he had one physical advantage: arms like steel. He was simply too grotesque to last. However, his endowment became the touchstone for the fame of Ben Bryn. Suffering from infantile paralysis as a child, Bryn was forced to push himself around on a wheeled platform. This put "tremendous power into his arms and iron in his soul." When he gained the use of his withered legs, "through sheer grit by heartbreaking exercises," he became a sort of fore-shortened Paul Bunyan, five feet tall and prodigiously strong.[3]

Ben Bryn survived a variety of insidious criminal masterminds, and his perils were published for several years in *Dime Mystery Magazine*. What Ben lacked in height (he was a mere five feet two) and lower body strength, he more than made up for with his good looks and charm, and fabulous upper body.

Dime Mystery presented Gray's Ben Bryn in "The Dead Hand Horrors" in its April 1939 issue. Once again, Bryn calls upon all his incredible feats of upper body strength. His foe is the wicked Zara whose skeleton right hand is pure bone and squeezes the life out of its victims. She spares no frills as she employs her vice-like appendage, hot branding irons, a pot of acid and other tortures in her escapades of horror. But the bone snapping is not one-sided. In one scene, when Zara is Bryn's captor, the detective states, "I have only to get this hand on your throat and you'd be dead in a second." "The Dead Hand Horrors" exemplifies why Russell Gray ranked with the best in his particular field of literary speciality.

In May 1939's "Flesh for the Monster," Ben Bryn returns to face a new menace. Victims are physically torn to pieces by a hideous monster, and Bryn appears to be the killer. It looks like he has "gone amok in a one man reign of terror." As the story opens, Bryn goes to a local hotel to make a social call on a lady friend. As soon as the detective disappears in the elevator, Egan, the hotel manager, turns to his friend George and comments on the handsome yet deformed Ben Bryn: "He mightn't have much altitude, but did you see those shoulders and arms? I once saw a guy he hit with his fist. It just wiped the guy's face away."

Dime Mystery featured Russell Gray and Ben Bryn once again in a saga of horrid rogues and gruesome crimes in its July 1939 issue. "Prey for the Creeping Death" showcases Bryn's tremendous shoulders and great power as the "one man police force" fights a hideous creeping death that consumes its victims in a slow, agonizing fashion. Burning, spreading acid facilitates terror and coersion. Voluptuous, sensuous girls and death abound. Yet, not to be outdone, "Bryn's fists make faceless those crooks who cross him."

Edith and Ejler Jacobson produced a popular defective detective with one of the most ingenuous deformities. He was Nat Perry and his affliction was hemophilia. The Jacobsons were a husband and wife team who sold a number of stories to the pulps, several of which chronicled the exploits of Perry. In recent years, Ejler Jacobson has been most prominently noted for his role as editor of *Galaxy* and *If* magazines. Nicknamed The Bleeder, Nat Perry faced a number of deadly assaults and death traps, any of which would have finished the average man. The irony was, of course, that the slightest scratch or cut, from a broken window for example, would have finished Nat just as effectively. At age fourteen, Perry was a hit and run victim, and police officer Harry O' Connor gave four blood transfusions to save him. Nat only had a broken leg, but was a "haemophiliac" and his blood would never clot. Now, at age twenty-nine, he was one of the shrewdest detectives in New York.

In *Dime Mystery*'s April 1939 presentation of "Funerals C.O.D.," the funeral business takes on a new dimension. And, the Bleeder swings his fists as if he has nothing to fear. Harry O'Connor ridicules his surrogate son and engages him in arguments of disapproval. But, deep down, O'Connor respects and loves his fearless son.

The tall, blond Bleeder makes a deadly discovery in July 1939's "They Die On Schedule!" The terror stems from an old Prohibition alcohol concoction that fails as a beverage but is the vehicle for horrible demises and destruction. Once again the Jacobsons outdo themselves in a tale exemplary of what the defective detectives were all about.

One of the formulaic appeals of all detective fiction for its audience, interestingly, is its portrayal of the "esthetics" of violence. Agatha Christie, that prim ambassador of the drawing-room mystery, evidences a wonderfully morbid fascination for the biological dynamics of poison, and quite often employs the most exotic assortment of fatal concoctions as vehicles for her discrete murders. "That gray and bloated face! That overturned decanter of brandy," Hercule Poirot or Jane Marple pronounces. "Obviously, Lord Plushbottom's evening aperitif was laced with (sniff, sniff: the smell of almonds) arsenic. Poor devil!" The hard-boiled cousin (distant cousin, that is) of Christie's classical detective hero, certainly an individual well-schooled in the arts of violence, is less the gentleman with his fascination for firearms. Blazing .45s cradled comfortably in his calloused fists effectively bark streams of hot lead into the stomachs, heads, arms and legs of those unfortunate hoods who happen to stand in the line of fire. "Die, you Commie bum," Mike Hammer screams through clenched teeth. "My roscoe's got another present for you . . . this one's for Velda!" Even that bureaucratic stalwart of the civil servant's union, the city cop, fondles with mixed affection his pump-action shotgun or snub-nose revolver. "Too bad these drug-smuggling creeps went for their weapons," Steve McGarrett says, placing dark sunglasses on his eyes. "Book 'em Dano when you sew them back together."

Of course the esthetics of violence in detective fiction isn't limited solely to the implements of death: it diplomatically includes the residence of death, his living room (if you will forgive the pun) that usually is tastefully decorated in Early American stainless steel morgue, subtly perfumed with essence of formalin. Peruse the library of death's living room, and amid the stacks of *New York Times*, hardcover collections of Edgar Allan Poe short stories and recent John D. MacDonald paperback bestsellers, you will discover a wide assortment of pulp magazines, including *Weird Tales, Black Mask* . . . and *Dime Mystery*. Selecting the February 1939 issue of the latter, and opening to Leon Bryne's tale "Society of Singing Death," we find the residence of death situated on a party dance floor:

Mrs. Farnsworth alone on the dance floor suddenly stopped as though rooted to the floor. A look of pain twisted her startled face. She trembled violently, emitted one scream, and clutched at her chest .... She had begun tearing at her clothes, shredding and ripping the gossamer lace that covered her matronly bosom. She was doing a mad dance of agony, far different from anything she had ever essayed on the stage. One minute she was standing there, screaming, writhing, and the next instant her torso seemed to disintegrate in a blinding, deafening crash.

Picking up the May, 1939 issue and turning to John Kobler's "Clinics for Killers," we find that death erects his residence squarely in New York's finest hospitals. Hospitals?—we question. Those institutions of healing and scientific good-will? Ah, yes, indeed, Kobler ironically replies, hospitals ... where, as anyone who has stayed in one will tell you, the patient is totally at the mercy of strangers. Even Peter Quest, the protagonist of Kobler's tale, himself in the hospital for an operation that will treat his glaucoma defect, discovers what it is like to be helpless in death's modern academy of healing. But as Hutchinson Memorial Hospital is the scene for Quest's attempted cure, it is also the scene of murderous intrigue, where doctors plot the death of clients for economic gain and where killers are trained with drugs, killers who leave a mess behind them:

A girl's nude body sprawled on the cold stone; the soft, swelling curve of thigh and breast was still warm. The once pretty face was contorted in a mask of unutterable horror. The head—Quest, who had seen many corpses, momentarily averted his eyes—the head hung by a shred of flesh. A knife had slashed through to the spine.

Subsequently, reversals of symbolically "good" medical establishments or party dance floors and cinematically graphic depictions of brutal murder were grist for the defective detective pulp stories. These motifs, which inventionally modify detective fiction's esthetics of violence, illustrate two major themes of the defective detective formula.

The first theme narrates the conflict between good defects and bad defects. Good defects are embodied by the detective hero. Peter Quest, as mentioned above, is glaucomic (his eyesight fails him just at the wrong moment, naturally) and strives to use his remaining health to fight crime. Interestingly, Quests wants to die in action, demonstrating a massive death wish (predating the Bronson films by some forty years). Dan Holden, Leon Bryne's detective hero, is defective as well, who becomes deaf while shooting it out with an evil confidence man (one of the confidence man's bullets struck Holden above the ear, forcing the need for a silver plate to be lodged in his head), and who devotes his time "hounding countless human parasites into the arms of the law—or into sudden, inexplicable death." Bad defects are exemplified by the villains of the stories, who employ torture and devices of mutilation as means of achieving wealth. Thus, the esthetics of violence in defective detective fiction centers not on the specific nature of the hero's abilities but on his handicaps, and not on the goals of the criminal but on his method of destructive killing.

The second theme of this pulp formula details the ironically manipulated reversal of socially virtuous, pleasing and benevolent settings, such as Byrne's dance floor, and Kobler's hospital. The goal of these, and other, writers of *Dime Mystery* was to horrify their readers, and one of their most effective methods of accomplishing this was to twist the common into the uncommon, the pleasant into the unpleasant, the beautiful into the gruesome.

One further motif reversal is a hallmark of these stories. A hold-over from the earlier weird menace formula, descriptions of the physical deforming of sensuous women underscore the horror of the conflict between good and evil, and, more immediately, the battle between the sexes. At a time when social, political and fiscal stresses threaten man's superiority and survival, as was especially real during the Depression, male-dominated society does not want the threat of female equality or superiority also. Such it has always been. For example, in the primitive world of the Amazons (alleged by the historian Herodotus in the fifth century B.C. to exist in the land of Scythia), the female society where men were used only for studding and then destroyed, the male-authored story showed the absurdity of this kind of society by making it necessary that the women warriors cut off their right breasts (thus becoming mutilated and imperfect) in order to do man's work (that is defending themselves and their society with the bow and arrow). In the defective detective society of the late Thirties, the best curved and padded of femininity are destroyed in most thorough fashions. Chests explode, breasts are mutilated and bare-bottoms are slashed. Wrists are bound and fresh skin is branded. Women represent the "finer" qualities of civilization, and their horrendous demises at the hands of snarling brutish men represent vicious attacks against society in general and against women in particular. Women on the pedestal may be worshipped, but they are also smeared with grafitti, defaced, slashed, disfigured because they, like God, are not serving the function for which men created them.

The world of the defective detective was indeed a strange one. Continuing the motif of the mythological hero thousands of years old, the outcroppings of the type emerged in the Thirties in a very imperfect and threatened society. The most effective manifestation of the hero, at least in the violence-laden genre of detective fiction, is at once more violent than the rest of society, less normal, yet more powerful than the adversaries. The power of evil is best overcome by greater power. There are few more revealing windows to the world of crime fiction of the Thirties than that of the defective detective.

Notes

Jones, Robert Kenneth, *The Shudder Pulps* (West Linn, Oregon: FAX Collector's Edition, Inc., 1975), p. 151.

[2]Ibid., p. 126.

[3]Ibid., pp. 156, 157.

THE DEAD HAND HORRORS

A Mystery Novel by
RUSSELL GRAY

*Zara was startlingly, breath-takingly beautiful—
and compelling. Yet her long black glove hid a
horrid implement of death!*

They dragged Lilis
toward the pot. . . .

CHAPTER ONE

The Mark of Death

THE telephone whirred harshly. Caroline Patten, seated on
the edge of a chair with her
hands clasped tightly on her knees,
stirred slowly and eyed the tele-

phone on the big oak desk as if it possessed a malignant life of its own. The brilliant light flooding down from the ceiling seemed to concentrate on her face. Two weeks ago it had been a kindly, rather youthful face of a woman of fifty. Now it was an ash-grey mask of fear in which only grey eyes were alive.

The telephone repeated its summons. She sat motionless, hardly daring to breath as her agitated eyes jerked about the library. This room, with its oak and leather furniture and cozy fireplace and ceiling-high bookshelves, had been her favorite in the Patten house. Now it was a room in which unspeakable menace lurked. She thought of running upstairs to her bedroom and locking herself in. But it would do no good. There was no escape.

Through the heavy panelled door she heard her niece, Selma, playing the piano in the drawing room. It was something gay from Chopin—something utterly incongruous at this moment of doom.

The third time the telephone rang Caroline Patten rose stiffly and moved like an automaton to the desk. She heard her brother, Aaron, barking into the wire from one of the upstairs extensions: "What's that? Whom do you want?"

A flat metallic voice said: "Caroline Patten."

"It's for me, Aaron," she told her brother listlessly.

There was a click as Aaron hung up. Then the metallic voice started again. Caroline Patten clutched the side of the desk with one hand to keep herself from collapsing. Yet all day she had known that this was coming. All day she had been preparing herself for the final, terrible end.

The voice stopped. She had to try twice before she could force her own voice past her throat.

"I told you I can't any more. You've got to be reasonable."

The metallic voice spoke briefly.

"Please!" Caroline Patten whimpered. "In the name of heaven, you can't! I've done all you asked . . . . Please!"

The voice ceased abruptly. The line was dead.

With trembling hands she cradled the 'phone. It was suddenly bitterly cold in the library, although the slight breeze which came in through the open windows was warm. She stood with her arms pressed closely to her sides, shivering, and a moan trickled from her bloodless lips. Slowly her right hand moved up and she stared at the thing which would remain engraved in the skin until the corruption of death rotted it away.

"Oh, God!" she wailed aloud. "Why me? I have led a blameless life. I have never harmed a living soul."

Suddenly her jaw set with resolution. Her spare frame straightened up, seemed to grow younger. She picked up the phone and said: "I want the police!"

Then the lights went out.

The phone clattered to the desk. She whirled with a terrified gasp toward the switch near the closed door. Light coming through the windows from a nearby street lamp sent ominous shadows flickering through the room. Nobody was near the switch; nobody could have opened and closed the door without her having heard it.

She stood rigid, as cold as death itself, her eyes probing the shadows to give them definite form. And then she saw the thing moving up from the high back of a leather arm-chair. A beam of light from the street, stabbing through a rift in the curtains, centered on the hand which clutched the top of the chair.

A hand! Dear God, there was no skin or flesh on it! It was a hand from the grave, a skeleton hand! And it had life!

She wanted to cry out, to scream at the top of her lungs and go on screaming for the rest of her life; but her constricted throat would not permit the passage of sound. A face appeared next to the hand —a living, human face. And yet the jutting cheekbones, the brown leathery skin, the upper lip drawn back from the teeth, might have been the face of death itself.

As from another world she heard Selma playing the piano, heard an automobile honking in the street, and above all heard her own husked breathing as she strove to force a scream past her lips. The scream came out at last, thinly, starting from somewhere deep inside her, trembling momentarily on her lips. But it never rose higher than a whisper.

The face and the skeleton hand disappeared, and an instant later a dark mass hurled itself at her from around the side of the chair. She felt herself slammed against the desk. The weight of a body forced her back on the desk top and the hard bones of fleshless fingers clamped about her throat. Her eyes bulged, but it was not so much from lack of breath as from sheer horror of the feel of those frightful fingers on her living skin.

She didn't struggle. She simply lay back on that desk top until merciful darkness closed in on her.

* * *

Ben Bryn sat in the quiet little restaurant facing the entrance so that he saw Selma Patten and her father as soon as they entered. He had never seen either of them before, but the time was right and the girl was as beautiful as the gossip columns maintained. She fixed blue eyes on him inquiringly and he nodded and stood up.

He had expected the surprise that came into her face as he rose to his feet. Seated, he looked like an extremely powerful man. But on his feet he stood exactly five-feet-two. Her eyebrows arched momentarily; then she smiled and came forward, followed by her father.

Her beauty hadn't been exaggerated. She had a small, delicately proportioned face, and he was glad to observe that she wasn't taller than himself. Taller women made him acutely self-conscious.

"Ah, this is a surprise," she said, and extended her hand.

As he held her small hand in his big palm, she quickly appraised him. He had a sensitive face, blonde curly hair and eyes as frank and as blue as her own. He tapered down from massive shoulders and a barrel chest to the hips and legs of a baseball player. The first shock at his shortness of stature gave way to approval.

She turned to her father. "Dad, I want you to meet Mr. Bryn, an old friend of mine."

Aaron Patten brushed his fingers over Bryn's palm, and then all three sat down at the table. At once Selma Patten started to chatter about the weather as if it were the only important thing on earth. She was plainly nervous.

Aaron Patten was nervous, too, but for a different reason. Stark terror lay deep in the back of his eyes which were continually glancing around at the other diners. He rolled a salt cellar between the fingers of his left hand until a waiter arrived with the food. He ate sparsely, without interest, and Ben Bryn noticed that he kept his right hand off the table as much as possible.

Suddenly Selma Patten said: "Daddy, I wasn't exactly telling the truth when I said I was surprised to meet Mr. Bryn here. I arranged this appointment with him this morning by telephone."

Patten's spoon clattered into the soup bowl. The terror came to the surface of his eyes as he looked at Bryn.

"Mr. Bryn will help you," Selma said quickly. "I knew that you wouldn't go to his office and that you would refuse to see him at home, so I had him meet us here. He's a private detective. . . . Daddy, please don't run away!"

Aaron Patten had started to rise to his feet. Selma clutched his arm, trying to push him down on the chair.

"A detective!" Patten muttered. "Selma, you don't know what you've done!"

"Daddy, you've got to stay," Selma pleaded. "I can't let the same thing happen to you that happened to Aunt Caroline. Daddy, for my sake, sit down!"

Mumbling crazily to himself, her father slumped down in the seat.

BEN BRYN leaned over the table. "Everything you tell me will be strictly confidential," he said in his gentle, slightly drawling tone. "Frankly, I believe that you are in grave danger. You can't be worse off if you let me help you."

Patten's head jerked up. "What do you know about it?"

"Not much. I know that two weeks ago your sister, Caroline Patten, was strangled to death by an unknown assailant immediately after she had telephoned the police. When the police entered the library of your home not many minutes later, they found her dead and the 'phone still off the hook. Investigation revealed that she had drawn every cent of a modest fortune from banks and vaults within a period of four weeks, not a cent of which has so far been traced.

"This much I found out today after your daughter called me. I have close friends, you see, among the official police. There are no clues to her murder. She had no known enemies; as she had impoverished herself, nobody could gain by her death. One thing, however, is puzzling the police—although they have not paid very much attention to it. That was a curious symbol which was found branded into the palm of her right hand; the outlines of a skeleton hand."

Patten was breathing heavily. Bryn went on: "Your daughter didn't tell me much over the 'phone. But I am assuming that she fears that you will meet the same fate as your sister." He turned to Selma Patten: "Why?"

Her voice was jerky with nervousness.

"For weeks before her death Aunt Caroline acted as if she were afraid of her own shadow," she said. "Daddy has lately been acting the same way. And—" She stopped suddenly, biting her lower lip.

Bryn said: "And one other thing. I think I know what it is. . . . Mr. Patten, may I see the palm of your right hand?"

Patten shriveled before Bryn's eyes. His face wasn't pleasant to look at. "No! You're signing my death warrant."

Patten's hand had been resting palm down beside his plate. Bryn's hand shot out and closed about Patten's wrist. He twisted the wrist and Patten's hand turned palm up. On the palm a tiny skeleton hand was branded!

Patten moaned deep in his throat. Selma was staring at the hideous brand with half-open mouth, her face the color of chalk.

"I'm sorry," Bryn said, releasing Patten's wrist. "I had to make sure. I'm going to help you fight this thing, whatever it is, whether you want me to or not."

Weakly, hopelessly, Patten nodded. "All right. Perhaps Selma is right. I can't stand it any more. I'll tell you everything. It began—"

His voice choked off. Patten had twisted slightly in his chair and was staring past his daughter as if he were seeing a ghost. Bryn followed the direction of his gaze.

There were very few people in that section of the restaurant. Two tables away a woman sat alone. She was looking lazily at their table through half-closed lids and she was smoking through a long onyx cigarette holder. A daring black evening gown clung to a sensuous figure. She wore black gloves to her elbows. Her skin was golden, her cheekbones high, her mouth thin and cruel.

"Zara!" Aaron Patten whispered. He turned his face to Patten. "It was a mistake," he said in a loud quivering voice. "I wasn't going to tell you anything. I was leading you on. . . . Come, Selma, we're leaving."

He got up to his feet. "Daddy, please!" his daughter pleaded. She pulled at him. Roughly he brushed her hand aside. His mouth opened suddenly and stayed open. His face froze into an expression of horror.

Selma screamed and knocked her chair over backward. Ben said: "What's the matter, Mr. Patten?"

Aaron Patten fell forward. His chin shattered one of the dishes on the table. Then his body slumped to the floor and lay still.

CHAPTER TWO

Satan's Daughter

A BRIEF examination showed Ben Bryn that Aaron Patten was dead. His eyes were open wide, staring, as if even in death he had not escaped the fear that had tormented him in life.

A woman was screaming shrilly, but when Bryn looked up from the body he saw that it was not the dead man's daughter. Selma Patten was holding onto the table in an effort to steady herself and was fighting bravely not to give way to hysteria. It was a fat woman diner who screamed. Now, other diners and waiters stood about the body in an awed semicircle.

The manager of the restaurant dropped down to Bryn's side. "Is he dead? Did he have a stroke?"

Bryn rose stiffly to his feet. "Dead," he announced grimly. "I suggest that nobody touch the body until the police arrive. There is a possibility that he was murdered."

A collective gasp arose from the onlookers. Selma moaned like a stricken animal.

"Murdered!" the manager exclaimed. "Why, that's impossible."

Bryn shrugged. "So it would seem. I said he *might* have been murdered. Anyway, call the police."

He turned to the table where the woman Aaron Patten had called Zara had been sitting. She was no longer there. Quickly he glanced about the restaurant. No sight of her. Then he was pushing through the diners and waiters toward the door. Startled eyes followed his progress.

Bryn went through the door and looked first toward the brightly lighted main street less than a hundred feet from the restaurant. Then he looked in the other direction and saw the tall slim figure of a woman hurrying along the shadows of the houses. He sprinted after her.

"What's your hurry?" he said when he reached her side.

She stopped, whirled to face him. Her thin mouth smiled instantly.

"The man in the restaurant?" she said in a husky, vibrant voice. "You wish to— become acquainted?"

"Sure. Then maybe I'll find out why you ran away the minute a man was murdered."

"You know he was murdered?"

A strong exotic perfume came from her. She was a good deal taller than he was and he had to look up at her. In the half-shadows of the dark street she was even more beautiful than he had at first thought. Not the fresh beauty of Selma Patten, but a beauty that was dark and heady and somehow sinister.

He said: "Which means, Zara, that we both know he was murdered."

She laughed. "You know my name. And I know yours, Ben Bryn. I know more than that about you. I know that as a child you were a victim of infantile paralysis which turned your legs into useless, withered appendages. For twenty years you pushed yourself about on a wheeled platform. You made a living selling newspapers and shoe laces. All your strength went into your shoulders and arms until today, according to rumors, you can perform incredible feats of strength with your hands. In spite of your handicaps you attended school at night and you evolved all sorts of exercises to strengthen your legs. Through sheer effort of will you developed your legs until they became as normal as any man's."

"That's pretty good as biography," Bryn snapped. "You probably read that in the papers. I was written up more than once. You and I, Zara, are going back to the restaurant. The police will want to have a talk with you."

She ran one black gloved hand down her golden-skinned cheek. "And if I do not wish to accompany you, you will force me?"

"You guessed it."

SHE swept him with her black eyes. "I do not like short men. But I like you. I am told that you are one of the most dangerous men in the country. Not only because of your strength, or because you can shoot accurately, but because you are foolishly brave. It must be because you suffer from a terrific inferiority complex. You have had a hard life and your lack of height bothers you, so you assert your ego by trying to be a man without fear. I have always been fond of brave men."

Roughly he gripped her upper arm. His fingers closed the least bit and she winced. He had to restrain himself from snapping her arm. He wanted to hurt her, to make her cry out with pain. With uncanny insight she had laid bare what he tried to keep locked up in his heart.

"Let's get going," he ordered harshly.

Docilely she fell into step beside him. He was rather surprised that she didn't offer more resistance, but he maintained his grip on her arm. As they neared the restaurant, he saw a police prowl car parked at the curb.

Soft feet pattered behind him. He start-

ed to turn just as a body threw itself on his back. Bracing his legs, he twisted— and suddenly horror froze him.

A hand had been flung over his mouth —a hand which had life and motion, yet which was devoid of skin and flesh. Nausea gagged him as he felt skeleton fingers clamp against his lips and teeth.

The sharp point of a knife pressing into the small of his back brought him out of his paralysis. His left hand reached around and grasped the left shoulder of his assailant. At the same time Bryn's right hand closed over the skeleton fingers on his mouth. Both of his powerful hands contracted. Bones snapped. A voice howled hoarsely in his ear. With a heave of his tremendous shoulders, Bryn hurled his assailant to the sidewalk.

He saw a small brown man lying on his back, the emaciated face contorted with pain as the normal left hand clutched at the broken fingers of the skeleton right hand. His lips worked soundlessly.

Bryn kicked the knife which had fallen to the ground into the gutter and stooped toward the brown man. Something small and round and hard jabbed into his back.

"Don't turn, Ben Bryn," Zara said, "or I'll put a bullet in your lung. Walk straight ahead."

Bryn cursed under his breath. Momentarily he had forgotten about Zara. He glanced over his shoulder. Zara's thin lips smiled.

"You know I would not hesitate to shoot if you made a single false move," she told him softly.

Less than two hundred feet away was the restaurant. Police were in there, but for all the good it did they might as well have been miles away. There had been no sound, save that single subdued howl of pain, during the brief encounter.

Bryn nodded and moved down the street. The brown man picked himself up, retrieved his knife, and, hunched over in agony, followed.

A swanky black limousine was parked near the end of the block. Two brown men sat in the front seat. At instructions from Zara, one got out of the car and pulled Bryn's automatic out of his shoulder clip. Then he got into the back seat and was holding the automatic on Bryn when Bryn got in. Bryn sat between the man who had his gun and Zara. The man he had crippled sat in the front seat and slumped down until only the top of his head was visible. Occasionally a faint moan of pain came from him.

The limousine drove through the city. Bryn asked: "Now what?"

"We could use your strength," Zara informed him. "It is regrettable that we cannot also use your intelligence. A slight operation on certain glands and you will be my slave. Mindless, unfortunately, but extremely willing."

BEN BRYN'S scalp tightened. Two guns were pressed into either side of him. His first move would bring death. Well, maybe that would be preferrable to what this she-fiend planned to do to him.

Bryn noticed that both Zara and the brown man on his other side held their guns in their left hands, and that, although is was summer, both wore gloves. The driver's hands were also gloved. An inward shudder went through Bryn. He had an idea what the right hand gloves of each of them contained.

Against his right thigh, arm and shoulder he could feel the pressure of Zara's warm body. A firm breast, half revealed by the low cut of her bodice, lay lightly against his upper arm.

"You are afraid," Zara gloated. "Really afraid for the first time in your life."

Ben Bryn forced a grin to his lips. "Maybe," he said. "But you ought to be afraid too. Look at my hand!" He flexed and unflexed the powerful fingers of his right hand. "I have only to get this hand

on your throat and you'd be dead in a second."

"You won't have a chance to. At the first move we'd both shoot."

Ben shrugged. "It would be a better fate than you have in store for me. And I'd take you along with me. Because I won't die at once. I'll live long enough to kill you with this hand. You should have had one of the guns trained on my heart; but it's too late to shift now." His voice dropped. "In a minute we'll both be in hell, Zara."

There was a taut silence. The brown man looked across at Zara for instructions. The smile was gone from her face. Small white teeth gnawed at her lower lip.

"Well, who makes the first move?" Bryn said. "Do I break your neck first or do you shoot first? Either way the result will be the same."

The limousine was now beyond the city limits, rolling along a dark, little-used road. The injured man raised himself in the front seat, but he did not turn around. The driver was looking back at them through the mirror. Seconds ticked off. Any moment there would be a break; the nerves of either of the two who held guns against Bryn would snap under the tension.

Finally Zara spoke in her low, husky voice. "You wish to make a deal with me?"

"No," Bryn said. "Go ahead, shoot."

Zara expelled a thin laugh through her teeth. Her breast flattened against his arm. "Your courage was not exaggerated. I confess I made a mistake in sitting too close to you. The death throes of a man as strong as you can be—deadly. Very well, you may get out of the car."

The limousine pulled up to the side of the road. Bryn did not move.

"You do not like to leave me?" she asked, showing her white teeth.

"I'd like nothing better. But if I have

to be shot down I prefer it to happen here where I can get my hands on your gorgeous throat."

"I give you my word no harm shall come to you—until after you have left us."

"Your word!" he mocked.

Her teeth were still bared, but the smile had given way to a snarl. "Eventually I shall kill you for that. At present I allow you to suggest how you will leave this car."

"Tell your chauffeur to start the car."

Zara gave the order and the limousine started moving. Bryn shifted his arm to the back of her neck. Panic flared in her eyes.

"You won't be hurt," he assured her. "My word should be at least as good as yours."

He leaned over and opened the door nearest her, pushing her along with him and keeping his hand on her neck. The brown man with the gun could still shoot him easily in the back, but Bryn knew that he wouldn't take the chance. The limousine was going along at a good speed with the open door swinging in the wind.

Bryn yanked the tiny automatic from Zara's hand, released her and jumped. He landed on his feet, went down heavily on his side, and lay there with the wind completely knocked out of him. The limousine rushed on.

CHAPTER THREE

The Headless Corpse

BEN BRYN staggered groggily up to his feet and flopped down again behind some bushes along the side of the road. Zara's .25 automatic was like a toy pistol in his huge hand as he waited for the limousine to return. Cars passed only occasionally; none was the one he expected.

After a ten minute rest he had recovered his breath. It was too dangerous to flag a car for a lift because one of them

might be the limousine. The night was so dark that he oculdn't see two feet in front of him, but there was nothing to do but grope and stumble through the darkness until he reached the outskirts of the city.

He hopped the first taxi he saw and returned to the restaurant where Aaron Patten had been murdered.

The restaurant was not open for business, but all the lights were on and there were plenty of people inside. A harness bull blocked his way.

Bryn mentioned his name. "I think I'm wanted in there," he said.

"I'll tell the world," the cop agreed heartily and stepped aside to let him pass.

The restaurant was jammed with homicide men and newspaper reporters and the restaurant staff and some of the diners who were being detained as witnesses The case was so important that Captain Duncan himself had come down to take charge.

"So here you are!" Duncan grunted as he saw Bryn pushing his way over to him. "I was thinking of sending out an alarm for you. Some of the waiters swore they'd seen you murder Patten and then take a powder."

Bryn dropped into a seat at the table where Captain Duncan sat. Aaron Patten's body was covered with a blanket.

"Where's Selma Patten?" Bryn asked.

"I sent her home with a couple of men. Poor kid's all broken up."

"Are you giving her protection?"

"Sure. First her aunt was murdered and then her father. She and her sister might be in danger too. Now let's hear your story, Bryn. How did you know Patten was murdered without looking him over?"

There was nobody near the table. Detectives were keeping the reporters and witnesses in the front part of the restaurant.

Bryn said: "I didn't know. Maybe the

witnesses who heard me told you something else—witnesses are like that—but what I said was there was a possibility he was murdered. He was scared to death of something, seemed to expect that something like that would happen to him; so, when he keeled over I had an idea it wasn't simply a stroke."

Captain Duncan nodded. "That checks with what Selma Patten told me." He fixed sorrowful grey eyes on Bryn. "You went tearing after a woman who sat at this table."

"Patten was about to tell me what was eating him up with fear. Then he saw this woman. None of us had seen her come in. Suddenly she was here, looking at Patten, and when he saw her he went to pieces. Then he died. When I got up from the body I glimpsed her leaving, so I streaked after her. She as much as admitted that she'd killed him." Bryn lit a cigarette, and asked: "How'd he die?"

"A poisoned dart, Doc Billings says. He doesn't know yet what the poison is, but it must have been powerful stuff."

BRYN expelled a line of smoke and watched it disintegrate. "She had a long cigarette holder in her mouth. I figured that was the way she did it."

"Man, getting anything out of you is like pulling teeth," Captain Duncan said. "You say you spoke to her. Why didn't you bring her in?"

"I started to, but I was careless. She had some accomplices with her, with guns, and they got me into a car. They were going to do something highly unpleasant to me, make me into an imbecile or something like that, so I decided to leave them. I had to jump from the car while it was doing thirty. The car went on."

"Just like that," Duncan grunted. "Well, some day I'll read the details in your memoirs."

Bryn said: "Her name is Zara. Second name, if any, unknown. She's an Eura-

sian, I think—about five-feet-eight, golden-brown skin, high cheekbones, slim, very beautiful. Mean anything to you?"

Duncan shook his head. "We'll check on her."

"Her henchmen are little brown men—natives of India, I should say She's no doubt from there too. Indian mother and American father or something like that. Talks English without any accent. Also—" He hesitated.

"Go on," Duncan urged.

Bryn rolled his cigarette between his fingers. "You wouldn't believe me. I don't believe it myself. Instead of a normal right hand, the little brown men have skeleton hands. I don't mean thin hands. I mean absolutely no flesh up to the wrists —just bones."

"Huh?" Duncan, and stared at Bryn.

"It's conceivable," Bryn explained. "A person can have the flesh of one hand removed and still remain alive. But here's something that will prove to you that I'm crazy. They can move those skeleton hands! No veins, no muscles in those hands—yet the fingers possess life."

Captain Duncan looked at Bryn for some time before he said: "Maybe you got a sock on the head when you got out of the car. You heard about the skeleton hand found branded on Caroline Patten's palm and you must have seen the same sort of thing on Aaron Patten's palm. You got smacked and dreamed about skeleton hands."

Bryn stood up. "All right, it's fantastic as hell. But isn't what you know of the rest of the case fantastic?"

"Somewhat. Those branded skeleton hands and the way Patten was killed. But on the whole it's just a variation of the old extortion racket. No doubt we'll find that Aaron Patten has lately been paying out large sums of money."

"Sure, extortion," Bryn agreed. "But there's more than just a gang of ordinary criminals behind it. There's a murder cult so utterly ruthless and horrible and, I might almost say, inhuman, that even a guy as hard as myself gets cold shivers just to think of them."

Captain Duncan got up too. He smiled down at Bryn from his foot of additional height. "First time I heard of Ben Bryn getting jittery. All right, what's the rest of the dope? The make of the car, where you were driving to when you jumped off and the rest?"

Bryn gave him the information, then left for the Patten house.

IT was a magnificent stucco structure in the most exclusive section of the city. As Bryn was going up the front steps a shadow detached itself from the darkness of the porch. Bryn dove for Zara's .25 which was in his pocket.

"Oh, it's you, Bryn," the shadow said. "Say, Captain Duncan was raising hell about you."

The light of a street lamp revealed the dim outlines of Detective Rosenbloom's features.

"I just saw him," Bryn told him. "Selma Patten is my client."

"Okay," Rosenbloom said and melted back into the shadows.

An incredibly tall and thin butler opened the door. His cadaverous face was drawn with fear. He wouldn't let Bryn in until Detective Clark, who was in the hall, came forward and said it was all right.

Selma Patten was in the drawing room. She jumped up when she saw Bryn enter and ran to him. Her lovely eyes were red with weeping and she clenched a moist handkerchief in one tiny fist. Bryn felt a strange fluttering within him at her nearness.

"Oh, Mr. Bryn, what happened to you? I was so worried. Did that horrible woman kill Daddy?"

"Yes," he said.

"Did you catch her?"

"She got away," he said. "But we'll get her. I can't tell you how sorry I am. In a way it was my fault."

She placed a small hand on the bulging muscles of his arm. "How could you have been prepared? Captain Duncan phoned and told me that Daddy had been killed by a poinsoned dart. How utterly horrible! First Aunt Caroline, now Daddy."

"And it won't stop there!" an hysterical female voice cried. "Either Selma or I will be next. They're determined to wipe out our family."

Bryn had seen the other girl as soon as he had entered. She had been seated on a couch next to a man in evening clothes.

The man held the girl close to him. "Now Lilis, get a grip on yourself. The police will protect you."

"No!" Lilis wailed. "I saw the fear that haunted Aunt Caroline and then Daddy. They would have gone to the police if they had thought it would do any good. I tell you they'll get us next!"

Selma led Bryn over to the girl and the man. She introduced the girl as her sister Lilis and the man as Herbert Simpson. Lilis was a somewhat younger addition of Selma, several inches taller, but with eyes as blue and features almost as lovely. Simpson was about thirty-five with a rugged, intelligent face. Bryn had heard of him as a successful stock broker.

"Not Ben Bryn, the famous detective!" Simpson said as he extended a hand to Bryn. "See, Lilis, everything will be all right. You have all the protection in the world now."

Once again Bryn was conscious of Selma's closeness to him. He wished he knew her well enough to place an arm comfortingly about her. "There's nothing for you girls to be afraid of," he said. "You're in no personal danger; and even if you were, the police have a line on the gang and will round them up shortly."

Subconsciously Selma swayed toward him. Her shoulder was against his as she smiled wanly up at him.

"I feel better with you around," she said softly.

The front door slammed open and a harsh voice roared: "Bryn! For God's sake, Bryn!"

Bryn rushed out into the hall. Detective Clark stood at the open front door. The cadaverous butler was moving noiselessly forward from the back of the house.

"Here, Bryn, on the porch!" Clark said. "God, it's awful!"

Clark waited until Bryn reached him, then stepped out to the porch. Bryn stopped in the doorway as if he'd come up against the wall. Propped up against each of the columns on either side of the steps were two men. The man slumped against the left hand column was Detective Rosenbloom. One look at his profile showed that he was dead.

Against the other column was another man—or part of a man. There was no head on the corpse.

Bryn took two steps forward and stopped again. From the knees of the headless corpse a waxen face with bulging eyes and an open hideously grinning mouth stared up at him. The corpse was holding its head on its lap!

CHAPTER FOUR

Ceremony of Death

BEN BRYN yelled; "Don't come on the porch! Stay in the house!"

But it was too late. Selma and Lilis Patten and Herbert Simpson were crowding through the door. The butled snapped a switch in the hall and light flooded the porch. Both girls screamed simultaneously. Bryn moved to Selma's side and caught her as she swayed. She didn't quite faint; trembling, she leaned against the curve of his arm and buried her face in his chest.

Clark was saying in an unsteady voice: "Look, Rosenbloom got it in the back with a knife. He didn't have a chance to make a sound. I was in the hall all the time and I didn't hear a thing. Then I came out here to ask Rosenbloom for a butt and I seen them like this." His voice broke. He muttered hoarsely: "Rosie was a swell guy."

Simpson had his arms about Lilis. Over her head he stared at the head which rested on the corpse's lap.

"That's Ingram Boniface," Simpson said. "You know, owner of the Boniface drug store chain. He lives in that white colonial house across the street."

Bryn looked at the white house. It was dark. All in it were probably asleep. In a little while it would be another house of mourning.

Gently he led Selma into the drawing room. Her face was deadly white, set as if in a trance. She didn't seem to hear his words of comfort. There wasn't much he could say anyway. No words could wipe away the horrible deaths of her aunt and father and the presence of that frightful corpse on the porch steps.

Leaving Simpson with the girls, Bryn returned to the porch. While Clark went inside to telephone headquarters, Bryn stayed with the two bodies. He was hardened to violent death, but that dead face grinning up at him from the corpse's knees did things to his stomach. He kept his eyes away from the face as he stepped around the body and gingerly lifted the right hand by the sleeve.

On the palm a tiny skeleton hand was branded.

Clark appeared on the porch. "There's a phone call for you, Bryn. A woman."

Bryn went up the steps. "A woman? Did she give a name?"

"No. Seemed to know you were here. Rang a moment after I'd called headquarters. The butler says to take the call in the library."

Bryn sat down at the big oak desk, leaned back in the comfortable leather chair, and said into the phone: "Hello, Zara."

Her husky, vibrant laugh came over the wire. "You *are* a detective. And I don't doubt that you are frantically trying to have this call traced on another wire."

"I'd be wasting my time," he said. "You're not that dumb. That was a cute memento you left on the doorstep. Was it for my special benefit?"

"You mean the late lamented Ingram Boniface? He was stubborn, miserly. I thought you would be interested in his fate and so I decided to have him brought to you. You see, Ben Bryn, I am really very considerate of you."

He said: "I'd give half of my life if your neck were between my fingers now instead of at the other end of this wire."

"How romantic, Ben Bryn! I want to see you. I want to talk to you. I shall have a car bring you to me."

"Not unless you want to have the driver commit suicide."

"You don't understand. I shall promise you safe conduct here and back. I kept one promise I made to you today."

"You couldn't help yourself," Bryn snorted. "What's the game? Are you trying to get me away from this house so that you can send your brown men after Selma Patten?"

"Ah!" she breathed. "So you care for that girl?"

At once Bryn regretted that he had mentioned Selma's name. He said quickly: "I hardly know her. But she's my client and it's my job to watch out for her."

"Ben Bryn, will you come? Why should we two be enemies? Even if you do not take my word that you will be unharmed, certainly you are not afraid."

"Sure I am," he said. "I have enough sense to be afraid of a poison snake. But I'll come. What do I do?"

"You leave the house and walk in any direction you please. Ultimately you will reach me."

There was a click at the other end of the wire.

SLOWLY Bryn cradled the handset. He leaned back in the chair and sat looking at the desktop. It was suicidal madness to go, but it was the only way to get to Zara before there were more murders. And she had to be stopped. He recalled the calculating inflection in her voice as she had said of Selma Patten: "So you care for that girl!" If necessary she would strike at him through Selma, and she would do it as ruthlessly and with as little conscience as the poisoned reptile to which he had likened her.

He searched through the drawers of the desk until he found a piece of twine. With it he carefully tied Zara's automatic to his thigh.

He heard the police arrive. Captain Duncan and several homicide men were standing at the foot of the outside steps when Bryn appeared on the porch.

"God!" Duncan gasped. "Twenty-seven years on the force and I've never seen anything to approach this for sheer horror."

Bryn went down the steps. "You'll find a skeleton hand branded on his right hand," he said.

Duncan's shoulders sagged wearily. "And they got Rosenbloom, too. What's that you reported, Clark, a knife in the back?"

Bryn hung around to answer Captain Duncan's questions. Not that there was much to be told, except Zara's phone call, and he made no mention of that. If police were sent to follow him, Zara simply wouldn't have him picked up, and it would ruin every chance of his getting to her before more damage was done.

He set out walking in no particular direction. It was near midnight and the streets were deserted. With each block the tension within him mounted until he felt perspiration pasting his undershirt to his skin. There were vicious criminals who took a pride in keeping their word. Zara might be like that—and she might not.

He regretted that he hadn't taken steps to procure another gun. If anything happened suddenly he could never reach in time the automatic strapped to his thigh.

A yellow limousine was suddenly rolling noiselessly beside him. A brown man sat behind the wheel. The back was empty. Knowing that an alarm would be out for the black limousine, Zara had sent another car.

Bryn stopped walking and the car stopped. He walked and the car moved. The chauffeur made no sign to him.

With a tight feeling about his heart, Bryn strode to the limousine and pulled open the back door. As soon as he seated himself against the cushions the car shot away.

He found himself wondering if Zara would be picked up along the way. Or if— Almost at once he knew; and then it was too late. Warning came in the form of realization that his brain was functioning sluggishly, that he had difficulty keeping his eyes open. He noticed that all the windows were tightly shut in back and that there was a glass partition between the driver's seat and the back of the car.

Bryn lunged forward to grasp the door handle. He got his hands on it, but he was unable to do anything about it. He sank to the floor, his hand sliding slowly from the handle . . . .

HE AWOKE as if from a deep, untroubled sleep. For a lazy minute he thought he was in his bed and wondered why the mattress was so hard. Then he opened his eyes wide and saw that he was lying on the floor. He sprang to his feet. A small electric bulb high beyond his reach showed him that he was in a small bare room. There were no windows. The door, which was of course locked, was made of steel.

Grimly he smiled to himself. Well, he had asked for it. Openly he had walked into the trap. He ran a hand over his right thigh. The small automatic had been taken from him.

Luckily his cigarettes had been left in his pocket, so he sat with his back against the wall smoking and waiting. It wasn't easy to wait. Zara obviously did not intend to have him killed in the immediate

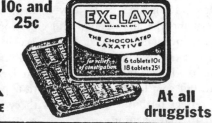

future, but that was small consolation when he recalled that earlier in the evening she had planned to make him into a mindless slave.

Suddenly the light went out. He flipped the cigarette against the opposite wall and rose to his feet, straining his ears for any hostile sound. A thin weird wailing, pitched on a single key and continuing indefinitely without a break, came through one of the walls. It had a peculiar chilling quality which worked its way into his bloodstream and turned his blood into icy rivulets.

A flat beam of light sprang into the room from one wall. Cautiously Bryn moved toward it. The panel of a space about six inches wide by three inches high had been slid open on the other side of the wall. Then the light from the panel vanished, but Bryn's fingers felt that the opening was still there. He did what was expected of him: he peered through the opening.

At first there was nothing but blackness out of which came that maddening wailing. Gradually out of the darkness a face formed, each separate feature seeming to drift together until it formed a unified whole. The face of Zara! Below the face a smooth throat appeared, then superb bare shoulders and the upper slopes of uncovered upthrust breasts. Then the materialization of the body stopped. The head and shoulders seemed to be an entity in themselves, without any torso or any need for one.

The disembodied head wavered in space, strangely white, strangely lifeless, and for a short while Bryn thought it was made of wax. Then the pupils moved in their sockets and the lips opened and closed in a weird incantation which was an accompaniment to the banshee wailing. Zara spoke in a language Bryn could not understand, but somehow her words had a hypnotic effect on him. He stood with eyes glued to that opening.

Hands took slow form in that blackness —skeleton hands which glowed with an eerie white light. They floated in front of the disembodied face of Zara in a fantastic sort of dance. And the flexing of the fingers showed that, although they had no flesh and no muscle, they lived.

Another face appeared suddenly—that of an elderly grey-haired man. His face was hideous with terror. From his lips came a crazy jumble of words. It was a desperate, hopeless, insane plea for mercy in which the words did not seem to hang together.

Slowly Zara intoned: "So die all those who refuse to obey Zara!"

The old man screamed once, and then the disembodied skeleton hands were on him, were clutching at his throat. He gurgled horribly, and his head sank to the floor, followed by the hands.

A woman screamed then, stridently. Bryn found himself pounding futilely against the wall. Who had screamed? It couldn't be—no, not Selma Patten!

"Quiet!" Zara ordered and the scream stopped as abruptly as if it had been switched off.

Zara's thin, cruel lips laughed. "Mary Rockland, you have seen how those who dare defy Zara can die. You have heard how, two weeks ago, Caroline Patten died; and tomorrow in the papers you will read how Aaron Patten and Ingram Boniface died and of how the body of this man, this Calvin Clinton, was found. What have you to say, Mary Rockland?"

Another face appeared out of the darkness. It was a face which often appeared on the society pages of newspapers—Mary Rockland, the copper heiress. She was young and noted for her beauty. She was not young now and certainly not beautiful."

"I'll do anything!" she cried shrilly. "I have money, much money!"

"Yes, you have money," Zara said. "Very well."

The glowing white tip of an iron appeared in midair. A skeleton hand seized it, bore it toward Mary Rockland. The girl was shrieking again. Her small white hand leaped into view below her face and other skeleton hands closed about the wrist.

The girl screamed louder than before as the white-hot branding iron was pressed against her palm. There was a smell of burning flesh.

CHAPTER FIVE

Mistress of Murder

ALL at once Ben Bryn was again standing in utter darkness. The panel had slid shut over the narrow opening. The screams of Mary Rockland died down, the thin eerie wailing melted away, and there was complete silence.

Bryn groped in his pocket for another cigarette. About all he could do was smoke —and wait.

He didn't have long to wait. The light went on and a minute later the steel door opened noiselessly. He went to the door. Nobody came in. He peered down a long dimly lit corridor which was empty.

Shrugging, he went down the corridor. He passed two doors, each of which was locked. The third door opened at his approach. When he had stepped into the room beyond, the door shut behind him.

He found himself in a tastily furnished boudoir. Amid numerous silk pillows on a divan Zara reclined. Her dress was midnight black and she wore those black gloves up to her elbow. Her thin lips smiled at Bryn.

He took a slow puff on his cigaret, expelled the smoke through his nostrils, and moved toward her. He said: "I'm sure that numbo-jumbo wasn't for my benefit. Phosphorus paint and trick lightning doesn't impress me."

"But you were impressed," she said.

"Yes." He crushed his cigarette out in an ashtray. "I was impressed by the fact that you are the most dangerous and ruthless and heartless fiend walking the earth. I'll have no qualms about killing you."

"I'm afraid you will have to restrain that urge for the time being. There are men who have rifles trained on you. Don't look; you cannot see them. They will shoot if you compel them to."

Quietly he asked: "And if I don't compel them to? I mean, why did you want me here? You could have killed me while I was unconscious. I'm sure you didn't think to scare the daylights out of me with your trick show and a display of ruthless murder."

"You are not the kind to scare easily, Ben Bryn. That is why you are alive now."

Languidly she rose from the divan. Obviously she wasn't wearing anything but that black gown and there wasn't much of that. It was made of some diaphanous stuff and clung to her like a second skin, bringing into sensuous relief every voluptuous curve of her body. The low-cut bodice covered little of her golden breasts.

She posed before him. "Am I beautiful, Ben Bryn?"

"As beautiful as sin and ten times as deadly."

She laughed huskily. "It is poor tactics to be frank with a man, but I shall be frank with you. There must be truth in the saying that opposites attract. I am dark, tall. You are fair and shorter than most men. But you are stronger than any man I have ever known and more courageous. Your curly hair, your blue eyes, something in your face that is at once hard and boyish—I confess that you trouble me strangely. That is why I wanted to see you again, Ben Bryn. I want you with me all the time."

"To be a partner in your murder cult?" he asked with a bitter twist to his mouth. "To be one of the performers in the shows to terrify rich people into turning their fortunes over to you? To kill for you?"

"Why not? There's millions in it. We can terrorize the wealthy of the city into giving us their money. The police are dull, stupid; we can be cleverer than they. I need a man like you, Ben Bryn. You are strong, fearless, intelligent. What can you make as a private detective compared to what I can offer you? Not only money, but—but myself . . ."

Her eyes were flashing with a strange, unholy fire; her splendid breasts rose and fell. He knew that she was mad as every criminal must be mad, but she was worse than any criminal he had ever known.

He said: "Do you think so little of me that you really imagine that I would accept your offer?"

HER face contorted with rage. "Look, Ben Bryn!" With her left hand she grasped her right glove and pulled it from her arm. He was prepared to see what was revealed, but the actual sight of that skeleton hand at the end of that perfect arm jolted him like a physical blow.

"Look, Ben Bryn!" she screamed. "Do you think one who has had to go through life like this will let anything stop her? It happened to me when I was a young girl. My father was a chemist. A cauldron of acid spilled over my hand and the flesh fell away. There was nothing to be done for me. It was fortunate I lived, they told me. Fortunate! Men loved me, many men, until they saw this—this horror. Then their love turned to disgust. Many times I thought of taking my life, but I had the courage to see it through. Do you think that anything can stop me now from getting what I want?"

Bryn stood very still. "So that was what turned your mind into that of a human fiend! Your brown men couldn't have lost the flesh off their hands through accidents. You did that to them, deliberately, so that others should share your misfortune. How did you manage to persuade them to dip their hands into that acid? Did you bribe them or drug them or lure them with your body? It doesn't matter. What matters is that you be wiped off the face of the earth."

She sank down on the divan. Her left hand dove among the cushions and came out with a gun.

Wearily she said: "You might try to kill me, Ben Bryn, before the rifle bullets get you. You might give your life just so that you can kill me. You are that kind of a man and perhaps that is why I love you. But you will come around to my way of thinking."

"Torture?" Bryn asked softly.

"No. I gave you my word that you would be unharmed and, strange as it may seem to you, I keep my word. But I did not say I would release you. I will keep you in that room with the peep-hole. You will see things in that other room." Her lips tightened with hatred. "You will see that girl, Selma Patten, brought in there, and eventually you will break. You will break or else—"

"Why, you—" He started to lunge at her.

"No!" she snapped, bringing up the gun. "Your death won't help her." He straightened up. "That's better," she said. "Now leave me and return to your cell to think."

For a full minute he stood there looking at her. His powerful hands opened and closed, opened and closed. Then, without a word, he turned, and strode out into the corridor.

Again the hallway was deserted. There was only one way to go. Behind him was Zara's boudoir in which hidden brown men waited with rifles; ahead of him the little windowless cell with the terrible peep-hole. Once the door of that cell shut behind him it would mean the end of hope. And through the peep-hole he would watch the horrible things Zara would do to Selma Patten and others.

SLOWLY he walked. It was like the one-way road to the death chamber, he thought grimly. Eyes, he knew, watched his progress. He reached the first of the two locked doors on the way to the cell. He had tried them when going to Zara's room, knew that they were locked, but he shook the knob again. The door was of heavy oak; it was doubtful if even his powerful shoulders could smash it down.

He passed on quickly so as not to arouse the suspicions of the watchers. He pressed his body close against the second door as if in examination of its strength. His object was to hide with his body what his hands were doing. His fingers closed around the knob, took a firm grip —and then all the power of his tremendous shoulders and biceps and wrists strained to turn that knob.

It was over in a matter of seconds. The lock snapped. Bryn pushed and the door flew open. As he plunged into the room he heard a cry of warning which seemed to come from the ceiling of the corridor.

Then Bryn slammed the door shut behind him. He was in an ordinary bedroom. The light was on. A naked brown man sat up in a bed. Bryn saw the yellow-whiteness of his skeleton right hand; saw the brown left hand streak under a pillow. Bryn hurled himself on the bed. He got his hands on the left arm, twisted, and there was a crack like a dry twig snapping. The brown man howled with pain. Bryn lifted him above his head and dashed him against the opposite wall. The brown man lay as limp as a rag doll.

Cries rose all around him. Feet pattered in the corridor. Bryn scooped up the revolver which the brown man had reached for. The room had two doors. One led to the corridor, one to what was probably an adjoining room. There were two windows near the ceiling. Obviously these rooms were in the cellar of the house. He wondered if he could squeeze his shoulders through one of the windows.

The door to the adjoining room flew in and a brown man stood framed in the doorway with a rifle in his hand. Bryn shot from his hip. A second or two later the other door opened and Bryn whirled, sending two slugs at a second investigating brown man.

Suddenly there was an utter, grave-like silence. Three dead brown men lay in the room—two shot to death, the third with nearly every bone in his body broken.

Bryn pulled a chair under one of the windows and mounted it. The window went up easily, but it wasn't wide enough to let him through. At any moment there would be another assault. Sticking the revolver in his belt, he gripped the sash and ripped it out. Then he started to crawl through.

Half of his body was out when a gun bellowed behind him. Fire stabbed into his thigh. With an effort he jerked the rest of his body through the window. The window was level with the ground. He tried to stand up and his wounded thigh gave way under him.

The prelude to dawn lessened the darkness enough to show the form which appeared around the side of the house. Bryn snapped a shot at it and the shape disappeared.

Only two bullets left in the gun! They would cut him down at their leisure as he lay there. Gritting his teeth, he started running. Behind him shots sounded. His wounded thigh was a ball of searing flame, but somehow he kept going.

It was wild country. Not many trees, but not far ahead he made out what seemed a vast area of bushes and undergrowth higher than his head. If he could reach it he had a chance.

He was some thirty feet from the bushes when a tommy-gun started barking. He heard the spat of slugs smacking dirt around him. Calling upon his last ounce of strength, he plunged in among the bushes.

But the tommy-gun went on spattering death. The brown men couldn't see him now, but they were raking the bushes. Bryn struck off at a right-angle. The bushes were so thick that he could hardly make his way through them. His clothes were ripped, his face and hands bloody.

He couldn't go any further. His wounded thigh refused to support him. He sank down to the ground. He passed a hand over the wound, and when he looked at the hand it was covered with blood.

His eyes closed against his will. He knew that he was sliding into unconsciousness, and that if he did he would bleed to death. With an effort of will he tried to keep awake, but it was futile.

CHAPTER SIX

Abducted!

IT WAS broad daylight when Ben Bryn opened his eyes. His wrist watch said ten after seven, which meant that he had been unconscious nearly three hours. Lifting himself on his elbows, he saw that his trouser leg about his left thigh was stained a thick reddish-brown. The material was pasted to the wound. That was what must have saved him from bleeding to death.

He tried to rise. His left leg was lifeless and he was weak as a kitten. Half-hobbling, half-crawling, he made his way out of the bushes. Those bushes had no doubt saved his life, hiding him from the brown men who must have taken a great deal of pains searching for him.

The house from which he had escaped stood neat and white about five hundred feet away—an innocent-looking cottage.

It seemed deserted, but there was no way of being sure.

He was on one of the highest points in the area and he could make out the narrow line of a dirt road in the distance. Several times he had to stop for long rests to keep himself from again passing out. His wound opened and started to bleed.

It seemed an eternity before he reached the road; actually it took forty minutes.

He flopped down on the road and lay there until a milk truck came along and picked him up. He showed his badge to the driver and explained that he had been wounded and slipped the driver a ten dollar bill to take him all the way to the Patten house. When they pulled up in front of the stucco house, Bryn called the patrolman and plainclothes man who were on the porch. They carried him to the house, barking questions at him.

All Bryn would reply was: "Selma Patten, is she all right?"

"Sure," the detective assured him. "We got four men in the house."

Herbert Simpson was on the porch. He said: "Take him into the drawing room. My God, that man should be in a hospital!"

"Never mind me now," Bryn said. "Go up and see if Selma is all right."

"But she'll still be asleep," Simpson protested. "I've been here all night, parked between Selma's and Lilis' rooms."

"Damn you!" Bryn said. "Do I have to go up those stairs myself?"

Simpson looked at Bryn and shrugged and left the room. One of the detectives went with him.

Lying on a couch, Bryn could hear Simpson knocking on a door overhead and calling Selma's name. Then he heard the door open and Simpson's startled exclamation. Feet ran in the upstairs hall and another door opened and Simpson yelled: "Lilis!"

Ben Bryn lay back, closing his eyes. Too late! He thought of Selma's slim loveliness and of Lilis, too, and a sick void formed inside of him.

Simpson burst into the drawing room. "Lilis and Selma are gone! It's incredible. There were four policemen and myself guarding the house." He flew at Bryn. "What do you know about this? How did you know they would be gone?"

BEN BRYN talked. He ignored Simpson, directing his words to Detective-Sergeant Morgan, whom Captain Duncan had left in charge.

Morgan snapped: "Right! We'll have that place raided in fifteen minutes."

He went to a phone and called headquarters. Then he put in a call for an ambulance for Bryn.

Late that afternoon Captain Duncan entered Bryn's hospital room.

"It's about time somebody came around," Bryn growled. "Nothing but doctors and nurses who can't answer civil questions and don't seem to read the papers."

"Take it easy," Duncan said, seating himself on the single chair in the room. "I hear that they dug a .38 slug out of your thigh and that you lost gallons of blood."

"A scratch," Bryn said. "Fortunately it only nicked a bone. I'll be out of here tomorrow."

The shadow of a smile creased Duncan's lips. "Ten days the doctor said. It'll keep you out of trouble." Then the smile vanished and Bryn saw that the captain's face was strained.

"Well?" Bryn demanded impatiently. "Did you find the girls?"

"No. We raided the house where you were kept prisoner. It was deserted."

"Of course," Bryn said. "They're mad, but they're not idiots."

"They left in a hurry. Took everything with them but one thing."

"I know," Bryn told him wearily. "The body of Calvin Clinton, the corporation lawyer. Probably propped up waiting for you at the door. That's Zara's grisly sense of humor." He paused and then added: "I saw Clinton die."

Duncan nodded. "Sergeant Morgan's report to me was complete. There was no sign of Mary Rockland. We've searched the city for her. She's in their hands, all right. They probably took her with them.

They won't kill her because she's worth nothing to them dead, and you've seen too much for them to take a chance in letting her go and paying them extortion money. I figure they'll hold her for ransom. They'll do the same with the two Patten girls."

"Maybe," Bryn said quietly.

Duncan got to his feet. "The girls were taken out through the back windows. The papers are raising hell with us. They say we should have had a cordon around the house. But there was nothing definitely pointing to their danger except that their aunt and father had been murdered after extortion threats. As far as we know, the girls were never even threatened. Still, I can't imagine how they got up to the girls' rooms. They couldn't possibly have lugged a ladder around with them."

Bryn thought: *Zara went after the girls because of me. She said she'd get at me through Selma . . . .* But he said nothing about that to Duncan.

"We'll find them," Duncan swore between tight teeth. "We're picking up everybody who looks like a brown man. We're stopping every limousine, although it might get us in trouble with our swankier citizens. There's a nation-wide dragnet out."

Bryn lay so quietly that Duncan thought he had fallen asleep. He tiptoed out of the room.

BUT Bryn's mind was wide-awake, raging inwardly at the weakness which kept him confined to bed. He, whose strength was a byword among the police and the underworld alike, was too weak to move under his own power. And the worst of it was that only he could get to the girls; if he were up, Zara herself would make the first move.

Days of mental anguish passed. Avidly he read the papers brought to him. The abduction of three heiresses was lead news. Only there wasn't any news. Zara, the brown men, and the three girls had simply ceased to exist.

At the end of the third day Herbert Simpson came to visit him. Under his arm he carried a package. His face was alight with excitement; his hands trembled with nervous tension.

"Bryn, I have a lead!" he exclaimed. "I think I can take you to this Zara."

Bryn sat up. "Go on, talk."

"There's no time to be lost if we want to save Lilis and Selma. I can't go to the police. It will mean the girls' instant death. You have to go with me. I hear that you're better than a whole police force by yourself."

"How'll I go, in my pajamas?" Bryn asked. "I've been trying to get out of here for two days now, but the damned doctors won't give me my clothes."

Simpson went to the door, glanced into the hall, returned to the bed and ripped open the package. "I thought of that. Here, these clothes ought to fit you."

"Good boy," Bryn said. He dressed hurriedly while Simpson kept a watch at the door. Bryn was rather surprised at how strong he felt. He had experienced his remarkable recuperative power before, but the doctors had almost succeeded in convincing him that he was in no condition to get up. He felt fine save for an unsteadiness in his legs.

Simpson announced that the coast was clear and the two men went quickly down the hall to the staircase. On the way down Simpson handed him an automatic. Bryn grunted with approval and slid the gun into his pocket.

Simpson's car was waiting in front of the hospital. As soon as the sedan got under way, Bryn said: "Now let's have it."

"Sure," Simpson said. "Here's the lowdown. There's a gun an inch from the back of your head. At the first move you make your brains will be spattered over my nice clean windshield."

Bryn twisted his head: The bore of a pistol pointed between his eyes. Behind the gun, smiling maliciously, was a malevolent brown face.

Bryn turned his head back to the front of the car. "And no doubt the gun you gave me contains blanks."

"That's right," Simpson said.

CHAPTER SEVEN

The Home of Horror

BEN BRYN reached forward to the dashboard, extracted the electric lighter and calmly lit a cigarette. Then he said:

"I suppose it serves me right. I wasn't figuring on you having somebody hidden in the back of the car. Of course—you didn't fool me up in the hospital room. I'd been waiting for Zara to make a move to get me in her power again. With all due modesty, I'm afraid the gal has a yen for me. As soon as you came in, I saw that you'd been sent to fetch me. You didn't care if I suspected you or not, because you knew I'd go with you anyway. I could handle you alone easily, but the chap back there makes it a bit inconvenient."

"Inconvenient is putting it mildly," Simpson said. His lips were pressed together; his skin stretched tightly from his cheekbones.

"You don't like this," Bryn told him. "You've never before led a person directly to his death. I figure you as having been only a fingerman. As a broker, you had a pretty good idea of your client's finances. You gave Zara the names of the best prospects for extortion. At first you thought it would be only extortion pure and simple, and maybe the first of the murders horrified you. But you were in it up to your neck, so there was nothing you could do about it. She forced you to help the brown men kidnap Selma. You were supposed to be standing guard outside their rooms. Probably you let down a rope ladder from Selma's window for the brown men to climb up. Also, you probably gagged and bound Selma first. Once the brown men were up there they told you that they were taking Lilis too, and there was no way you could stop them without giving yourself away. How'm I doing?"

"I should have known it would lead to murder," Simpson said hoarsely. "Even if it hadn't been necessary to murder, Zara and her men would have killed just for the fun of it. They're kill-mad. But I'll get out of it yet. Zara promised me. I'll get my share and then I'll marry Lilis who'll inherit the whole of the Patten fortune."

Bryn flipped his cigarette out of the window. They were well into the country now.

"So that's it," Bryn said. "Zara told you she'd release Lilis if you brought me to her. Lilis will never know you were involved because I'll be dead; or, if Zara has her way, I'll be forced into becoming part of her murder cult. What temptation did Zara use to get you in with her at first? The prospect of a lot of money, her gorgeous body—or both? Didn't her skeleton hand turn your stomach the least bit?"

"Shut up, damn you!" Simpson cried.

"Would you have me killed before we reach there? You know that Zara ordered you to bring me in alive. Suppose I forced the chap in back to kill me? That would be a great joke on you. Zara would be sore as hell."

Simpson looked panicky. "You wouldn't try to make a break, would you?"

"No. I'm anxious to see Zara—and Selma."

Then there was silence save for the purring of the car. For more than an hour they drove on the broad highway. Presently the car swung onto a dirt road and after a mile or two turned into what was hardly more than a cowpath. Two miles

of extremely bumpy riding brought them to a ramshackle farmhouse.

Zara and a couple of the brown men were waiting for them. She wore another one of her black, exotically fitting evening dresses and elbow-high black gloves. The brown men held guns in their left hands. Their yellow-white skeleton right hands hung at their sides.

"Welcome, Ben Bryn," Zara greeted him, with her slow smile. "I should be angry at you because you killed three of my men. I could, however, be persuaded to forgive you."

"Don't bother," Bryn snapped as he got out of the car.

"You still refuse to be reasonable?"

"Call it what you will."

Her smile vanished. Without a word she went into the house. Guns prodded Bryn and he followed. Simpson waited outside.

INSIDE the house Bryn was forced to be seated and his arms and legs were tied to the wooden chair. Zara stood over him.

"You know that we have Selma Patten here," she said. "Once again I make this offer to you: Come in with me. Be my partner and more than my partner."

Bryn said nothing.

"Have it your way," she said. "Selma Patten will be brought in here. I promised you a few days ago that through her I would break you. This is your last chance to save her and yourself."

"If I give in, will you release Selma and Lilis Patten and Mary Rockland?"

She looked at him a long time. "I am not a fool, either, Ben Bryn, as you know. Already you are thinking of betraying me. I shall have to keep a hostage to guarantee your good behavior."

Wearily Bryn said: "All right, you win."

Once free, once Zara's guard and that of the brown men were relaxed, he would have at least a chance of rescuing Selma and the others.

Zara gave an order in an alien tongue and two of the brown men left. Several minutes later they returned with Selma and Lilis Patten.

The girls were dressed only in sheer sleeping pajamas. They appeared unharmed, but the terror and uncertainty of three days' imprisonment and the horror of the skeleton hands had turned their complexions to the color of green chalk and etched harsh lines on their lovely features. With a cry Selma pattered on bare feet across the room to Bryn and threw herself on him. Something choked him at the feel of her body against him.

"It'll be all right," he whispered. "I'll get you away."

Zara strode over to them, grasped Selma by the back of the neck, pulled her away from Bryn and slapped her sharply across the face with her boney right hand. Then she hurled Selma brutally to the floor.

"I was a fool!" Zara spat out at Bryn. "I humbled myself before you, begged for your love, forgot my pride. And when a few minutes ago you consented to give in, you were already planning to betray me. You shall not have that chance. You'll suffer, Ben Bryn, you and that girl whom you prefer to me."

She barked a command. Two men gripped Lilis by each arm. She started to scream shrilly, writhing in their grip. Selma lay sobbing on the floor. The brown men dragged Lilis toward a huge iron pot which stood against one wall of the room.

With a sinking heart Bryn realized what was in that pot. "For God's sake, Zara, you can't do that!" he cried.

"Go on, squirm!" Zara gloated. "I want to see the hardboiled heroic Ben Bryn beg for mercy. First we'll let the girl you love watch what will happen to her sister. A little at a time she will be dipped into that acid which eats the flesh off bones. She'll go mad just watching, but even that won't be the end for her. She'll be next, and you'll see her, a living, agony-crazed monster with her torso and face unimpaired, but with the hands and arms and feet and legs of a skeleton."

She laughed insanely. "My skeleton hand revolts you, does it? Wait until you see what is left of your sweetheart!"

Bryn knew that argument was useless. Desperately he strained at the cord which tied him to the chair. While one of the brown men held the thrashing body of Lilis, the other grasped her wrist with a normal hand and a skeleton hand and slowly forced Lilis' hand over the lip of the iron pot.

The door opened and a voice roared: "Stop!" Herbert Simpson held a blue automatic in his hand.

THERE was an abrupt cessation of movement in the room. Even Bryn stopped fighting his bonds. Selma ceased whimpering. Lilis cried: "Herbert! Thank God!

The two brown men holding Lilis straightened up. There were two other brown men in the room, one standing over Selma, the other near Bryn—all, probably, that were left alive.

Zara said: "Don't do anything silly,

Herbert. You're in this as much as any of us."

Simpson's eyes were smouldering pools of rage. "You said you'd let Lilis go if I brought Bryn here. I kept my end of the bargain."

Zara's lips smiled; but the rest of her face had become ugly with the fear of death.

"We have to protect ourselves, Herbert," she said. "This girl knows too much." She looked at his face and then shrugged. "Very well, we'll let her go. You may take her, Herbert."

"You are trying to talk me into disarming," Simpson said in a strangely detached tone. "You said you can't afford to let Lilis go and you don't intend to. You're going to die, Zara. By killing you I'll atone to some degree for the ungodly things you and my greed for money made me do."

The skeleton hand of the brown man who stood over Selma jerked upward. The silver of a knife flashed through the air and its blade buried itself in Simpson's chest. Simpson staggered backward and his gun started bellowing.

Bedlam followed. Selma and Lilis and Zara were shrieking and Simpson kept shooting from the floor and two of the brown men held exploding guns in their hands. Bryn threw the chair to which he was tied to the floor and concentrated every ounce of strength on his bonds. His powerful muscles bulged; effort contorted his face; the cord knifed through his skin and into his flesh.

And then the cord parted against the pressure of his tremendous strength.

The shooting had stopped. Simpson lay dead in rapidly forming pools of his own blood. Two other bodies lay on the floor. One, the brown man who had thrown the knife and had been shot dead by Simpson. The other, Zara, writhing in agony, clawing at a jagged red splotch which dyed her right breast.

Bryn saw that he wouldn't have a chance to get the cord off his legs. Two of the brown men were kneeling on either side of Zara; the third was throwing himself at Bryn, chopping down at his head with the butt of a revolver.

Bryn twisted his body aside and the butt of the gun struck his shoulder a glancing blow. Bryn drove his big fist up into the brown man's face. He felt the jar all the way up to his shoulder. The brown man's face was gone. Blood sputtered out of shattered cartilage.

Bryn flung himself toward the revolver which the brown man had dropped. The chair dragged after him. He saw one of the two remaining brown men level his gun at him. Bryn grabbed up the revolver, but knew he would be too late. As he brought the gun up, he expected to hear the report which would blot him out of existence.

All he heard was the click of the hammer on an empty chamber. The brown man had emptied the revolver into Simpson!

Then his own gun belched death and the brown man with the gun went down. He shot again and then once more he heard the futile click. This time it was his own revolver.

THE last of the brown men grinned hideously, and pulling a knife from his belt advanced slowly on Bryn. Bryn threw the empty revolver. The brown man ducked and the gun shattered a window behind him. Lilis was still screaming and Zara continued to moan. The brown man stopped three feet from Bryn. His arm went back to flick the knife. At that distance he couldn't possibly miss and Bryn, hampered by the chair to which his legs were tied, was helpless.

A pajama clad figure skimmed over the floor. Small white arms wound themselves about the brown man's legs and the brown man went down, face forward, into Bryn's reach. Bryn grabbed the wrist of the hand which held the knife, twisted, then got his other hand around the scrawny brown throat. The brown man's neck snapped.

"Good girl, Selma," Bryn said.

Then her warm trembling body was in his arms and the feel of her through the thin pajamas and the nearness of her made his head swim.

Whimpering, Lilis was coming over to them. Bryn reluctantly released Selma and pulled the cords off his legs. He went over to where Zara lay.

Her eyes were open. Her breasts rose and fell with the pain of her breathing.

"I am dying, Ben Bryn," she gasped, and there was a wry smile on her thin lips. "You are the finest man I ever knew, Ben Bryn, and the most courageous. What a team we could have made together. But you wanted it this way and —and you won. Goodbye, Ben Bryn."

Her eyes closed. A spasm shook her splendid body and she was still.

Bryn rose to his feet and turned to Selma. "Is Mary Rockland still alive?"

"She was locked in with us in a room in the cellar."

He went down to the cellar and freed Mary Rockland. Then he hurried the three girls out of that charnel house. He remained behind and bent over one of the dead brown men, examining the skeleton hand.

Close inspection showed him what he had not been able to see during the brief and distant glimpses of the skeleton hands —that fine steel wires were attached to the joints of the fingers. Some ran to the wrist, some to the elbow, some to the shoulder. By flexing wrist, elbow or shoulder the wires tightened and produced motion of the fingers, much in the same fashion as puppets are operated by the pulling of strings.

With a grim smile he dropped the arm and left the house. Selma Patten was waiting outside for him. Her sister and Mary Rockland were already seated in Herbert Simpson's sedan.

"Look at that sunset," Selma said, moving close to him. "I thought I'd never see another."

The western sky was streaked with brilliant purples and oranges. "Looks swell," Ben Bryn agreed.

Together they moved toward the sedan. He found that his arm was about Selma's slim waist and that she was leaning intimately against him. There are moments in life when one feels with a kind of intense physical sensation how good it is to be alive. For Ben Bryn this was one of those moments.

THE END

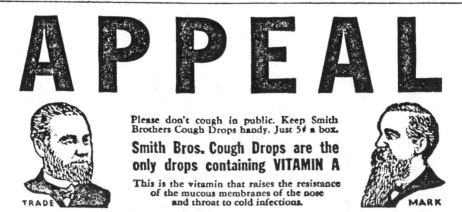

FLESH FOR THE MONSTER

Only one man in the state had the incredible strength to tear human beings apart as Alice Foley and Leland Ansley had been found horribly slain. And that man was Detective Ben Bryn—who seemed to have run amok in a one-man reign of terror!

CHAPTER ONE

The Thing in the Bedroom

THE short, broad-shouldered man who walked across the hotel lobby carried a box of flowers almost as tall as himself. He said to the bored young man behind the desk: "Miss Alice Foley, please."

The hotel clerk stroked a thin mustache with the side of his thumb and looked down at the short man from his superior height. Having nothing else on which to pride himself, he had developed a contempt for men who were shorter than himself.

Superciliously he asked: "Who shall I say is calling?"

The short man turned friendly blue eyes up at him. He had removed his hat,

revealing blond, curly hair. His features were finely chiselled, sensitive.

"Ben Bryn," he said.

The clerk turned to the switchboard,
trying to remember where he had
heard that name before. A minute later

It was a man . . . he had been
murdered in the same way. . . .

he returned to the desk. "She wants you
to go right up, Mr. Bryn. Room seventeen-o-nine."

As soon as Bryn's broad back had disappeared into an elevator, Egan sidled up
to the desk. His appearance shrieked hotel detective, even though he didn't wear
a hat and smoked cigarettes instead of
cigars.

Egan expelled smoke and said: "Know
who that was, George?"

The clerk shrugged.

"Said his name's Ben Bryn."

"He's the private dick," Egan announced with something of awe in his voice. "He mightn't have much altitude, but did you see those shoulders and arms? I once saw a guy he hit with his fist. It just wiped the guy's face away."

The clerk wasn't impressed. "Yeah, that's right. I read about him in the Sunday supplement. So that squirt's the terror of the underworld? Hell, he looks as if he'd be scared of his own shadow."

"I wouldn't go by looks," Egan said. "Gunmen have tried that, and woke up knowing different—or they didn't wake up at all. They say he had a pretty tough time as a youngster. Had infantile paralysis, and for twenty years pushed himself around on a wheeled platform. That's what put the strength into his shoulders and arms. Then he did exercises which made his legs return to normal. Bet he's here on a case. Who's he seeing?"

"Alice Foley, the cute trick that's got seventeen-o-nine. You're a hell of a detective, Egan. He's on a date. Did you see that box of flowers he was lugging? I'd go after her myself if she'd give me a tumble. Her old man died a couple of months ago and left her a pile of dough."

Egan sighed. "Why be a shamus if you have blue eyes and curly hair?"

Ben Bryn knocked at the door of seventeen-o-nine and waited. After half a minute he knocked again. Still no answer. That was odd. Alice had told the clerk to tell him to come right up. She should have expected him within two minutes at the most. He knocked a third time, loudly. After another brief wait he turned the knob. The door swung inward under his pressure.

Light streamed through the open door of the bedroom into the large, richly furnished living room. Nobody was in the living room, and the bathroom, he could see through the open door, was dark and empty. That meant that she was in the bedroom, but why hadn't she answered his knock?

"Alice," he called.

When the sound of his voice melted away, there was a profound silence, broken only by the thin, muted sounds of traffic in the street seventeen stories below. Probably she had left her rooms for a minute to visit somebody in the hotel. But why would she do that if she knew he was coming up?

Bryn placed the box of flowers and his hat on a table and pulled a silver cigarette-case from his pocket. No telling how a woman will act, especially one who had too much money for her own good and might not think too highly of a mere private investigator. Still, she had sounded eager enough when he had invited her to dinner and a show.

He struck a match, but it never reached the tip of his cigarette. He must have been aware of the smell the moment he had entered the room, but he had been giving too much thought to Alice's apparent absence to pay any attention to it. Now, standing stock still with the match almost touching his cigarette, the sweet, cloying odor assailed his nostrils. It smelled something like a slaughter house, something like—

"Alice!" he yelled.

He strode across to the open bedroom door. Just inside the threshold he stopped. He was used to the sight of death, but what he saw in the bedroom made his stomach churn.

THERE was blood all over the room. It spattered the walls and the mirror of the vanity table; it stained the silken cover on the bed and the expensive rug on the floor. And scattered about were pieces of flesh.

At his feet was all that was left of Alice Foley. Tatters of a blood-soaked evening gown and chemise still adhered to the remains of what could scarcely be recognized as a human torso. Only the head was untouched save for blood which smeared it. The face was turned up to him—a face incredibly placid except for the bulging, staring eyes.

Alice Foley had been literally torn to pieces.

"Alice!" Ben Bryn said for the third time since he had entered the apartment. This time his voice was husky with horror.

He stepped into the bedroom. And suddenly the lights went out and the door slammed behind him.

He whirled, his right hand streaking intuitively for the gun under his armpit, which, of course, he was not carrying tonight. But even had he had his gun, he would not have been able to get it out, for a monstrous shape hurled itself at him from the wall. The only light in the room now came from a feeble moon low in the sky, but it was sufficient to barely outline the form. Bryn put everything he had into a left jab into his attacker's midriff. He heard an agonized grunt, felt the charge stop momentarily—then something like a thunderbolt exploded under his jaw.

It seemed to Bryn that he flew upward from the floor, then backward. Haze possessed his brain. Another violent blow, this time against his temple, and he went down heavily. He felt raw, blood-soaked flesh under him, knew with a sense of horror that he had fallen on Alice Foley's mangled corpse, and tried to force his semi-paralyzed muscles to get him on his feet.

Through super-human effort he was halfway up to his feet, when abruptly consciousness was completely blotted out. . . .

Ben Bryn opened his eyes to look up at the worried face of Dr. Barley, the medical examiner. He started to rise, felt pain lance his head, but he sat up anyway. He was on the couch in the living room. The place was jammed with homicide men who had suddenly become very quiet. They were staring at him queerly.

Bryn fingered his throbbing skull, felt bandage. His brain was in a whirl. He tried to remember what had happened, suddenly straightened up as he saw the dried blood on his hands, saw blood caked on his jacket and shirt. Not his own blood.

"My God!" he said. "Alice!"

Nobody said anything. And now he saw what it was in the eyes which stared at him—loathing and a murderous anger.

He put his feet on the floor, fumbled in his pocket for his cigarette-case. He couldn't find it. "Anybody got a smoke?" he asked.

None of the homicide men moved. Dr. Barley took a package from his pocket and tossed it on Bryn's lap. Bryn pulled one out with a blood-caked hand and lit it. He couldn't understand why they were all looking at him like that. Maybe it was shock because of what they had seen in the other room. Hot rage rose in him. He thought of Alice Foley, her trim little figure and pert little nose and dancing eyes. God, if he could only have another chance to get his hands on the monster!

Captain Grant Duncan, chief of the Homicide Bureau, came out of the bedroom. He strode across the room, planted his rangy figure in front of Bryn and stared down at him.

"All right, Ben," he snapped. "Let's have your story."

Bryn said: "I had a date to take Alice Foley to dinner and a show. I met her at a party a month ago. I'd taken her out a couple of times since. I came up here. She didn't answer my knock, but the door was open. I found her in her bedroom, or what was left of her. You've seen her."

H̲E PAUSED, shuddering, thinking again of how lovely she had been. He went on: "I was going into the bedroom when the lights went out and the killer was in there with me. I was a fool. I should have thought of the possibility that the killer might be hiding behind the open door. I couldn't get a good look at him because only the vaguest kind of light came from the moon, but he looked as big as the room itself. And he had enormous strength. I socked him in the midriff, but it didn't do more than make him grunt. Then he hit me twice with his fists and knocked me out."

"Knocked you out, eh?" Captain Duncan mused, rubbing his lean chin. "With his fists?"

"Yes. I didn't think anybody could, but he did." Again he felt the bandage on his head. "Wait a minute. I didn't go quite out. He must have sapped me while I was groggy."

"With a lead pipe," Duncan told him gloomily. "And the pipe was in your hand."

GRADUALLY Bryn was beginning to understand why they were looking at him like that. He blurted: "Good God, Captain, you don't think I knocked myself out?"

"It could be done," Duncan said. He turned to Dr. Barley. "Doc, an ordinary man, even a very strong one, let's say, couldn't kill a girl like that?"

Dr. Barley shook his head. "Not even a frail little thing like Alice Foley. Kipling once wrote a story about a gorilla who killed a girl. He said it was as if somebody had torn up a lot of paper and scattered it all over the room. Only it wasn't paper. Yes, a gorilla could, but not many men."

Slowly Duncan asked: "Doc, you know Ben here. You have an idea of how strong he is. Could he have done it?"

Dr. Barley nodded wordlessly.

Bryn leaned back against the couch. He wished his head would stop throbbing. "Why can't somebody else be as strong

as I am?" Bryn said. "Or stronger?"

Duncan ignored that. He said: "About a minute after you spoke to the desk clerk, the elevator operator brought you up here to the seventeenth floor. Alice Foley spoke to the clerk, telling him to send you up. You mean to say that a minute, or maybe two minutes, after she spoke to the clerk she was dead?"

"That's just what I'm saying," Bryn stated. "The killer could have got her as soon as she hung up, or maybe he forced her to answer the phone. Then, probably, he strangled her or broke her neck to keep her from crying out and did the rest to her. Then I came in and he waited for me."

"He'd be covered with as much blood as you are," Duncan said. "He would have been seen trying to get out."

"Maybe he went to one of the rooms on the floor. Did you look?"

Captain ran his tongue over his lips and rubbed his chin. Then he gave an order that all rooms on that floor and several floors above and below be searched.

Bryn said: "Who found the corpse and me?"

"The hotel dick, a guy named Egan. A woman next door phoned that she'd heard somebody cry out. She's a respectable old woman, so don't get any ideas about her. If it's the way you say it was, she heard you or the other guy yell. If you killed Alice Foley, maybe she had a chance to scream. When the report came in that Ben Bryn had gone kill-crazy, I decided to come up myself."

Bryn took another cigarette from Dr. Barley's package. "Why would I want to kill the girl?"

"I don't know—yet. A lover's quarrel, like so many killings. You wanted to get rid of her for some reason or other."

"But we weren't lovers. I told you I'd taken her out only a couple of times."

Duncan said: "That's your story. Maybe it's true. Or maybe you thought we'd trace any other method of killing her to you and decided to make up a story about a human monster and knock yourself out with a pipe."

Bryn rolled the cigarette between his fingers. "Look, Captain. You've known me for some time. On occasion we've worked together. Do you think I could murder a girl in cold blood and as brutally as that?"

Duncan looked at a spot on the ceiling above Bryn's head. "I'm trying not to think that, but I can't help it. Sorry, Ben, but I'm charging you with the murder of Alice Foley."

CHAPTER TWO

The Second Corpse

FOR eight hours they worked on Ben Bryn in a basement room in headquarters. The wrecking crew had a reputation for being tough, but they had never been as tough as this. Many of them had known and respected him, but they had seen the thing that had been Alice Foley and they went at him in a kind of frenzy.

Bryn took it stoically, without anger, knowing that things looked pretty black for him but not too black. There wasn't enough evidence to get a conviction or even an indictment.

Dully he repeated over and over. "You haven't shown me why it couldn't be a frame."

"A frame!" a detective spat out. "That's the squeal of every rat."

"What's my possible motive?"

"That's what you're going to tell us," another detective said, and they went at him again.

They didn't smack him or use the rubber hose. Even though there were six of them, and they had him more or less at their mercy, they were still in awe of his physical strength. But their nagging was harder to stand than any blows would have been.

Throughout the night Captain Duncan drifted wearily in and out of the room. The last time he entered he announced in a tired voice: "All right, boys, let up. There's a mouthpiece outside who has papers for his release."

"Damn the lawyers!" a detective said between his teeth. "He'll go out and tear somebody else to pieces."

"I don't think so," Duncan stated flatly. "If he killed the Foley girl, it was in a fit of rage, and we'll get him for it yet." He went over to Bryn. "Maybe the way you tell it is true. It could be. That's why you're being sprung, because some big shots who think a lot of you don't think there's enough evidence to hold you. I hope to God they're right."

Bryn didn't say anything. He stood up on unsteady legs and brushed past Duncan. Upstairs in the lobby a swarthy man waited for him with firm mouth smiling thinly. Bryn had never before spoken to him, but he recognized him as Victor Clayborn, a rather well-known criminal lawyer.

Clayborn extended a hand and pumped Bryn's arm. "It was an outrage, Bryn!" he said. "Did they do anything to you down there? If they did, I'll set the department on its ear."

"Never mind that," Bryn told him. "How did you come in? Why the interest in me?"

Clayborn smirked with secret knowledge. "A friend of yours dragged me out of bed a couple of hours ago. Since then I've been burning up the town."

"A friend?"

"You have a great many. I was asked to keep the name confidential, and, of course, an attorney's ethics forbid—"

"Thanks," Bryn said and started for the street.

Clayborn hurried after him. "If there is anything else I can do—"

"No," Bryn said. "You can't help me find Alice Foley's murderer."

Dawn was breaking when Bryn stepped into the street. The air was clear and fresh and felt good in his lungs. In spite of his disheveled appearance and the dried blood on his clothes, he decided to walk home in order to get the cramp out of his bones and the fog out of his head. Once a patrolman on the other side of the street stared at him with interest, but didn't cross over to question him.

Fifteen minutes after he had left headquarters, Bryn slipped into the apartment house where he lived. He took a hot shower, scrubbed himself thoroughly, then turned on the cold water full force. He hadn't slept in twenty-four hours, but he had no time for sleep now. Feeling considerably revived by the shower, he set about preparing breakfast. He turned on the radio for the six-thirty news broadcast to hear what the press had to say about the murder of Alice Foley.

H E WAS frying eggs in the kitchen when the news came on. The first item was about the murder, about himself being found on the scene of the crime and being held by the police. Then the announcer drifted into the troubles of Europe.

Suddenly the announcer's voice rose excitedly. "Here's something that came in a moment ago, folks. It's a flash. At about six o'clock this morning—that is, thirty-five minutes ago—Ben Bryn, the private detective who was being held by the police for the brutal murder of Alice Foley, was released because of insufficient evidence. Seven minutes after he walked out of police headquarters, Leland Ansley, a wealthy building contractor, was murdered in his home in precisely the same way as Alice Foley. Ansley was torn to pieces by a man of prodigious strength."

Bryn slid the eggs onto a plate and went into the living room in order to hear more clearly. His heart was thumping.

"Police are convinced that Ben Bryn committed this crime, and are certain now that he had also murdered Alice Foley. A silver cigarette-case bearing the initials B. B. was found a few inches from the corpse, apparently having been dropped by the killer. In addition, a patrolman states that he saw a man answering Bryn's description hurrying along the street a block from Ansley's residence. The time has been established as being a few minutes after the crime was committed. Police state that Bryn, who is noted for his physical strength, was one of the few men alive who could literally tear apart a man like Ansley, who weighed one hundred and sixty pounds.

"Rhea Ansley, wife of the murdered man, was asleep in the adjoining bedroom when she was awakened by a falling object, probably a chair knocked over in Ansley's room. She called out and, hearing no reply, got out of bed to investigate. She opened the door connecting the two rooms in time to glimpse a shape slipping out through the window. Her screams roused the servants who immediately called the police.

"Police advance the theory that Bryn, who has often killed desperate criminals in the line of duty, has become possessed by a homicidal mania. Considerable criticism is due to fall on Judge Robert E. Michaels who signed the writ of habeas corpus, and on District Attorney Clemens who forced Bryn's release by asserting that there was insufficient evidence against Bryn for an indictment.

"That's all for now. Keep your radio tuned to this station for further news about these horrible crimes."

Bryn clicked the radio off. For all of a minute he stood motionless, staring at the radio cabinet, his body bathed in perspiration. Whoever was behind the two murders had wrapped a neat frame around him. The timing had been perfect. Both murders had been planned in advance. It had been known just when he would visit Alice Foley, and while he had been unconscious his cigarette-case had been taken from him to plant at the scene of the second murder. If only he had taken a taxi from headquarters, he would have an alibi; but nobody had seen him except the cop who had observed him hurrying home.

Damnable perfect. There was only one way to save himself and that was to find the murderer. What a chance, with everybody in the city watching out for him, with the police probably having been instructed to shoot to kill at the sight of him.

The telephone jangled. Mechanically Bryn picked it up.

"Mr. Bryn? Oh, thank God you are at home." It was a woman's voice, tense, obviously frightened.

"Yes?" Bryn said.

"I just heard on the radio about the murder of Leland Ansley. They're accusing you. I know you didn't do it. I think I can help you."

"How?"

"Because, you see, I know who the murderer is."

He gripped the phone tighter. "Go on."

"I can't tell you over the phone. You must come here, at once. My name is Joyce Daily. I live at Three-twenty-one Parkview Place. Please hurry, Mr. Bryn, because I—I'm in danger of my life."

"Why don't you call the police?"

"No!" Joyce Daily cried. "I haven't enough evidence and—and you'll see when I've spoken to you."

"All right," he said. "Just one more thing. As you seem to be convinced of my innocence, did you hire Victor Clayborn to spring me?"

"Victor Clayborn? I—yes, of course. I was the one. You'll come at once?"

"Yes. But why—"

He heard a click and the wire was dead.

HE WENT into the bedroom and put on a shoulder harness and stuck a .45 automatic into the holster. Flicking through a telephone directory, he found that Joyce Daily really did live at the address she had given him. He stopped off in the kitchen to eat the cold eggs and drink a cup of steaming coffee. He drank looking out of the kitchen window.

A black sedan stopped in front and plainclothesmen tumbled out. They didn't make much attempt at secrecy, certain, no doubt, that he would not be foolhardy enough to return to his apartment. But they had to try every angle.

He took the fire stairs up to the roof. They would find his blood-smeared clothes in the apartment and figure that he had been home to change and then had fled.

The apartment house was seven stories high. Smack up against it was another house two stories lower. He dropped to the lower house, landing on his feet with a considerable jolt, and went down the stairs. He knew that the entrance of this other house was around the corner. He went out the front entrance into the deserted street and hurried away in the opposite direction from the police car.

The address Joyce Daily had given him wasn't more than six blocks away, but he did the distance rather slowly. His short, stocky build made him too easily recognizable. He walked along the sides of buildings, ducking into doorways whenever anybody passed. Fortunately it was still too early for many people to be on the street.

The house in which Joyce Daily lived was one of a neat line of two-story stucco structures on the block. For several moments he stood at the corner surveying the street, figuring out from the number of the corner house that Three-twenty-one must be the third house down. He went up the driveway of the corner house, found himself in a fenced-in back garden and climbed two wire fences until he was in the back of number Three-twenty-one. No sound came from that house, or from any of the others.

Bryn tried the back door. It was locked, but a skeleton key opened it without difficulty. Noiselessly he went through the downstairs rooms. No sign of life. Had he arrived too late?

On his toes he ascended the carpeted stairs. At the head of the stairs he paused. He had no way of knowing which was Joyce Daily's bedroom, but he had an idea that it would be one of the rooms facing the street. Softly he moved to the first door, placed his ear against the panel. Faint snores came to him. He went to the next door and again listened.

At first he heard absolutely nothing. Then his straining ears caught a muted, stifled sound, as of somebody trying to speak through a gag. Pulling his gun out and placing it in his left hand, he pushed the door in.

A large man stood at a window looking down into the street. One of his huge arms was wound around a girl clad only in a nightgown, pinning her arms to her side. His other hand was clamped over the girl's mouth.

CHAPTER THREE

The Masked Man

AT BRYN'S entrance, the man who held Joyce Daily spun toward the door. His entire face was covered by a black mask. Bryn had assumed that the slayer of Alice Foley and Leland Ansley was some sort of moronic sub-human monster, but there was nothing freakish about the man he confronted.

He wasn't more than six feet tall and probably didn't weigh more than two hundred pounds, yet that body, as Bryn knew from experience, was solid muscle, possessing a strength which was perhaps greater than his own. His clothes were expensive and well-fitting, and although Bryn could not see his face, he sensed ordinary human intelligence behind that mask.

For a long moment the two men and the girl were rigid. Then Ben Bryn said: "Surprise! Did you imagine I would fall for that gag? Why would a girl like Joyce Daily be listening to a radio at six-thirty in the morning? She was obviously being forced to phone me. This was a continuation of the frame-up formula. You were watching for me through the window. As soon as you saw me you'd kill Miss Daily. No doubt the police have already been tipped off. I was to be trapped here."

The masked man said nothing. Joyce Daily gazed at Bryn with brown eyes in which terror and relief mingled. Held there against the big body of the masked man and clad only in a sheer silk nightgown, she looked like a frightened child.

Bryn said: "Release her."

Still the masked man did not move. Bryn brought his gun up. He could easily send a bullet between the eyes of the mask, but he had to capture this man alive in order to clear himself. The masked man must have known it. As if he were lifting a doll, he raised Joyce Daily a foot from the ground and held her in front of him.

"That won't do any good," Bryn said. "I can get the lower part of your legs. I can cut you to pieces with .45 slugs without touching the girl. And there'll be enough of you left to turn over to the police. In three seconds I start shooting."

The masked man acted then. He threw the girl at Bryn.

There was so little preliminary motion behind the act, so little apparent effort required by the masked man to hurl the one hundred and five pound girl ten feet through the air, that Bryn was taken wholly by surprise. He saw the white, squirming body of the girl coming at him, and yet was helpless to do anything about it. His gun was useless. He tried to sidestep, couldn't quite get out of the way.

Warm flesh struck the side of his chest. A soft arm lashed his face. He staggered back a step or two, but didn't fall. The girl's screams filled the room, clashed against his eardrums. She hit the floor with a dull plop and the screams were suddenly choked off.

The whole thing took three or four seconds. The masked man was no longer in the bedroom. Bryn went through the door into the hall, heard feet pounding down the stairs. The front door had opened and slammed shut by the time Bryn had gone halfway down the stairs. When Bryn got the front door open, he saw a grey sedan roaring away from the front of the house.

Bryn decided not to risk a shot after the car. There wasn't much chance of doing any damage; a shot could only rouse the neighborhood and bring the police sooner. He went back into the house.

He dashed up to Joyce Daily's room. She was on her feet, breathing hard. He heard a voice call, "Miss Joyce, are you all right? Who screamed?"

He closed the door, turned the key. "Tell them you had a nightmare," he whispered.

"Why, I—"

"Do as I say!"

F ISTS were pounding on the door. "Miss Joyce, did you scream?" a woman's voice demanded. Then a second woman shrilled: "Let me in, Joyce!"

She looked at Bryn with a puzzled expression, then nodded. She went to the door.

"I'm all right. I had a nightmare and awoke screaming."

"But I heard feet on the stairs and the front door slam," the first voice insisted.

She bit her lips. "I started to go downstairs for a drink. Then I changed my mind and came back. It was my door you heard slam. Now will you please let me go back to sleep?"

There was a whispered consultation in the hall.

Finally the voices moved away and Bryn heard doors close.

Bryn asked: "Who were they?"

"Our housekeeper, Mrs. Marin, and my Aunt Kate with whom I live."

"Are they the only ones in the house?"

"Yes."

He went to the window, looked out, and turned to Joyce Daily. "Are you all right? Were you hurt?"

"I just had the wind knocked out of me."

He stood looking at her. She was a delicate little thing, with large brown eyes and perfectly proportioned features and figure. If he had not realized the trap, she would now be gruesome bits of flesh and blood spattered over the room. Bitterly he cursed himself for having let the killer get away.

Under his scrutiny, she became aware that she was clad only in a sheer nightgown. Crossing her arms over her half-exposed breasts, she went to a closet and got into a housecoat.

She said: "Thank you for saving my life, Mr. Bryn. I had to phone you. He held me, told me he'd tear me apart if I didn't, and that he'd do the same thing to my aunt. I was crazy with fear. I—"

"That's all right," Bryn told her. "You couldn't know that he was going to kill you anyway."

"But why? I never saw him before in my life."

Bryn tensed at the window. Two autos were coming up the street.

He spun toward her. "The police! Can you hide me here? In the cellar perhaps?"

Her eyes opened wide. "But I don't understand. I can prove that you're innocent."

He gripped her arm. "Please take my word for it. The police mustn't know that I was here. And don't tell them about the killer. If your aunt or the housekeeper mention the screams, tell the police the same story about the nightmare. You've got to trust me. We're both in danger."

She smiled wanly. "Yes, I trust you."

He unlocked the door, whispered over his shoulder: "Come down to the cellar after you've got rid of the police. And don't let a soul know I'm down there."

He went down the stairs quickly, noiselessly. He was opening the door to the cellar in the kitchen when the front bell rang. Through the kitchen window he glimpsed men turning the back corner of the house and making for the back door. He closed the cellar door behind him and went down the steps.

By the light of matches he looked around. The only place to hide was behind a couple of trunks and if the police decided to search the house, he wouldn't be very safe. But if Joyce Daily played her part well they wouldn't bother to search.

Standing there in the dim light, he listened to feet moving over the floor above, listened to a jumble of voices, doors opening and closing, the sound of motors in the street. Once the cellar door was pulled open and Bryn slid back behind the trunks with pounding heart. He heard one man say to another:

"Guess it was some guy's idea of a joke." Then the door closed and feet moved away from the kitchen.

Presently the police departed. A silence settled over the house, broken after a while by the sound of breakfast preparations in the kitchen. Hours passed during which Bryn sat on a trunk and burned cigarettes.

IT WAS pretty close to noon before he heard the light steps coming down for which he had been waiting. A voice whispered: "Mr. Bryn?"

"I'm still here."

Joyce Daily came down with a tray of food. "I'm sorry I couldn't come sooner. I thought it best to get the other two women out of the house. I persuaded them to go downtown shopping."

"Good girl," Bryn said. He took the tray from her and placed it on the trunk and pulled over two wooden boxes. He sat down on one and Joyce Daily sat on the other.

"You've been swell," Bryn told her as he started on the food. "I suppose you want to know what it's all about."

"I have an idea," she said. "I know Alice Foley and Leland Ansley were murdered by the man from whom you saved me. He told me that when he made me phone you; he even described how he had killed them." Her frail shoulders quivered. "And I heard from the police just now that they were sure you were guilty. Of course I know you aren't. Several times I was at the point of telling them the truth so that I could prove your innocence, but you had asked me not to. I can't understand why."

He patted her hand. "Don't you see that your word alone would not prove me innocent? Nobody but you and I saw the killer. The police think they have pretty conclusive proof against me. They'd have the idea you were my girl friend who'd made up that story with my help in order to save my skin. They'd think the same thing even if you had only told them the killer had been here and been scared away by their arrival, without mentioning my presence. Cops know their business. They'd have searched this house and have found me."

"I see," she said. "And you want to be free so that you can find the murderer because he killed the girl you loved?"

"I didn't love Alice Foley, though she was a swell kid. Yes, I want to get my hands on the killer because of what he did to her and because, frankly, I want to save myself. And there's another reason: while the killer is alive, you're in danger. I don't want to frighten you, but it's best that you know the truth."

She sat forward on the box, her hands clasped before her, the clear skin of her face taut.

"Nobody can gain by killing me," she said quietly.

"Did you know Alice Foley?"

"Slightly. Her father and mine had been business partners."

"And where does Leland Ansley fit in?"

"His father had been my father's partner, too. I'd thought of the connection at once, but I can't see where it means anything. The iron mine which they had owned in Minnesota had been played out years ago. My father left me the shares, but they are worthless."

Slowly Bryn stirred his coffee. "Were there any more partners?"

"O**NE** more. Howard Douglas. He died some years ago, but his widow is alive. She lives in this city. If you think anybody would try to murder us for the possession of that useless mine, you're wrong. Even if the mines were worth anything, no outside party could get hold of our shares.

"The four men were very close friends when they discovered the mine. They were Patrick Foley, John Ansley, Howard Douglas and Father. They'd been poor men; together they had gone through a great deal of struggle and privation and heartbreak before they succeeded in making the mine pay. So they had resolved that no outsiders, no banks or speculators, would ever get control of the mine. Possession, they decided, must never go outside their families. So they had signed papers to the effect that ownership of the mine could be transferred only once, to the nearest of kin, to a wife or child after the death of any of them. When the person to whom the shares were transferred died, the shares of that person would be divided equally among the remaining owners. This would prevent any sort of speculation or sale or control by an outsider."

"So now," Bryn said, putting down his coffee cup, "Alice Foley's and Leland Ansley's shares will be divided between you and Mrs. Douglas. And if you die, Mrs. Douglas gets the whole business."

She nodded solemnly. "But I think we're wasting time discussing this, because Mrs. Douglas surely wouldn't have anything to do with murder and because the mine is worthless anyway."

Bryn stood up. "The fact remains that either the man in the mask or somebody directing him wants you three out of the way. I've simply been chosen as the fallguy. The killer probably meant to finish the murder orgy with you. He intended to kill you as soon as he saw me enter the house. I think he delayed killing you so that you could scream just after I entered the house. Then he could have said that he'd been passing, had heard you scream, and had rushed to your rescue—too late. He would then say that I attacked him, and he had to kill me in self-defense. That would have been perfect from his angle. The three people he wanted out of the way for some reason or other would be dead. I would be blamed. Fortunately, I was the one to spring the surprise."

"And you think he'll try again?"

Bryn nodded and started to stride back and forth. Suddenly he stopped. "Over the phone you said you'd retained Victor Clayborn to spring me. Is that true?"

"No. With that fiend standing beside me, I was ready to answer yes to anything. I'd never heard of Clayborn."

Bryn said: "Somebody was anxious to have me released, no doubt the murderer. While I was being held by the police, Ansley's murder couldn't be pinned on me, nor could yours." He snapped his fingers impatiently. "I've got to get out of here."

"But how can you with all the police looking for you?" she protested.

His eyes twinkled suddenly. "What's your aunt's figure? Is she rather plump?"

"No," Joyce replied, obviously puzzled. "She's tall and thin." She shot a quick look at him. "Oh, I see. Our housekeeper, Mrs. Marin, is just about your build. Rather big in front and in the shoulders." She smiled. "You'll make an interesting woman."

CHAPTER FOUR

Ordeal of Strength

JOYCE DAILY said: "My dear auntie, stop walking so jauntily. It isn't becoming for a woman of your years."

Ben Bryn let his feet lag. It wasn't hot out, but he was beginning to perspire under the brown wig which Joyce had found in the attic, and the heavy make-up felt as if it were cracking his face. Mrs. Marin evidently had big feet, but her shoes were still too small for him.

"And keep your hands out of sight," Joyce cautioned. "No woman has hands to big and hairy. Otherwise you make a very sweet matron—from a distance. Fortunately you haven't that severe manhunter face. You look almost kindly."

Ben Bryn growled: "I still don't like the idea of your coming with me. There's bound to be fireworks sooner or later."

"But you told me yourself that you were afraid to leave me alone," she pointed out. "I'm sure I'll be safest with you."

He hugged her hand which was tucked through his arm. In front of a newsstand he stopped and picked up a couple of eve-ning papers. His right hand started to move to the side of his skirt as if he were about to dip into his trouser pocket for change. Joyce grabbed his arm and opened her handbag and paid for the papers. In the handbag he carried lay his big automatic.

Photographs of Ben Bryn were smeared over the front pages of every paper, accompanied by detailed descriptions. "Monster" and "fiend" were some of the milder terms applied to him. The newspapers were hysterical over what they stated was his one-man campaign of terror and declared that not a single life in the city was safe while he was at large. Editorials vigorously attacked Judge Robert E. Michaels and District Attorney Clemens as having been responsible for his release.

"The beasts!" Joyce cried. "They've condemned you without giving you a trial."

"That's the way of newspapers," Bryn said as he dropped the papers into a refuse can.

In a short time they reached an office building in the business section. Letters on a frosted window on the fourth floor said: VICTOR CLAYBORN, ATTORNEY-AT-LAW.

After a ten minute wait they were admitted into an inner office. Clayborn sat behind a desk.

He rose and came toward Joyce with an outstretched hand. "I have never had the pleasure of meeting you, Miss Daily, but I knew your father quite well." Then he looked at Bryn and waited for Joyce to introduce him.

Bryn said: "You're my lawyer, Clayborn. Look close and you'll see who I am. Ethics require that you protect your client, even from the police."

Clayborn's eyes popped. He backed away from Bryn until he was stopped by his desk.

"You needn't be afraid of him, Mr.

Clayborn," Joyce said. "I know he's not the murderer, but there is no way of making the police believe it. The real murderer tried to kill me and Mr. Bryn saved my life."

Clayborn sidled around the desk and dropped heavily into his swivel-chair. He pulled open a drawer.

"Don't try to go for a gun," Bryn warned. "I'm faster and better than you."

"All right," Clayborn said thickly, shutting the drawer. "What are you after?"

"The answer to just one question: Who hired you to spring me?"

"I promised—"

"My God, man!" Bryn interrupted. "This means my life and the life of this girl. Everything may depend on the answer." He dropped his voice. "You're going to tell me, Clayborn, if I have to choke it out of you."

Clayborn ran a dry tongue over his lips. Weakly he said: "Mrs. Theresa Douglas."

Joyce Daily emitted a little cry. "No! She couldn't—"

"She was the one," Clayborn asserted. "I handle all her legal business. Now, for God's sake, will you leave? Suppose you're found here!"

"You're not telling the police about my disguise," Bryn said quietly. "You wouldn't want me to hunt you down after I'm declared innocent, would you?"

Clayborn's swarthy face paled by a couple of shades. "I swear I won't say a word. Now please go."

Bryn fixed his steady blue eyes on Clayborn and the lawyer cringed in his seat. Then Bryn smiled and took Joyce's arm and they left.

IN THE hall Bryn said: "He's too scared to talk—I hope. That's the chance we have to take. Now for Theresa Douglas."

"She can't be involved," Joyce said.

"She's a sweet old woman who wouldn't harm a fly."

Bryn shrugged. "We'll see."

Theresa Douglas lived in an ultra-modern bungalow on the outskirts of the city. Bryn and Joyce Daily drove there by taxi.

"Remember, you do all the talking," Bryn whispered to her as they went up the flagstone walk. "I don't trust my voice to sound feminine. Bring up the subject of this horrible Ben Bryn and quizz her about hiring Clayborn. There's a chance we'll learn other things, too."

"If we come through this alive, I'll make a fine detective," she commented.

There was no answer to Joyce's ring. "That's odd," she said. "There should be at least a servant in the house."

Bryn tried the doorknob and to his surprise the door opened. They stepped into the house.

"Perhaps she's been killed, too," Joyce whispered tightly.

Bryn said nothing. Cautiously they went through the living room, found themselves in a tiny foyer into which the bedroom doors opened. Bryn pushed one of the doors open and looked into a bedroom.

"Looks as if we're up against a blank wall," he muttered gloomily. "At least temporarily."

Then Joyce shrieked.

She had opened the door on the opposite side of the foyer, and he whirled to see her swaying against the door-jamb. Her shriek had died into gasping whimpers. He leaped to her side, threw an arm about her, and looked into the room.

He had known at once what he would see in this bedroom, but he had expected the body to be that of a woman. It was a man. He was a less horrible sight than Alice Foley had been, because he was, on the whole, in one piece. But he had been murdered in much the same way. His neck was obviously broken and one of his arms had been torn from its socket. There was a lot of blood.

The dead man had been past sixty, grey-haired, retaining even in death some of the dignity which had distinguished him in life.

Bryn said hoarsely: "Judge Robert Michaels! Where in heaven's name does he fit in? As far as I know, his only connection with this mess is that he signed the writ of habeas corpus for me."

Joyce moved away from the open door in order to shut out the sight. "Judge Michaels was going to marry Theresa Douglas, or so it was rumored," she said in a thin voice. She held tightly to Bryn. "Suppose the police catch you here, they'll blame you for this, too. You said yourself my word mightn't be enough."

"It seems the trail leads only to corpses," Bryn observed bitterly.

They walked across the living room with his arm about her waist. Suddenly she stopped and stared at a photograph on the grand piano. It was the picture of a young man clad in swimming trunks.

His face was handsome; his thin lips were twisted in a cynical half-smile. He was big, powerfully built. Across the bottom of the photograph was scrawled: *"To Mom from Clyde."*

"That must be Clyde Douglas, Theresa's only child," Joyce muttered. "I haven't seen him since he was a small boy. He's been out in California all these years."

There was a tense silence as both continued to stare at the photograph. Joyce clutched convulsively at Bryn's arm.

"It might be . . . Do you think—"
Slowly Bryn said: "It's possible."

"More than possible." A voice behind them chuckled. There in the doorway stood the young man of the photograph.

EARLY that morning he had been wearing a mask, but there wasn't any doubt about the big, solid, muscular body,

about that barrel chest. This was a man powerful enough to tear a human being to pieces.

Clyde Douglas kept on laughing. "How thoughtful of me to have persuaded my mother to visit relatives for a few days, and to have given the servants the day off. I reasoned that you might come here. And how thoughtful of you, Ben Bryn, to have brought the charming Joyce Daily with you. Joyce, you understand, came here to visit Mother and you followed her here in order to kill her. Judge Michaels also dropped in and you murdered him. Fortunately I arrived in time to kill you, you human monster; but alas, not in time to save either the Judge or Joyce."

Bryn moved in front of Joyce. Softly he said: "Do you think you can do it?"

There was something hideous about the boyish grin on the face of the man who had killed three innocent people with his bare hands within the last twenty-four hours.

"I flatter myself that I can," Clyde Douglas smiled. "I know of your reputation for strength, Bryn. In fact, that's why I chose you for my dupe. No doubt against ordinary men your strength means something. But not to me. Of course, you are probably cowardly enough to try to pull a gun on me. I don't need any."

With an impulsive gesture of contempt, Bryn tossed his handbag through an open door.

"My gun was in there," he explained. "I don't need one, either. Let's go." He kicked off the tight shoes, and his matronly coat, in order to allow himself more freedom of movement.

"Wait!" Joyce cried, stepping between the two men. "Clyde, we used to play together when we were children. Why should you want to kill me?"

"To prevent you from cheating me out of a fortune," Clyde Douglas stated without emotion. "Because of a crackpot agreement our parents and their two partners signed many years ago, not a cent from the iron mine will come to me. My father transferred ownership once already, which means that when my mother dies her share would be divided between you and Ansley and Alice Foley. But with you three dead, mother gets it all—in which case she will legally be able to leave it to me."

"But the mines are valueless," Joyce protested.

"Until recently they were. But a new process has been invented which will make millions of tons of low-grade ore marketable."

Joyce looked at him with revulsion. "You beast! Your mother—"

"Leave her out of this!" Clyde Douglas burst out. "She knows nothing about the mine. She doesn't know I killed anybody and she'll never know."

Bryn asked: "Where does Judge Roberts fit in?"

Douglas scowled. "Like a fool I told him about the value of the mine. I went to him for legal advice, and he assured me that I hadn't a chance of getting a penny unless the three others died before my mother did. He knew I'd killed Alice Foley and Ansley, but he said nothing. Not that he would have had any proof. He was playing his own game. After Joyce was dead he meant to dig up some proof and give me away to the police. Then he'd marry my mother and—"

Clyde Douglas moved while he was still talking—moved so swiftly that both Bryn and Joyce were taken completely by surprise. Every nerve and muscle taut, Bryn had been waiting for the attack, but he had expected Douglas to leap at him and not at Joyce.

Douglas hurled himself at Joyce, and before she could make a step or utter a sound, one of his big hands swung at her. At the least he would have broken her jaw had not Bryn marred his aim. But some of the damage had already been done. Douglas' fist grazed Joyce's chin and knocked her against the piano. She crumpled unconscious to the floor.

Cursing harshly, Bryn went after the bigger man. Douglas had made sure that Joyce would not be able to flee during the fight.

BRYN bore in with both fists. Douglas gave ground, sparring. It was obvious that he did not want to box. Twice he tried to get his hands on Bryn and twice Bryn rocked him with lefts which would have lifted the head from the shoulders of an ordinary man. Douglas only shook his head and smiled and came in again. At the third attempt he got his arms around Bryn and squeezed, and then Bryn knew that he was closer to death than he had ever been before.

Those weren't flesh-and bone arms which were crushing Bryn's bones, which seemed to be forcing his heart through his ribs. They were arms of steel, and the torso against which Bryn's fists flailed seemed to consist of granite. Any other man would have been finished then and there, but Bryn's own strength was far from ordinary.

Bryn allowed himself to fall backward, bringing his knees in Douglas' stomach with an impact which made the bigger man grunt. Douglas' grip loosened and Bryn rolled free and bounced up to his feet.

Again the two men faced each other, Douglas towering above Bryn by nearly a foot. Bitterly now Bryn regretted the bravado which had made him toss his gun away. It was not only his life for which he was fighting, but the life of Joyce as well.

But this was no time for regrets. Once again they were locked in conflict and then they were rolling on the floor. The next few minutes would forever remain a vague blur in Bryn's memory. There were no tricks of wrestling, no science. This was a struggle of two primitive, ruthless, merciless beasts fighting to the death.

The smile had been wiped from Douglas' face, which was now blood-streaked. Instead he was plainly worried. He had met a man who was nearly his own match in strength, and who more than made up for that difference in an all-pervading determination, in the consciousness that he was fighting for an innocent girl. . . .

And then at last a man was staggering to his feet—alone. The dress he had been wearing hung in tatters. His face was a pulp. He felt as weak as a kitten. With an effort he staggered over to where Joyce Daily lay, grasped the side of the piano to keep himself from falling.

"Joyce!" he muttered weakly.

She looked up at him and he realized that her eyes must have been open for some time.

A sense of relief gushed through him. "Are you hurt?"

She smiled wanly up at him and felt her chin. "When I came to I thought my jaw was broken, but I guess it's just bruised."

The smile vanished as she looked at the form of Clyde Douglas on the floor. "Dead?" she whispered.

Bryn shook his head. "Somehow I managed to break his right arm and then it was all over. I had to leave him alive to give him a chance to confess so that I'd be cleared."

Then Bryn slid slowly to the floor at her side. She leaned over him, crying: "You're hurt!"

He grinned feebly. "Just weak as a new-born baby. Be a good girl and phone the police."

When she returned from the telephone, she found Ben Bryn sitting astride of Clyde Douglas. Douglas had regained consciousness.

"The police will be here in a few minutes," Bryn was saying. "You'll tell them them everything or—"

Bryn grasped Douglas' broken arm. Douglas shrieked, "Yes, yes, I'll talk!" Then he passed out again.

Some time later Captain Duncan burst into the house at the head of a squad of police. A full confession signed by Clyde Douglas was waiting for him. Ben Bryn was lying on the couch with his head on Joyce Daily's lap. Tenderly she was sponging his face.

When Captain Duncan had finished reading the confession, he went over to the couch and stood looking down at Bryn.

"Can't tell you how sorry I am, Ben. But I had to do my duty as I saw it."

"Forget it," Ben Bryn said. "And run along. Can't you see the young lady doesn't want to be disturbed?"

THE END

A Full-Length Novel

PREY FOR THE CREEPING DEATH

by

RUSSELL GRAY

"Let me plug this guy," Willy growled. "Then we can get to work on the girl."

Unless Ben Bryn could halt, somehow, the relentless and horrible march of that creeping plague, it was curtains for him—and for the girl who had trusted him!

CHAPTER ONE

Summons from the Dead

BEN BRYN read the note twice. The writing was scrawled, shaky; obviously the hand had been unsteady. Was it a hoax of some kind?

Perhaps a trap? His hand moved to the telephone on his desk, hovered above it for several moments, then he changed his mind. He scowled over the note again.

Dear Mr. Bryn:

In the name of heaven, come to me as soon as you have read this! I dare not go to see you and I dare not telephone you. I write this locked in my room with the windows bolted. I shall slip this letter under the door and Pauline, my maid, has been instructed to drop it into the mailbox.

You may not be able to save me from the horrible creeping death. I think that no power on earth can—now. I am burning up alive! But the worst of all is dying like this alone, without making an effort.

Hurry, Mr. Bryn! Heed what is probably the last plea of an old woman.

Desperately,

Marianne Carson

Ben Bryn stuck the letter in his pocket and went across the street to the office of the *Evening Advance*.

As he moved across the city room, men and women glanced up from their desks at his short, stocky figure. Some looked after him with curious eyes; others nodded to him. He stopped in front of a desk behind which an attractive brunette was hunched over a typewriter.

"Hello, Helen," he said.

Helen Forrest rose languidly and extended a slim hand. "I suppose it is foolish for my heart to do a handstand in the hope that you have come here to see me," she said in her liquid voice. "I'm not a woman to you. I'm simply society editor of the *Advance* and, as usual, you want information."

Ben Bryn's clear blue eyes twinkled. "I'm as susceptible as any man to beauty and charm."

She studied him between half-shut eyes. She was the willowy type and she knew that tall women made him uncomfortably conscious of his lack of height. He himself stood only five-feet-two, although the first impression of him was one of great power. It was a correct impression, for his tremendous shoulders, his smoothly muscled biceps, his large hands possessed a strength of which the underworld whispered in awe. Yet there was nothing cumbersome about him. His shoulders tapered down to the slender hips and legs of an athlete.

For twenty years of his life those legs had been useless appendages as the result of infantile paralysis. His youth had consisted of pushing himself about on a wheeled platform and selling newspapers and shoelaces. That had placed strength in his shoulders and hands and iron in his soul; and when a series of exercises he had evolved had eventually developed his legs to normal, that strength and that iron had made him the most feared criminal investigator in the state.

"What can I do for you?" Helen Forrest asked with a weary sigh.

"Who and what is Marianne Carson?"

Her sleepy eyes opened all the way. "My dear man, she's beyond the range of your profession. She's a respectable dowager, very much society; has successfully married off two daughters and a son and now lives in solitary splendor in an ancient mansion attended by a maid and a cook."

"Nothing shady in her past? No ugly gossip?"

"Not a whisper. And now that she's over seventy, she wouldn't care if there were."

"Thanks," Ben Bryn said. He was frowning as he walked out.

HE took a taxi to the address on the letterhead. As he was going up the walk of the neat colonial house, he saw the black crêpe on the front door, and it gave him an ugly start. Marianne Carson had written of the "creeping death" and here, not an hour after the delivery of her letter, the symbol of death was on her door.

A pretty girl in a trim maid's uniform came to the door. Her eyes were swollen with weeping.

"I'd like to see Marianne Carson," Bryn said.

"She—she's dead," the maid stammered.

Bryn nodded. "Are you Pauline?"

Her head jerked up, and suddenly she looked frightened. "Yes. Why?"

"I'm Ben Bryn. You mailed a letter addressed to me last night."

At the mention of his name the fear left her. "Come in." When he was in the hallway, she said: "For two days Mrs. Carson had been acting strangely. She locked herself in her room, even kept the windows shut in spite of the warm weather. She refused to come out for meals. She would open the door only wide enough for me to slip the tray through, then she'd quickly slam it. Last night, about eleven, she called me on the extension phone and said that in five minutes she'd slide a letter through under her door for me to mail. It wasn't more than thirty minutes later that the fire started. The poor thing! It's such a horrible way to die!"

"The fire?" Bryn said.

"She always insisted on smoking in bed. I guess she went to sleep with a cigarette in her hand. Cook and I had gone to bed when we heard her scream. We rushed to her room and found smoke coming through the cracks of the door. We tried to get in, but the door was locked. Cook rushed downstairs for an axe and I nearly went crazy standing out there listening to Mrs. Carson's frightful screams sinking lower and lower. And all the time I heard flames crackling.

"Finally cook came back and chopped an opening through the door. The bed was a mass of flames and the poor thing was still on the bed. Just then Mr. Powys came and we managed to put out the fire with pails of water from the bathroom,

but it was too late to save Mrs. Carson. She—"

"Who's Mr. Powys?" Bryn interrupted.

"Lace Powys, Mrs. Carson's brother."

"I thought Mrs. Carson lived alone."

"She did, but Mr. Powys dropped in."

"You said it was around midnight?"

The maid shot him a quick look. "I guess it is odd, now that I think of it. He very seldom comes here."

Bryn said: "I'd like to see the body."

"Upstairs in the second room to your right." The maid shuddered. "If you don't mind, I don't like going up there again."

BRYN ascended the stairs. The first door he came to was nothing but a splintered frame on hinges. Obviously this had been Marianne Carson's room. A glance was enough to show him the havoc the fire had wrought. The room smelled acridly of burned feathers.

The door to the second room was closed. He pushed the door inward and the first thing he saw was the long hump covered by a sheet on the bed. He strode in, pulled the sheet down. The pit of his stomach went abruptly hollow.

The face was not recognizable. There was no hair on the head. And the rest of the body was a blackened horror.

"Who the hell are you?" a voice behind him demanded.

Bryn turned leisurely. He saw a lanky man of about fifty-five glowering at him through horn-rimmed glasses.

"Lace Powys?" Bryn asked.

"That's right. Who gave you permission to come in here?"

"I'm a private investigator," Bryn said quietly. "Mrs. Carson hired me yesterday by letter. She was in fear of her life. Evidently that fear was justified.

"She died as the result of an unfortunate accident," Powsy snapped. "Clearly she's no longer your client. Good day."

BRYN replaced the sheet. "I'm not sure of that," he said. "She was burning up alive when she wrote me, but it wasn't from the fire in the bed. That came later. For some days she had been burning up slowly in some hideous fashion; that's why she had hidden herself. And she had locked herself in her room because she was afraid something like this would happen. Her bed was put on fire to hide the signs of what was done to her." ·

"You're crazy!" Bowys barked. "My sister was locked in her room. Nobody could get in there."

"Maybe," Bryn said.

He brushed past Powys and went down the stairs. Powys ran after him, demanding: "What do you intend to do now?"

"Gather some necessary information. Then I'll be back."

Powys' blustering manner changed suddenly. He seemed to shrivel before Bryn's eyes until he was only a very frightened and very helpless old man.

"No!" Powys whined. "For God's sake, don't come back here!"

Bryn fixed him with his steady blue eyes. "Why not?"

Powys caught his breath in a tortured sob. His tall frame shivered. Then he turned abruptly and strode away.

Bryn let himself out of the house and went reflectively down the walk. As he reached the edge of the walk, a man with great sloping shoulders and a bull neck stepped out from the tall hedges which surrounded the house. The man's right hand was sunk in his right topcoat pocket. Beyond him a sedan was parked at the curb. A man with a slouch hat pulled low over his forehead sat behind the wheel. The motor of the car was idling.

The big man said: "We don't like snooping. How about you stepping into that car and having a talk with me and my pal?" He pushed the barrel of his gun significantly against his pocket.

Bryn had his hands at his side. There wasn't a chance of him getting at his own gun. And no doubt the man in the car had a gun on his lap.

"I'm particular with whom I ride," Bryn said.

The big man came a step closer to Bryn. His right side was nearest Bryn. He muttered between his lips: "Okay by me if you want to get a belly-full of lead right here."

Bryn's fist drove up for a distance of twelve inches into the right forearm of the big man. A second later the big man's brain telegraphed his finger to pull the trigger, but by that time it was too late. The gunman's right arm and hand were useless. Bryn's blow had broken some of the small bones, had paralyzed the nerves.

The big man yelled stridently. Bryn jabbed up with his left, missed the jaw and laid open the left cheek, sending the big man in a heap against the hedge.

THEN Bryn was diving around to the other side of the hedge as the gunman in the sedan opened fire. Bryn jerked out his .45 automatic and crawled to the break in the hedge. The big man had had enough strength left to run around to the other side of the car. The sedan was already in motion; the big man was clinging to the running-board on the farther side.

Bryn had time for two shots. The first splintered the windshield inches from the driver's head; the second missed completely. The sedan skidded around the corner and was gone.

Bryn stood up, brushing himself off. His knuckles tingled pleasantly. The man he had hit had been at least twelve inches taller and must have outweighed him by more than fifty pounds, but it hadn't done him much good. Bryn's fists had the pulverizing power of a rock crusher.

People were pouring out of the houses on the block and, not wanting to be bothered with questions, Bryn hurried up the street. Glancing around at the Carson house, he saw the face of Lace Powys at a second floor window.

When Ben Bryn reached his office, he found a girl pacing agitatedly before the door. He came up behind her, asked in his soft voice: "Looking for somebody?"

She spun, crouching a little, as if she were about to leap into instant flight. Stark terror glinted in the depths of her eyes.

Then she straightened up and gasped with relief. "You're Ben Bryn?"

"Right. You wish to see me?"

"Yes."

He unlocked the door and led her into his office, pulled one of the leather chairs from the wall for her. She was a remarkably pretty girl. Yet there was an unnatural pallor on her smooth cheeks and the pupils of her eyes were dilated.

She stood facing him, gripping the back of the chair, and there was a mute plea in her hazel eyes as they met his sympathetic blue ones.

"Mr. Bryn," she said, her voice catching, "I want you to save my life."

CHAPTER TWO

The Death Brand

THE girl sank down in the chair, as if her limbs had suddenly lost all power to hold her up any longer. She buried her face in her hands and her shoulders heaved.

Ben Bryn placed a big hand gently on her arm. "Of course I'll do everything in my power to help you."

She turned a tear-stained face up to him. "It's not only that I'm afraid to die, or even the horrible way in which I'll die. It's the terrible strain, the suspense, the waiting."

"What makes you so sure you'll die?" Bryn asked.

"This," she said.

She stood up and started to unbutton the top of her dress. When she had the top buttons undone and started to slide the neck of the dress down over her shoulders, Bryn opened his mouth. He closed it again without saying anything, sat there watching her keenly.

Her naked shoulders were like polished marble. She pulled her dress down until the upper slopes of her firm, rounded breasts were bared. A jagged, brown, blistered splotch marred the curve of her right breast, extended narrow tentacles into the valley between her bosom.

"You've been burned!" Bryn exclaimed, jumping to his feet. "My dear girl, you should go to a doctor."

"No," she said dully. "Doctors can't help me. Perhaps you can. I don't know. I'm crazy with fear." She moved against him, clutching at his arm. "You have to help me, Mr. Bryn! You can't just let me die!"

"How did you get that burn?"

"I don't know. Two days ago I woke up and I found it on me. It was just a tiny spot at first. Then it started to grow."

Bryn said, "Some sort of fungus, perhaps. A close friend of mine is a skin specialist. I'll give you his name."

She stepped back. "I knew you wouldn't believe me. But you have to! Will you do me one favor? Come to my apartment with me?"

He had become convinced that the rash, or whatever it was, had caused her to have delusions of persecution. The pain might have temporarily unhinged her mind.

"I'm rather busy on a case at present," he told her. "If you'll go to see this doctor—"

WITH a sob she turned away from him. Listlessly she buttoned her dress, then went toward the door. Her shoulders drooped hopelessly.

"Just a minute," Bryn said.

It had occurred to him that perhaps the attack on him outside the Carson house was tied up in some way with this girl's presence. Somebody wanted to kill him; he hadn't any idea why, except that it was connected with the death of Marianne Carson. Possibly this girl had been sent here to lead him into a trap. Looking at her, so sweet and distraught, he hated to admit her capable of anything like that, but he had had too much experience to trust in appearances. Sooner or later he would again come up against whoever wanted to kill him, and he had learned that the best defense was an offense.

"I've changed my mind," he said. "I'll go with you."

She brightened up perceptibly. Her figure straightened. For a moment he felt a qualm for suspecting that she might be a stooge for killers. Then he shrugged and walked out beside her.

For a while they sat in silence in the taxi. Then Bryn said: "Tell me about yourself."

"My name is Sibyl Day. You might have heard of my father, Norman Day, the tire manufacturer."

"Does he know about that burn and your visit to me?"

Sibyl Day shuddered. "He's dead. I returned home yesterday and found him murdered."

He stared at her. "Did you report it to the police?"

"I dare not."

"Suppose you tell me the rest."

"You won't believe me," she said wearily. "Not until you've seen what I'll show you, and even then. . ."

HE asked no more questions. Presently the taxi pulled up in front of an apartment house. The elevator took them up to the twelfth floor. Bryn loosened his gun in its holster as she unlocked the door. He flung the door open, brushed past her, strode in first. He went through the foyer into the sumptuous living room of the duplex apartment. There wasn't a sign of anybody.

"No servants?" he asked.

"They were discharged. Now I'm living alone with—with—Come this way."

Warily he followed her, keeping his hand near his gun. She led him down a hall, then opened a door and stepped into a room. Bryn stopped dead in the doorway. Only a short time ago he had entered a bedroom in another house and had seen the same kind of a long hump on the bed covered with a sheet. He went to the bed and pulled the sheet down a little way.

The grey-haired man who lay there must have been dead for a couple of days. Even death had not relaxed the expression of unendurable pain. Bryn flicked the sheet all the way to the footboard and a gasp of horror escaped his lips.

From knee to neck, Norman Day's scrawny body was a mass of charred, blistered skin tissue. Like Marianne Carson —with one difference. Marianne Carson had obviously been burned by fire, whereas Norman Day's body looked precisely like that raw, blistered splotch on Sibyl's breast.

Ben Bryn covered the body with the sheet and turned to the girl. She stood against the wall, quivering, her hands crossed on her breasts.

He put an arm about her. "You poor girl," he said. Gently he led her out of the bedroom into the living room. He saw a decanter, poured stiff drinks for the girl and himself.

They sat side by side on the couch. He said: "I see what's on your mind. You think that a burn similar to yours started on your father's body and spread until it killed him."

"I *know* that's what happened," she told him hollowly. "I spent the week-end with a girl friend at Little Long Lake. Two days ago my chest started itching.

I paid no attention to it. When I awoke yesterday morning, the itching had turned to pain and I noticed the splotch on my skin. I thought it might be an infection of some kind and decided to see a doctor after I returned home.

"When I entered this apartment yesterday afternoon, I found that the servants were gone. I unpacked, took a shower, and after a while happened to wander into my father's room. He was on the bed, naked, evidently having torn his clothes off in his agony. He looked the way you have just seen him—horrible. I guess I must have fainted.

"The ringing of the telephone brought me to. I went to the extension phone in the room and picked it up. A ghostlike voice spoke at the other end of the wire. The voice warned me not to go to the police; not, in fact, to tell anybody about Dad's death; that I could remove his body for burial only if I could arrange it so that nobody but myself became aware of the fact that he was dead. The voice said that if I disobeyed in the slightest degree, the burn would spread over my body until I died as frightfully as Dad had. Then there was a click and I was alone with Dad's body."

There was a silence. Bryn's arm tightened about the girl's slim quaking body.

"A little later, I saw a letter on the dresser," she went on. "Here it is."

She opened her handbag and handed Bryn an ordinary sheet of typewriting paper on which was typed:

Enclosed is the jar of salve. You are a greedy old man. Perhaps you delayed too long. In that case you will have to purchase a stronger salve from us at double the price.

Again we remind you not to inform a soul of your affliction. Your only hope lies in complete silence and application of the salves we send to you.

One other word of warning. If you are foolhardy enough to go to the police or any other source for aid, remember that you have a daughter whom you love. You would not like to have her a victim of the creeping death!

"The creeping death," Ben Bryn muttered to himself. That was what Marianne Carson had also called it in her frantic letter!

SIBYL said hoarsely: "After the voice spoke to me on the phone, I opened my dress and saw that the burn had spread still further. I went almost crazy with fear. The voice called again, told me that if I sent ten thousand dollars in cash to a certain post office box I would receive a salve that would cure me. I thought the salve hadn't helped Dad because he'd delayed too long. I rushed to my bank before it closed and withdrew the money. My mother left me an independent income. I sent the money by special delivery.

"Then all the rest of the day and last night I waited. It was a nightmare. I dared not go to anybody for help, because I was depending on that salve. Early in the morning the salve arrived by special delivery. I applied it to the burn, which had continued to spread during the night. The salve soothed the pain somewhat, but not enough, and after an hour or two I noticed that the burned area was larger. Frantic, I took the jar to a chemist and had its contents analyzed. The report was that the salve, for which I had paid ten thousand dollars, could have been bought in any ten-cent-store. The salve was nothing but cold cream!"

Ben Bryn's big hands opened and closed convulsively. His eyes turned into twin balls of blue ice.

"The fiends!" he muttered. "What I'd give to get my hands on them!"

The front door slammed open and feet hurried in the foyer. Instinctively Bryn pulled his arm from about Sibyl, but not before a young man appeared in the doorway. Bryn realized that that gesture must have looked quite incriminating to the newcomer.

Sibyl said: "Why, Tom, what are you doing here?"

The young man advanced across the room, glowering at Bryn. He was built like a football guard.

"I might have known I couldn't trust you," he growled at Sibyl. "I tried to get you by phone all morning. I saw you leave your house and followed you here—and find you like this."

Sibyl rose to her feet. "Tom Meers, how dare you make such insinuations?"

"I have eyes," the young man snapped. "I had an absurd notion that you were a decent girl. Now I find you're no better than—"

"Just a second, friend," Bryn broke in. "I don't like your tone of voice and I don't like what you're saying."

"You don't, eh?" Meers whirled on Bryn. Maybe you'll like this." He swung his fist down at Bryn's jaw.

Bryn side-stepped the blow, caught the bigger man's arm as it lashed past his face. He twisted Meers' arm behind his back, captured his other arm, then lifted him. A look of astonishment passed over his antagonist's face. He had known few men who could beat him in a fight, and this man was handling him almost as easily as he would a child.

Cursing, Meers started to struggle. Bryn carried him across the room, through the open front door and dumped him into the hallway. Meers lay panting on the floor, incredulity and hatred mingling in his eyes as he stared up at Bryn.

"Next time you'll talk civilly to a lady or you'll be hurt," Bryn said and slammed the door.

Sibyl Day stood in the living room, her breasts rising and falling, her hands clasped in front of her.

"Maybe I shouldn't have done that," Bryn said. "I should have given you a chance to explain. But I didn't want him

to start anything in here which would bring people. I'd rather nobody knew for a while what happened to your father."

"There's nothing to explain to him," Sibyl Day stated. "He's jealous and hot-tempered. I'm rather fond of him, but he can't get it into his head that I don't want to marry him."

Several minutes later they left the apartment. Tom Meers was gone.

CHAPTER THREE

The House of Murder

BRYN took Sibyl to his friend, Dr. Stanley Behren, a famous skin specialist. Impatiently he paced up and down the confines of the waiting room while Dr. Behren examined the girl. When at last they came out, Bryn hurried over to them, his eyes question marks.

"Nothing serious," Dr. Behren, a tall man with a Van Dyke, shrugged. "The young lady seems to have been burned by some caustic acid. Frankly, Ben, I can't understand her attitude. She refuses to tell me how the acid was spilled on her."

"But I did tell you," Sibyl protested. "No acid could possibly have been spilled on me."

"Never mind that," Bryn interposed. "Look, Stan, assuming that a drop of some sort of acid fell on her, would it gradually spread?"

"Certainly not," Dr. Behren stated.

"Have you any idea what the acid is?"

"No way of telling off-hand," Dr. Behren replied. "Some not-too-strong form of vitriol; something like that. What's it all about, Ben?"

"Tell you some other time," Bryn said, and taking Sibyl's arm, he led her outside to a waiting taxi.

Back in the cab, she started to claw at his arm again and her voice became high-pitched with mounting hysteria. "You see, even the doctor doesn't know. It'll spread and spread until I die!"

"Nonsense!" Bryn snapped. "If you want me to help you, you'll have to be sensible. Somebody put drops of the acid on you while you slept."

"But it spread, and even now it keeps on spreading," she argued. "Nobody has been near me for twenty-four hours." Her voice rose. "It's hopeless, I tell you. It's something hellish, a curse. I'm doomed."

"Cut it out!" Bryn's voice lashed out like a whip. She stared at him a moment, then subsided into a pathetic bundle deep in the seat.

He made his voice gentle. "Look here, Sibyl. You said you'd trust my judgment. Well, I'm taking you up to my apartment and I'm having watch kept over you day and night. Nobody and nothing will be able to get near you. I'm certain that the burn will not only stop spreading but go away entirely."

She nodded and leaned against him like a little girl coming for comfort to her father.

When they were in his three-room apartment, he made two phone calls. Within a half hour Billy Pierce and Dolly Dennis, whom he occasionally employed as his assistants, showed up. Pierce was a dapper little man with the fighting qualities of a gamecock. Dolly Dennis was big and buxum and red-headed, and could handle her fists and a gun better than most men.

"These are the instructions," Bryn said crisply. "Both of you are staying with Miss Day in this apartment day and night until further orders. You're sleeping and eating here, and at least one of you will always be awake and have a gun handy. Nobody comes near Miss Day; nobody sees her or even talks to her. And I'm locking up the liquor and you're not to buy any."

"What's the dope, Chief?" Billy Pierce asked. "A kidnap threat?"

"Worse than that," Bryn told him. "I haven't time to go into details now."

Sibyl Day went with him as far as the door. She put a small hand in his big paw and smiled wanly up at him.

"I feel better already," she said softly, "knowing that you're watching over me."

He squeezed her hand and went out.

Ben Bryn rang the doorbell of the Carson house without getting an answer. He went around the back of the house, found the back door also locked. But all the ground floor windows were wide open, so he lifted himself through one of them.

Noiselessly he walked through the dining room, then the drawing room. As he was about to step into the downstairs hall, he heard the whirr of a telephone dial. He leaned around the doorway, then stepped into the hall.

"Fancy meeting you here, Helen," he said.

HELEN FORREST spun, her hand jerking behind her head with the handset phone as if she were about to throw it. Almost at once her fear-contorted features returned to normal and she smiled languidly.

"Playing bogyman now, Ben?" she drawled. "You almost scared me out of my skin. I was just about to call my paper."

"I suppose you saw Marianne Carson?"

Helen made a wry face. "Don't remind me of it. I might have taken it easier had I been prepared for the sight. I knew from your questions that I could find a story here. I came as soon as I could get away. Nobody answered my ring, so like a good newspaper woman I climbed through the window and looked around. Is it murder, Ben?"

"What makes you think so?"

"Why'd you be around if it wasn't?"

"Who would have the most to gain by her death?" he asked, evading an answer.

Helen Forrest shrugged. "I wouldn't know, except—well, everybody in her family is pretty well heeled except one

brother who was the family black sheep
and got cut off from the gravy. Marianne
rather liked him, though, and the rumor
was that she'd leave her money to him."

"Lace Powys?" Bryn asked.

"I said you knew everything. Did he
do it, Ben?"

Bryn shrugged. "I'm not sure. Even
if he did—"

He broke off and stared at Helen. She
was scratching abstractedly at the deep-
cut neck of her dress.

"Does anything hurt you?" he asked.

Her hand dropped to her side. "Oh,
it's nothing much. I think I have a skin
rash of some sort."

"Do you mind if I see it?" he asked,
suddenly tense.

She smiled. "Why, Ben, this is so sudden. Of course, if you want to—" Her
fingers went up to the neck of her dress,
then stopped abruptly.

High up in the house a woman's voice
rose shrilly.

Bryn dashed up the stairs with Helen
at his heels. When they reached the first
floor, the voice was still above them.
Bryn took the stairs up to the attic. He
heard a woman shouting:

"You killed Mrs. Carson! I saw you
in the house before the fire started. I
saw you slinking in the hall before I went
to bed. You killed her for her money."

"Shut up, damn you!" a man said.

And then a second woman screamed:
"He's got a gun! My God, don't shoot!"

The door of the attic room at the head
of the stairs was open. Bryn saw the
maid, Pauline, and an elderly woman, no
doubt the cook, gaping at Lace Powys
who had an automatic in his hand. Powys'
face was working convusively and he was
gasping: "It's a lie! I'll kill you if you
say another word! I swear I'll kill you!"

Bryn had his own gun out. He snapped:
"Drop your gun, Powys. I have you covered."

Powys spun toward the door. He had

aged several years in the last few hours.
He backed against the wall, started to
bring his gun out, then realized the futility
of it and dropped the gun on the floor.

"He killed Mrs. Carson!" the cook
shrieked. "He burned the poor old woman
in her bed!"

"Did you!" Bryn asked quietly.

"I had to!" Powys wailed. "She was
dying anyway. There was no hope for
her. It was a quicker way, even an easier
way, out for her. They made me do it!"

"Who made you?" Bryn asked gently.

"I don't know. Please don't make me
tell you more!"

Bryn said: "Unbutton your shirt."

Powys dug his back against the wall,
cringing. "No! Haven't I suffered
enough? Have mercy!"

WITH a swoop of his powerful arm,
Bryn pinned both of Powys' arms
behind his back. Powys fought like a
frenzied woman, clawing and thrashing,
but Bryn handled him easily. With a couple of downward motions of his fingers,
Bryn ripped open the front of Powys'
shirt.

The man's chest was a hideous mass of
blistered skin.

The three women cried out in horror.
Bryn released the man and straightened
up. Powys slumped to the floor, moaning.

And then, above the moaning of the
man, Bryn caught the sound on the attic
stairs outside. It was a tiny squeak which
might or might not have been made by
leather on the uncarpeted steps. Gun held
in his right hand, Bryn moved along the
wall to the open door. All sound in the
room ceased as eyes focussed on him.

With a sideward twist of his body, Bryn
hurled himself through the doorway. Then
he pulled himself up short as he confronted, not more than two or three feet away
from him, the gunman he'd hit outside the
house a few hours ago.

The man had a gun dangling along his

side. His mouth jerked open soundlessly as he saw Bryn's automatic pointing at him and realized that he couldn't get his own gun up in time.

But Bryn had other plans. You can't get information out of a dead man. So he brought up his left hand instead. His fist crashed into the big man's face with all the force of his great strength. He felt the jar of the impact all the way up to his shoulder. The big man went backward down the stairs.

At almost the same instant the roof seemed to fall down on the back of Bryn's head. He clawed the air for support, felt his legs buckle under him; then he was rolling down the stairs. Darkness blotted out his senses before he had reached the bottom.

CHAPTER FOUR

Spreading Death

COLD water revived Ben Bryn. He opened his eyes and found himself looking up at the florid face of Lieutenant Hummel of Homicide. He started up to his feet. Hummel got an arm under his shoulders and helped him up.

"Take it easy, Ben," Hummel said. "You got an awful smack on the head and tumbling down those stairs didn't do you any good."

Bryn saw that he was at the foot of the attic stairs. There were uniformed cops and plainclothesmen in the hall and he heard voices in the attic above and the rooms below. Near his feet the big man he had knocked down the stairs lay in a crumpled heap. He hadn't any face left. There wasn't anything but bloody, jumbled features. This wasn't the first time Bryn had seen the damage his fist could do when he put all his strength behind it.

"Dead?" Bryn said to Hummel. "I'm sure my sock didn't kill him."

"Not quite," the lieutenant said, "though I'd rather be kicked in the face by a mule any day than have you take a smack at me. What finished this guy was falling down the stairs. His neck is broken."

Bryn rubbed his bruised bones. He put his hands to the back of his head and felt dried blood. "Almost broke my neck too. How'd you get here?"

"Helen Forrest phoned. As soon as the guys who killed Powys scrammed, she ."

"Powys is dead?"

"Yeah. There were three of the killers. One of them is that chap there. Another one was waiting against the outside of the door and slammed his gun down on your head. Helen Forrest was coming out to see what was up and she saw it. Then the guy who knocked you out smacked her down with his fist and went into the room. By this time the third killer was coming up the stairs. The maid and the cook saw the rest. Powys was kneeling on the floor, pleading for his life. One of the killers just stepped up to him, put his gun against Powys' forehead, and let go. Then they beat it."

Bryn said: "Know who this guy I socked is?"

"No idea. You ruined his face, but we might dig something up on his prints. You'd think we could get some sort of description of the two other rats, but you know how frightened people are. We got three different and contradictory descriptions from the three women."

"They made no attempt to touch the women?"

Lieutenant Hummel shook his head. "Looks like they were only after Powys. I think the only reason they didn't finish you off when they passed your body was that they either thought you were dead or that they were in too much of a hurry. The screams and the shots could be heard for blocks." The lieutenant paused. "Well, Ben, what's it all about? There's still another corpse in the house, you know. It used to be old Mrs. Carson."

"Come downstairs and I'll give you the dope," Bryn said wearily.

In the drawing room Pauline and the cook were recovering from a pretty bad case of hysteria, while a police stenographer was painstakingly writing down their disjointed statement.

"Where's Helen Forrest?" Bryn asked.

"I let her go to write the story for her paper," Hummel told him as he beckoned to the stenographer.

When Bryn and Hummel and the stenographer were seated at the long dining room table, Bryn started talking.

Twenty minutes later he was concluding: "They had drained all the money, they could out of old Mrs. Carson. They knew, in common with a lot of other people, that she would leave her money to her brother. So the burn appeared on Powy's chest and started spreading and then they got in touch with him. They wanted the old lady out of the way now because that was the only way they could get the rest of her money through Powys, but they didn't want the police to know she'd been slowly murdered. They ordered Powys to go into her room and put her bed on fire.

"He did it because it would end her suffering sooner and because he would get her money and because he'd gone nearly crazy with fear. So he got into her room with a skeleton key, ignited the bed, then slipped out and pretended that he had just arrived.

"The killers didn't trust him. They knew his nerves would give way and he'd start talking under pressure. When they saw me slipping into the house, they came to put both of us out of the way."

HUMMEL put his small grey eyes on Bryn and for half a minute their steady gazes held. Then Hummel said: "You've always co-operated with the police, Ben, and we've given you breaks in the past. Why did you hold out on the fact that Mrs. Carson had been murdered?"

"I didn't know it until a little while ago. I had no reason to believe that she hadn't really been burned as the result of an accident."

"Not even after the letter she sent you?"

"That was no proof."

Hummel sighed. "All right. Why didn't you tell us about Norman Day?"

"I didn't have a chance," Bryn said. Then he smiled wryly. "I better give it to you straight. I didn't want the cops to start messing around Sibyl Day. Not only is she on the verge of going to pieces, but I am certain that she'll be in danger if she is away from my protection for even a moment."

"Even if we take care of her?"

"Yes."

Hummel said: "You haven't much confidence in us, have you?"

"That's not it. I'm really scared of these fiends. Not for myself, but for Sibyl Day and their other victims, if any are left alive. I think I'm doing what's best for her. Look here, Lieutenant, I know you can find her if you want to. But I'd like you to release her as a material witness in my custody for a day or two."

Hummel shrugged. "It's not up to me, but I guess I can swing it. We've always found we can trust you."

Bryn went to the office of the *Evening Advance* and learned that Helen Forrest had already left. Nobody knew where she had gone. She had complained of what she thought was a skin rash on her chest! Bryn knew the dread significance of that. But why should the killers go after her? She had no money. The fact remained, however, that she was in danger of a hideous death.

He stopped off at her apartment, found that she wasn't in. Then he went to police headquarters and told Lieutenant Hummel that he feared that Helen Forrest had become another victim of the fiends. Hummel growled, "Why didn't you tell me at the Carson house?" and sent out an alarm for her.

Bryn spent the next few hours at police headquarters and in the district attorney's office, giving all the information he could, in addition pulling strings to have Sibyl Day placed in his custody. Several times he telephoned his apartment. He learned to his satisfaction that the burn on her chest had ceased to spread.

So far so good. But most of the job was still undone. With the fiends at large, Sibyl's life continued in danger, as did his own life and the lives of whatever other victims there might be in the city unknown to himself and the police.

And Helen Forrest had not yet been located. There was a city-wide search for her now.

It was about ten o'clock at night when Bryn let himself into his apartment. Billy Pierce was standing alongside the door, gun leveled at Bryn.

Pierce grinned and returned the gun to his holster. Good boy, Pierce. Took no chances.

"How is she?" Bryn said.

"Quite some pain, but it's not spreading any more, like I told you over the phone. Dolly's in the bedroom with her, sleeping with her. The way Dolly sleeps, a mouse couldn't walk across the room without her hearing."

L IGHTLY Bryn pushed the door of the bedroom open. A dim nightlight was burning. He moved lightly toward the bed on which Sibyl and Dolly were sleeping. Because of the heat of the night, Sibyl had pushed the blanket down to her waist. He stared down at her, at her face calm now in sleep and very lovely. The low bodice of her nightgown showed the ugly blotch on the upper curves of her young breasts.

Poor thing, Bryn said to himself. Then he thought of those others, of her father and Marianne Carson and Lace Powys. What mental and physical agonies they must have suffered before death had at last released them! A hard, cold core formed in the pit of his stomach.

He noticed that Dolly's eyes were open, that one of her hands was under her pillow where she no doubt kept her gun. Dolly was smiling up at him.

"Okay," Bryn whispered. "You can sleep tight. Billy and I will be in the other room all night."

Bryn stretched out on the daybed in the living room and slept soundly until two-thirty when Billy Pierce awoke him. Then Pierce slept and Bryn sat deep in an armchair, every sense alert.

The night passed uneventfully. At seven o'clock Bryn went into the kitchen to brew coffee. He was leaning against the stove, moodily watching the coffee percolating, when Sibyl Day's screams shrilled out.

Bryn slammed out of the kitchen, reached the bedroom door at the same time as Billy Pierce. Both men had their guns out. Bryn pushed the door inward. Only Sibyl and Dolly Dennis were in the bedroom and both girls were rolling on the bed, apparently struggling.

Bryn picked Dolly off the smaller girl and dropped her on the floor. Sibyl was writhing on the bed, clawing at her nightgown, and her mouth was open in an endless scream. He pinned her arms down, and shook her.

Dolly had risen to her feet; her ample bosom heaved under her pajamas. "Her screams woke me up," Dolly panted. "She looked like she was tearing herself apart, so I tried to stop her. She fought like a wildcat."

Sibyl's screams had turned to whimpers. She subsided, breathing heavily.

"It's spread!" she moaned. "Oh, God, I knew nothing could save me!"

Bryn had been modestly averting his

eyes from her exposed breasts. Now he looked down at her and his blood ran cold. The blistered blotch had spread until it covered all of her breasts and extended ragged fingers down to her waist.

"Holy Gee!" Billy Pierce exclaimed. He strode to the window, turned with wide eyes, and said: "It's five stories to the street and nothing but straight wall—and it's two stories to the roof. Only a spider could climb up here."

"It's impossible," Bryn muttered. "Dr. Behren told me that that burn didn't conceivably spread. Nobody could have gotten into this room except—" Automatically his gaze rested on Dolly Dennis.

"What are you looking like that at me for, Chief!" Dolly cried. "You don't think I—"

"I don't know," Bryn said slowly. "By this time I don't even trust myself."

CHAPTER FIVE

Killers' Trap

THE telephone whirred. Bryn went wearily into the living room and picked up the handset. In the bedroom Sibyl was moaning, not so much from the pain as from the maddening conviction that she was doomed to hideous death and that nothing anybody could do would save her.

"Hello?" Bryn muttered into the mouthpiece.

A voice spoke at the other end of the wire, but it wasn't words that it uttered. Bryn heard a choked mumbling.

"Hello?" he repeated impatiently.

Then out of the thin, gasping mumbling he distinguished a single word. "Ben," the voice said. And then again: "Ben . . . Ben. . . ."

He tensed, pressing the phone against his ear. Another name came to him, thinly, as if from the grave. "Helen . . . Helen Forrest . . . Ben . . . save. . . ." The voice melted away.

"Helen!" he cried. "Where are you? What's happened to you?"

He heard her panting agonizingly. Then words came again, stronger, as if she had called on her last reserve of energy.

"Bungalow . . . Grove Road . . . I'm dying. . . . Come quickly."

Ominous silence followed. Bryn cradled the phone, stood biting his lower lip in indecision. Sibyl's moans came out to him. Yet there was another girl who needed him even more.

"What is it, Chief?" Billy Pierce asked anxiously.

"You and Dolly stay here with Miss Day." Bryn snapped. "Do what you can to relieve the pain. And don't let anybody in."

He hopped a taxi and dangled a five dollar bill before the driver's eyes to encourage the breaking of traffic regulations. Last summer he had been out to Helen Forrest's summer bungalow several times. He'd forgotten about it. Fool not to have told the police to look for her there.

The cab reached the bungalow in forty minutes. Bryn raced up the walk, shoved open the front door.

HELEN FORREST lay on the living room floor. She was nude and her body was twisted into a contorted heap. Near her lay the telephone. She was no longer smooth and white and lovely to look at, but a horror of raw, ugly, burned splotches.

"Helen!" Bryn exclaimed, dropping down to her side.

Her eyes opened. The pain faded from them, she forced a brave smile to her lips.

"Too late, Ben," she moaned. "I . . . I'm finished. . . . It took an . . . eternity . . . to crawl to the phone."

He gathered her tortured body in his arms. "What happened to you, Helen?"

"The . . . itching grew worse. . . . I went . . . to bed. . . . I awoke at night

. . . burning up. . . . Nobody heard my screams. . . . Finally I . . . I crawled in here . . . called you"

"Why did you come here?" he asked.

"I . . . he. . . ."

Her strength gave out. She kept moving her lips, but only indistinguishable sounds came out. Suddenly a tremor ran through her body and she was dead.

Gently Ben Bryn placed her on the couch. Hot rage choked him as he stood looking down at her.

All at once he stiffened. Although her torso was a horror of frightful burns, her face was unmarred. So were her legs and the lower parts of her thighs. The burns started in a semicircle just above her breasts!

H E WENT into the bedroom, saw the bed a chaos as the result of her agonized struggles. He saw tatters of silk on the bed and the floor, remnants of her nightgown which she had torn in her pain. Picking up one of the pieces of silk, he rubbed it against the back of his hand. He felt nothing. Then he applied the material to his tongue. With a grimace he pulled it away. His tongue burned.

He returned to the living room, picked up the phone, called his apartment number. He heard the buzz at the other end of the wire. Three, four, five times the buzz was repeated. He turned rigid, hardly breathing.

At last the operator said: "Sorry, your party doesn't answer."

"Are you sure?" he asked tensely. "Have you the right number?"

He hung up and called again. Once more there was no answer.

Then he was running out to the road. Madly he cursed three passing drivers who refused to stop for him. Then a small truck picked him up. As soon as the truck came to an empty taxi, he transferred.

After what seemed an eternity, he burst into his apartment. Billy Pierce was seated at the desk talking into the phone.

"Where is she?" Bryn yelled. "What happened?"

Pierce dropped the phone on its cradle and turned a white face toward Bryn. "God, Chief, I've been trying to locate you all over. They're gone, both Dolly and Miss Day. I came back and the apartment was empty."

"You fool!" Bryn raged. "Why did you leave them alone?"

"All I did was go down to buy some lotion for her burns," Pierce exclaimed in agrieved tones. "I wasn't gone more than ten minutes."

Bryn strove to get control of himself. "Sorry, Billy. I know that it wasn't your fault."

Bryn went to the bedroom door and looked in. Pierce came up behind him.

"No sign of any struggle," he said. "It beats me how they got in here without Dolly being ready for them; even then, they'd have had a hell of a job taking her. . . . Say, do you think, after all, Dolly's in with 'em? I don't believe it, but—"

"No," Bryn said dully. "Dolly's all right. Come on, Billy."

They questioned the elevator operator but he had not seen either Dolly or Sibyl.

"I see how they did it," Bryn said as he and Billy stood in front of the apartment house. "They got into the apartment, put guns on Sibyl and Dolly, made Sibyl dress, took the girls down the stairs to the basement and then out the back door around the side of the block where they had a car waiting."

"Yeah, but how'd they get through the locked door with Dolly in there with a gun?" Billy Pierce puzzled.

"I have an idea how that happened," Bryn said. "You go to headquarters and tell Lieutenant Hummel everything you know. Tell him also that Helen Forrest was murdered in her bungalow."

"Jeez!" Pierce exclaimed. "And where are you going, Chief?"

"To get the killer," Bryn said in a voice so quiet that it belied the fury within him.

The day before at headquarters Bryn had learned that Pauline, the former Carson maid, was staying temporarily at her parents' home, and he had automatically jotted down the address.

He took a taxi to the tenement house. There were no names under the doorbells. He had to inquire at several apartments on the ground floor before he learned that Pauline's parents lived on the fourth floor, rear.

He went up slowly, cautiously, stopping on each landing to peer up and down the dimly lighted stairs and to listen for any suspicious sound. It was this caution which saved his life. Out of the shadows on the third floor landing a shape detached itself. A voice said: "This is as far as you go, shamus." Bryn saw the gun in the man's hand.

BRYN hadn't time to go for his own gun. He left his feet as soon as the gunman had started talking. His broad body skimmed over the floor; his wide shoulders struck the man's hips an instant after the gun blasted. The gunman hadn't had a chance to bring his gun down far enough, and the slug smacked into the wall three feet above the floor. The gunman crashed down heavily on his back with the wind knocked out of him.

In a moment Bryn had kicked the gun from the man who had tried to shoot him down. He heard steps pounding up from the floor below. Lifting the stunned killer in his arms, he looked down over the railing. A man was running up with drawn gun. Bryn raised the gunman in his arms, held him over his head and hurled the body down at the man who was coming up. The hurtling body struck the other, and both went tumbling down the stairs in a jumble of arms and legs.

Then Bryn was rounding the staircase,

his own gun in his hand, cold fury raging within him. They must have followed him here from his own apartment. While he had been inquiring below as to where Pauline lived, one must have come up here while the other remained below, planning to trap him between them. It was plain that they did not want him to get to Pauline.

As he flew down the stairs, the gunmen were untangling themselves. One of them shot wildly up at him, and then Bryn's gun barked. The one who had shot stumbled backward, but kept his gun pointed up at Bryn, striving desperately for strength for a second shot. Bryn's gun belched another slug and the wounded man fell forward on his face.

Meanwhile the second gunman, the one Bryn had thrown down the stairs, had fled. He was already out of sight around the curve of the staircase. Bryn pounded after him. Between the second and first floors Bryn caught sight of him, but by that time tenants had begun to pour out of their apartments and Bryn couldn't risk a shot for fear of hitting one of them.

The gunman slammed out through the front door and into the street. When Bryn himself reached the street, the gunman was out of sight. He might have run into the next house or dived into a waiting car.

Bryn holstered his gun and went up the stairs. Tenants shrank away from him. He flashed his badge, said, "Get a cop," and continued upward. On the second floor landing he passed the body of the man he had shot. Dead, all right. He went up to the fourth floor and saw Pauline among the excited group huddled at the head of the stairs.

"Oh, it's Ben Bryn, the detective," she said with relief.

He took her arm lightly. "Where's your flat?" She nodded toward an open door in the rear and he led her in there, shutting the door behind him.

PAULINE said: "Mr. Bryn, I didn't have a chance to thank you yesterday for saving my life. Can you imagine, it was that horrid Lace Powys who burned poor Mrs. Carson! I always said—"

"Look, Pauline," Bryn broke in, "you can thank me by telling me what laundry the Carson household used."

"Laundry? Gee, what's that got to do with what's been going on? You detectives ask the craziest questions."

"Don't you want to tell me?"

"Sure. The Sunbrite Hand Laundry."

"What's the address?"

"Somewhere on Monarch Road, I think. Glad to help you out, Mr. Bryn, but I don't see—"

"Have you been giving your laundry to them for a long time?"

"Only a couple of weeks."

"Why did you change to that laundry?" She didn't look at him. "Well, I—"

"That's all right, Pauline," Bryn said. "I'm not going to arrest you because you got a rake-off from the driver. That's how he got the Carson order, by giving you—well, let's call it a commission?"

Pauline faced him defiantly. "Well, everybody does it."

"Sure," he said. "Thanks for the information."

She looked after him with a puzzled expression as he left, wondering at the queer methods of detectives.

As he had expected, the name of the Sunbrite Hand Laundry was not listed in the telephone directory. He flagged a taxi and told the driver to roll slowly along Monarch Road. It wasn't until they were almost in the suburbs and the houses started to thin out that he found what he was looking for.

It was an unpainted frame building flanked on either side by empty lots. A badly lettered sign over the front door said: SUNBRITE HAND LAUNDRY. Bryn got out of the taxi, paid off the driver.

The door was locked. Bryn peered through the dirty store window. All the equipment of a hand laundry was in there —counters and bins and ironing boards. The building consisted only of a store. He could see every inch of it from the front window.

The place looked absolutely empty, but he wasn't quite satisfied. The door was locked only by a Yale lock fastened to two iron staples, one imbedded in the door and one in the frame. He hooked his powerful fingers through the lock and pulled. Slowly the staples came out. He dropped the staples and the lock to the ground and turned the knob.

Behind a bin he saw wooden steps leading downward. As he peered down into the uncertain light below, he heard a vague, muffled moan. Stiffening, his hand went to his gun.

He didn't quite reach it. Hard steel dug into his back. He knew at once that somebody had been crouching behind the counter, that at the slightest motion on his part he would die instantly.

Bryn twisted his head and looked into the handsome face of Tom Meers, the young man he had thrown out of Sibyl Day's apartment.

CHAPTER SIX

The Burning of Hell

TOM MEERS called down the steps: "We have company, Willy. I told you Bryn would come here and come alone. He's not the kind to work too closely with the police."

A short, slim man came up the steps— one of the two who had tried to trap Bryn in the tenement house. He stopped two steps below Bryn, grinned wolfishly, and leveled his gun at Bryn's heart.

"Get away from behind him, Tom," the man named Willy said. "My slug might go right through him."

"Not yet," Meers said. "I have a better

idea." He reached over Bryn's shoulder and extratced his automatic. "Go down, shamus," he ordered. "I have two guns on you and Willy has one, so don't try anything."

Bryn went down the steps. Willy moved backward in front of him, Meers descended right behind him. Bryn found himself in a small, dimly lit cellar.

He lurched forward, swearing harshly, at the sight of Sibyl Day's slim figure dangling by her wrists from a beam in the ceiling. A filthy rag was in her mouth. She stared at him with horror-widened eyes.

"Hold it!" Meers barked, and Bryn pulled himself up short. His immediate death would not help her and evidently Meers and his friends did not intend to kill him at once.

Near Sibyl's feet he noticed a burning charcoal brazier in which irons glowed white-hot. The cellar was divided in two by a thick plank wall. Wood and shavings were piled knee-deep on the floor.

With an effort Ben Bryn kept his voice calm as he said: "I figured it was you or somebody like you, Meers. Only somebody that Sibyl knew well and trusted could have taken her out of my apartment. You and your thugs took the fire stairs up to my apartment so as not to be seen. You rang and told Dolly Dennis who you were and, probably, that you had an urgent message for Sibyl. After a consultation with Sibyl, Dolly let you in. Sibyl had no reason not to trust you. She didn't love you, but regarded you as a close friend. Once inside the apartment, you pulled a gun on Dolly and let in your pals who were waiting outside. The rest was easy."

"That's not so brilliant," Meers commented.

"All right, here's the rest of it," Bryn said.

He was talking to gain time. Realizing now how foolhardy he had been not to have left a message with the police as to where he was going, he could only hope desperately that Pauline would think of telling the police that he had asked for the whereabouts of the Sunbrite Hand Laundry. The chances were, however, that it wouldn't occur to her to mention it.

Bryn told Meers: "I don't suppose this laundry did much business; it was concerned only with getting the business of a certain few people. This was easily accomplished by bribing the maids. Not being a chemist, I'm not yet sure what you, or whoever of your gang ran the laundry, put on the undergarments. Probably something like sulphur trioxide, which can easily be rubbed on the garment.

"Sulphur trioxid forms sulphuric acid when united with water. In this case, when ' united with perspiration. The weather has been hot. By limiting the area on which you spread the stuff, you could more or less limit the burn. For instance, rub it only on the bodice of a nightgown or a chemise and a slight acid burn appears. Spread more of it on the next garment the victim wears and the burn spreads.

"Diabolically clever, save for one flaw. You could sell the tortured victim a salve at an enormous price, but you couldn't sell any salve that would immediately cure the burn. And you couldn't prevent the victim from wearing other undergarments which had been treated in your laundry. Otherwise you might have been able to extort even more money from them."

Tom Meers shrugged. "That knowledge isn't going to do you much good now."

WHIMPERS tore through Sibyl Day's gag as her slender form swung from the ceiling. Bryn's eyes shifted frantically about the room. No chance for a break with those guns pointed unwaveringly at him. Would the police come?

He said: "What I can't understand is why you killed Helen Forrest. She wasn't rich enough to be an extortion victim."

Meers scowled darkly. "She forced me to. Nobody knew that she was my mistress. I was growing tired of her, wanted to get rid of her, but I hadn't planned to kill her. Then yesterday morning while she was rummaging through my coat for cigarettes, she found the ten thousand dollars in cash Norman Day had sent me for the salve. She knew I hadn't much money and kept asking embarrassing questions about where all that cash had come from. Then when you started digging up some of the details, I was afraid she'd become suspicious of me. She was a friend of yours and might talk to you. I hustled her away from her office yesterday, took her out to her bungalow, said I had to hurry away on business and that I would probably return later that night. Needless to say, I didn't. The nightgown she wore took care of her."

"And now you're about to kill another girl you cared for," Bryn said through tight lips. "My God, man, haven't you a spark of humanity left?"

"Sibyl never returned my affection. Now she'll make me rich."

Bryn eyed the charcoal brazier. Why was Meers heating those irons? He looked at Sibyl swinging there and his scalp tightened. Was it worth taking a chance against those two armed men? The odds were suicidal and there was still hope that the police might come in time.

WILLY had been shifting uneasily on his feet. "What's the idea of wasting time?" he growled. "Maybe the cops will find this place. Let me plug this guy and then we can get to work on the girl."

"You're right, we've been wasting time," Meers agreed. "Though I'm sure Bryn is so damned conceited he decided he could handle us without ringing the police in. Shooting's too good for him. Remember he killed George and Tim."

Meers jabbed one of the two guns in his hands into Bryn's back. Willy unlocked the heavy plank door to the other cellar room.

"Okay, Bryn, in there," Meers ordered.

Bryn hesitated. Then he stepped forward and went into the other room. The door slammed shut behind him. Almost buried in the shaving strewn on the floor lay Dolly Dennis. She was tied and gagged.

Meer's mocking voice came through the planks. "Let's see you break out of there, Bryn. Even if you manage it, all you'll accomplish is to walk into our guns. As a matter of fact, I'm being kind to you. I'm saving you the sight of what will go

on in this room. You saw the burning brazier in the other room and the hot irons in it. They're used for persuasion. Willy you can make a mummy obey orders with hot irons. The idea is to persuade Sibyl to make out a will in my favor. Later it can be witnessed by reputable citizens who are not too reputable to do certain things for substantial bribes, and the same will be true of a rather respected lawyer.

"Sibyl, I made sure to find out, has no living relatives. She not only has a considerable sum of money in her own name, but a great deal more which was left to her by her father.

"Of course it will be necessary for Sibyl to die after that, along with you and Dolly Dennis. As soon as Sibyl writes out the will, gallons of kerosene spread over this shack will make it into a tinderbox. Naturally your deaths will be blamed on the gang that killed Norman Day and Mrs. Carson and Lace Powys, but it won't matter, because nobody but you suspects me of being linked with the gang. As for the will, that will arouse little or no suspicion, for it is known that Sibyl and I were very close friends and she had nobody else to leave her fortune to. I have let it get about that Sibyl and I planned to be married in the near future."

BRYN felt a vast emptiness inside of him. He and Sibyl and Dolly would die like trapped rats in the fire. The police, if they came at all, would probably arrive too late.

In the other room there was the sound of ripping fabric and harsh male laughter. Dolly Dennis stared up at Bryn with a fear-contorted face. Through the wall came thin, mewling sounds as Sibyl's gag forced her screams of agony back down her throat. Her torture had begun.

Glancing frantically about, Bryn's eyes fell on the single high, grime-covered window through which light trickled. He went to it quickly, released the window from the hook which locked it and swung it up.

The opening was barred.

Of course! They wouldn't have placed him in this room with an unbarred window. But bars were to imprison ordinary men. Often he had given a demonstration of his strength before friends by twisting iron bars. He tugged, moved the bar slightly in its cement casing, but all the power of his mighty muscles couldn't pull it out.

It was one thing bending an iron bar when it was free and he had plenty of leverage. It was ten times more difficult pulling out a bar firmly incased in concrete and when he had to reach above his head to grip it. Desperately he looked about for something to stand on. The little room was absolutely bare.

SIBYL'S moans continued in the other room. Bryn's blood turned to ice as he visualized what the poor girl must be suffering.

He strode over to Dolly Dennis, ripped the gag from her mouth, set to work untying her bonds. She smiled courageously up at him.

"Guess I got it coming to me for letting that Meers guy in," she said. "But I'm sorry I got you in this mess, Chief. Looks like we've reached the end."

"Not by a damned sight," he stated between his teeth.

As he was pulling the last of the ropes off her, he heard Meers' exclaim triumphantly; "Good! She'll write out the will now. Take her down, Willy."

Only a couple of minutes left at the very most!

Bryn said to Dolly: "If you got down on your hands and knees under that window, could you hold up my weight? I need leverage to get at those bars."

"I'll try, Chief."

He took off his shoes, mounted on her

back, holding part of his weight up by grasping the bars. But when he pulled back on one of the bars, her back sagged under him and she went down on her stomach.

"Guess I wasn't set," Dolly apologized, panting. "Try again."

Again he stood on her back, and this time he exerted every ounce of muscle. Once more Dolly gave way under him; the bar, however, was now definitely loose in its casing. The next attempt sent him sprawling heavily on his back, but his fingers were around the bar which he had torn out.

Meers' voice chortled: "Everything's set. Dump her on the floor, Willy. Spill the kerosene all over the place and upstairs in the bins. When you're ready to drop a match upstairs, call down to me and I'll light the shavings here. I want the place to go up in flames all at once like tinderbox."

Bryn was attacking the second bar. Sweat soaked his underwear and poured from his face. Beneath his feet Dolly was moaning:

"We can't get out in time! Oh, God, we'll roast alive!"

TWO attempts removed the second bar. But at least two more bars had to be pulled out before Dolly's buxom body and his own broad shoulders could squeeze through.

He worked at those bars like mad. Dolly beneath him was taking terrific punishment, but no further sound came from her. Time after time he tumbled off her back.

And then, just as the fourth bar came free, he heard Willy's voice in the store above: "It's all set up here. I'm dropping the match."

Quickly Bryn pushed Dolly through the window. For breathless seconds she was stuck in the frame, then with a mighty effort squeezed through. He lifted himself

with a silent prayer that his shoulders would make it. He got one shoulder through, couldn't quite pull out the other. Dolly had her hands about his chin, sobbing as she tugged at him. He could already hear the cackling of the flames—or was it his imagination? And Sibyl was lying in those kerosene-drenched shavings!

MOMENTARILY he paused to catch his breath. Then he again fell to squirming, wriggling, trying to contract his bulk. Somehow his second shoulder tore through. It was a matter of seconds to pull the rest of his body through the opening.

He started running as soon as he was on his feet. The window opened to the rear of the building. As he raced around to the front of the store, Willy was just coming out of the door. He saw Bryn a second before Bryn's fist broke his jaw. Willy went down abruptly and lay still. Bryn hurdled his form and dashed into the store.

Tom Meers was coming up the steps. His mouth fell open stupidly when he saw Bryn and he took a single step downward, at the same time diving in his pocket for his gun. The flames below threw an eerie light on his big body and hate-distorted face.

Bryn simply threw himself at Meers. The two men went down together, landing in the flames. Bryn bounced to his feet, saw Meers rising and still trying to claw for his gun. Bryn dove in, sinking his left fist into Meers' midriff. Meers grunted hollowly and his legs collapsed under him. Flames licked at him.

The cellar room was already an inferno. That dry timber and shavings soaked in kerosene had taken only seconds to blaze furiously. And lying almost in the midst of the flames was the white, writhing body, tied and gagged, of Sibyl Day.

SWINGING her up in his arms, he mounted the steps which were already on fire. Flames met him at the head of the stairs. A matter of only a few steps through the hungry flames, and then he was out in the fresh air.

Arms took Sibyl Day from him. Dazed, he looked at Lieutenant Hummel's florid face and at Billy Pierce standing at Dolly Dennis' side, and at a crowd of uniformed and plainclothes police.

A single agonized shriek rose above the roar of the fire.

Bryn whirled and headed back for the store. Hummel and Pierce hurled themselves at Bryn at the same moment.

"It's death to go back in there," Hummel rasped.

"But Tom Meers is down there!" Bryn cried. "My God, you can't let any human being die like that!"

Hummel said between his teeth: "That's the fate he planned for the three of you. Dolly Dennis told us in a couple of words what it was all about. He'd burn anyway in the chair. And it's too late to save him. You'd never come out alive."

Ben Bryn allowed Hummel and Pierce to lead him away. He realized that parts of his jacket and trousers were smoldering, that his hands were beginning to blister.

Billy Pierce was saying enthusiastically: "Even if we hadn't come, Chief, you could have handled it all right by yourself. I'd been talking to Hummel when the call came in that you'd just rubbed out another killer. That Carson maid is a dope. She didn't tell us what you'd come to see her about till Hummel started questioning her. But, hell, Chief, you didn't need us. You're a one-man police department by yourself. . . . What do you say, Lieutenant?"

"That's putting it just about right," Hummel grinned.

Ben Bryn moved over to where Sibyl Day sat in a police car. She was covered up to her neck in policemen's coats. A police chauffeur was about to drive her to a hospital.

"I don't want to ask you how you feel," Bryn said. "Poor kid, what you must have suffered. I'm sorry I couldn't get to you sooner." Bryne patted her hand and looked down at her wan little face.

She smiled wanly in spite of the pain that must have wracked her body. She leaned forward and placed her lips against his mouth and her small, soft hand moved tenderly over his face. She sank back and the car started to move.

Ben Bryn stared after the car with an utterly bewildered expression on his face. Little by little a broad, happy grin appeared on his face. Behind him Dolly Dennis and Billy Pierce and the cops were snickering, but Ben Bryn didn't care.

THE END

FUNERALS==C. O. D.

A murder=mystery novelette filled with tense drama and ending with a chill=packed punch!

by EDITH & EJLER JACOBSON

Wing somersaulted over him, landing on his head beyond the desk.

It had all the earmarks of the most despicable racket ever devised by man . . . or monster. And Nat Perry, very vulnerable detective known to the underworld as "The Bleeder," was in a fair way to crush it—if he could comb the hearses out of his hair!

CHAPTER ONE

The Third Hearse

PLAINCLOTHES Inspector Harry O'Connor walked out of the commissioner's office, fighting for control of that odd smarting in his eyes. Younger men nodded uncomfortably as he passed, as though it had not been their inclination to nod at all. The old detective returned no salutations. They could think as they pleased, and be damned to them.

Still, the commissioner had been thinking the same thing. Harry wondered why his superior hadn't been tougher. It was no secret that many a younger officer had been busted for exchanging favors with Aaron Bluff—which was exactly what Harry O'Connor had been doing! Bluff was the nightclub king of New York—until the cops closed his hot spot on a public nuisance charge, pending a checkup for something worse. But that didn't faze Bluff. He had "loaned" money in important directions. O'Connor smiled to himself. . . . It was a damned good thing the commissioner hadn't seen him with Bluff the other night—in the *hearse.* . . .

He had been a long time in harness,

Harry thought with sudden desperation, and every year the going was harder. Just a little more time, he prayed, time enough to finish the biggest double-cross in history. And then, if he had to, he'd go out like a man. The thought ran over and over in his mind, a bitter, secret thing. It had gone that way all through his interview with the commissioner, so that he had heard only the trend, and not the phrases, when he was spoken to. Wait, all of you, till you see my diary. Maybe, by that time, you'll be burning Aaron Bluff for the murder of a damned old fool who used to be a city detective. But you'll be burning him for plenty besides, and when you're through, I'll be waiting for my innings at him in hell. . . .

"Pop."

Startled, Harry looked up at the slender blond young man at the curb. He was a quiet-looking fellow, and his face was calm, but there was more trouble in his eyes than Harry liked to see. Was Nat against him, too? Nat Perry, the kid whose life he had snatched from Fate's maw, the kid he loved? He looked at a black coupe parked by the curb. "Buy a new car?" he asked lamely.

Perry shook his head. "No—smashed the other one up. I rented this till the green one gets repaired." His voice was gentle, concerned, as though he were talking to a child, and it made O'Connor furious. Hell, it wasn't Nat's place to care for him! Nat was twenty-nine, a grown man, one of the shrewdest detectives in New York—but to Harry, he had been a son; and he was still a kid. "Pop, I want to know something: How did I happen to see you with Aaron Bluff last night?"

O'Connor snapped, "Probably because you snoop too damned much." Perry swallowed, and frowned a little, as though he couldn't believe it. He'd have to take it that way, O'Connor thought, and a sudden panic made him want to tell the young man the truth. Once he'd been Nat Per-

ry's hero, and he had been prouder of that than of anything in the world.

He had reason for that pride. He'd given Nat Perry everything, and his first gift had been life itself. There'd been no hope for that fourteen-year-old they found in the wake of a hit-and-run driver until Patrolman O'Connor gave him four blood transfusions, and imbued him with a fighting will to live. Only a broken leg; but Nat Perry was dying of broken skin. He was a born haemophiliac; his blood could not clot, and never would.

AND now that fourteen-year-old was a man; a smoother-spoken, quieter man than O'Connor had ever been, and it was O'Connor who had reared him. A man who stood insistently before him, with faint damnation in his puzzled face.

"But, Pop, why pick a hearse for a conference? It's a good place for privacy, but what's private between you and Bluff?"

Harry shut his eyes, and opened them again. It wouldn't have been Nat's way of getting at Bluff, he thought — it wouldn't have to be. The Bleeder, they called Nat in the underworld. And they were afraid of him. No one was particularly afraid of Harry O'Connor any more.

Sixty's not so old, he told himself, but he didn't believe it, not when he looked at Nat. He should have quit—but he couldn't quit! Not with the terrible knowledge inside him that every case he'd touched for the past five years had been successfully closed only because the Bleeder was tacitly and inescapably behind him. He had to prove, even to himself, that he hadn't borrowed too much time from eternity . . . that he was still useful.

Best for Nat if I go, O'Connor thought. I got him into this kind of work in the first place. Without meaning to, or wanting to, I'm keeping him in it. He is the Bleeder, and his name was a name to reckon by, and always before, he had been too clever and too careful to die. But some day, if he stayed in it long enough, he'd hit the short end of the law of averages, and there'd be a broken old man mourning Nat Perry's sharp young wits and quiet young courage. Better if I go first, O'Connor thought. . . .

What was wrong with the boy? Why must he still be staring with that odd heart-broken look on his face, and the spring sunlight full on his bared yellow hair? I'm a city detective—O'Connor told himself, as he retreated into the shadow of the white building—I have a right to my own ways without explaining them to a whipper-snapper of a private dick. He said, "What's wrong with Aaron Bluff? He's done me plenty of good, and I mean good." The words seemed queer to be coming from his own throat, but so many things about himself puzzled him now that he was old. "Beat it, you. And keep your face clean."

Nat Perry got into the black coupe, and drove away. That's what I've done with my life, O'Connor thought, watching the black coupe, and a certain pride came into him, so that his back stiffened and his eyes grew clearer.

NATHANIEL PERRY knew, two blocks before he reached Bluff's offices at Forty-second and Lexington, that he wasn't going to enjoy the interview. Aaron Bluff wasn't the kind of man he liked to deal with. They had never pinned anything on him big enough to fight—at least, not big enough for Nat to fight. The Bleeder knew his own vulnerability, and he disliked risking his life merely to prove how mean a man could be.

At Fortieth Street, he saw a sombre black vehicle in his rear vision mirror. The sight reminded him anew of last night. What had Harry O'Connor to do with Bluff—in a hearse? The answer must have been obvious to the commissioner,

but Nat Perry wasn't the commissioner. Bluff had a payroll, and O'Connor must be on it. But Nat had known O'Connor too long to accept a thing like that.

Suddenly, the puzzle went crazy in his head. He couldn't think of it clearly, because just now he couldn't think of anything clearly. He always drove with his windows closed, which was one more item in his necessarily careful system of life. But clear warm air had been seeping into his coupe a minute before. Now, the warmth was abruptly gone. He was chilled to the bone and the breath left his lungs like air from a split balloon.

Death! He had been close enough to it before to recognize it. But now, there was no reason to die! He shouted, yet could not hear his own voice. It was like a dream, from which he was trying to wake. A shape moved past him, out in the sun-streaked avenue, and he knew it was the hearse he had seen in his rear vision mirror.

A hearse—for him? In a last defiant gesture against mortality, he tried to level his automatic toward the evil faces peering from the driver's seat of the hearse. But he had no strength. His gun arm slacked, the pistol clanking against the window.

Something roared thunderously in his ears, and a rush of wind made his crazily-pumping heart do dizzier tricks. For a second, he saw nothing at all.

When his brain cleared, he found himself slumped over the wheel, the automatic clutched weakly in his hand. His front bumper was kissing a traffic stanchion, and someone was bellowing from another car that he didn't own the road. A triangle of glass was missing from the front corner of his left window, and, three blocks north, a hearse was losing itself into traffic.

That hearse. . . . Some unreasoned clarity of purpose formed in his numb awareness, and his hand darted toward the gear shift. He had some idea of checking on the interest that driver had shown in him, but suddenly his body stiffened, and he leaned backward. He had been about to lean against something bright and gleaming that lay in his lap—it was the glass triangle, broken out of his window.

That, too, meant death. Something about that piece of glass brought Perry's thinking back to focus. He still felt cold, and more than a little shaky, yet he knew with lucid certainty that he had stepped into something. What, he didn't know. Probably the same thing Harry was in. His heart shouldn't have kicked up like that—there was no reason for it. Whatever else was lacking in his blood, it was pumped by as sturdy a muscle as any man's.

He was still shaky, five minutes later, when he looked down a short corridor at the large plate glass door enscribed:

AARON BLUFF, INCORPORATED

Suddenly, the things he had meant to say to Bluff seemed ridiculous. He had business with the man—as vital business as he'd ever had with anyone—but it had ceased to be anything they could talk over.

It would be pointless now, to ask Bluff why he interviewed policemen in hearses. Pointless, because Nat had already been answered in a way. Not a nice way. He had met a hearse, on his way over, and he had come closer to death than he liked to. If Aaron Bluff had written him a letter about it, he could have been no more sure that Bluff had tried to kill him.

But he couldn't accuse the man of that. He couldn't accuse him of anything—yet. He kept watching that glass door. Aaron Bluff, Incorporated. Incorporated what? What was Bluff's business these days? Nat wracked his memory, and discovered the surprising fact that Bluff had no business, as far as he knew.

THE glass door opened briefly, and a girl was coming down the corridor. There was grim concern in her face. What-

ever Bluff conducted behind that door, she knew about it. She might be his secretary, on her way to lunch; a client, or even a girl friend—it didn't matter.

Nat touched her elbow. Before he could speak the girl jumped away from him like a startled mouse. Her fear waxed to something like panic in the space of seconds. She ran from him, called to an elevator operator to wait, and hurried into the car as though there were a mad dog behind her.

Now, more than ever, Nat wanted to talk to her. He took the next car down, caught sight of her in the lobby. She was slender, too well-dressed to be Bluff's secretary, and not pretty enough to be a girl friend—of his. She couldn't have been more than twenty, and Bluff's affairs seldom involved innocents. Then who was she?

She entered a black limousine parked at the curb. Nat was close enough to hear her tense instruction to the chauffeur. "Dr. Etterley. Dr. Carl Etterley. Hurry!" He was not close enough to stop her.

As the limousine nosed out into traffic, Nat's rented coupe ground to a start. A bus swung out in front of him. He cut around it and then straightened out, just behind the limousine again.

No voice sounded from the larger car, but a second's glimpse told Nat that the girl in the tonneau was screaming. She beat against the shatter-proof windows with frantic gloved fists, her mouth a scarlet oval of terror in a blanched face. That wasn't fear—it was torture!

He pulled alongside, remembering his own recent experience in a closed car, and shouted at the chauffeur. There was no response, and a second shout froze in Nat's throat. He had seen that chauffeur less than an hour before, driving a hearse!

The coupe's chromium nose veered leftward, forced the limousine to stop at the curb. Perry leaped clear. When he opened the door of the tonneau, he knew he was too late. The girl's body sagged in his arms when he tried to lift her out, and horror had frozen onto her cold face forever. There was a coldness inside that car that didn't belong in a closed car on the hottest Thursday in May.

Nat turned to the chauffeur—but the chauffeur wasn't there. Everything had happened so quickly, so quietly, that an idle crowd was just beginning to gather around the limousine.

Through a clearing in the crowd, he saw a hearse rounding the corner.

The sight made him get back to his own car, quickly. Others would tend to the dead girl—any help he might have given her was useless now, and he couldn't even identify her. He pulled away, turned into the side-street, but the hearse was gone.

He was almost unnerved. Aaron Bluff —and three hearses. Maybe the same hearse, seen three times. Why had the girl died, as he had been intended to die? And what was her business with Bluff? What had been Harry's business with Bluff last night in that sombre death-cart?

It occurred to Nat that Bluff shouldn't have expected a visit from Nat Perry. There was only one man who could have told him of the possibility of such a thing. And that was Harry O'Connor.

There was an answer to everything, and he had the peculiar feeling that it was all contained in a little jagged triangle of glass which had come from his car window. There had been something about it, something more significant than just a deadly object for a haemophiliac to have in his lap. He realized that. But he didn't know the answer.

CHAPTER TWO

The Corpse Died Twice

HE PARKED in the East Thirties, and consulted a grimy telephone directory in a grimier drug store. Dr. Carl Etterley had offices on Park Avenue, and he lived on East Eighty-ninth Street. At the office, a feminine voice told Nat that the doctor was at home. He didn't 'phone again—he couldn't get what he wanted over a wire.

He didn't know the girl's name, but her doctor would. And her doctor might know other things. Doctors usually do. Maybe Dr. Etterley knew why a girl of twenty, who looked as though she belonged in another world, apart from Bluff, had been worth somebody's while murdering.

Maybe he knew what a girl like that could possibly have to do with a man like Aaron Bluff.

She had been an expensive-looking girl, and she'd had an expensive doctor. The apartment house on East Eighty-ninth Street had a lobby that might have been a ballroom. The uniforms fitted the doormen, and there was indirect lighting in the elevator. Nat rang the bell of apartment 8-A. It sounded three lilting musical chimes. They were very pretty, but not pretty enough to down Nat's rising ire when he heard footsteps and received no answer.

He rang again. This time, he heard nothing but the chimes.

Something was wrong. A doctor, even the richest doctor, is on call twenty-four hours a day, and anyone who lives with him knows it. If there were footsteps, there should be an answer. Nat took a small wire spring from his pocket; with it his dextrous fingers could open anything short of the mint.

A woman in a silk dress walked through the corridor. She saw a tall well-dressed young man fumbling with what appeared to be a key. She smiled sympathetically, and walked on. Nat smiled back. When she rounded the corridor, the lock was open.

It was mid-afternoon, but the foyer was dark. So were the other rooms—green shades had been pulled against the afternoon's heat. It was very cool, cooler than mere shutting out of sunlight could have made even an airy apartment on that hot day. It was almost chilly. And there was no one at home.

That chill—he'd felt it twice before during the afternoon. Once in his own car, and once when he opened the door of a limousine. A tremor of anticipation rose in him as he drew the blinds in one room after another, looking for the person whose footsteps he'd heard outside. He found the studio portrait of a handsome woman of thirty on the grand piano in the living-room. "To Carl, all my love, Bea." And the frame was draped in black.

Here was death again, death softened, death that could be displayed on a grand piano. Apparently Dr. Carl Etterley had been recently widowed. Perry thought of that other display . . . three of death's vehicles, that had passed before him since his abortive visit to Aaron Bluff. He had a sudden mental image of Bluff as a distributor of fashionable death—it had to be that way. He stepped into the next room.

Stretched on a candlewick bedspread, there was a handsome stoutish man who looked sick in the sudden sunlight. His limbs were tensed, as though in secret pain, and the carefully shaven skin of his face was the color of a frozen pond. Over the left breast pocket of his dressing gown was the maroon monogram C. E., and the letters did not stir.

"Dr. Etterley!" But it would take more than a cry to wake Dr. Etterley. A shove would not do it, nor the touch of a warmer hand on his. There was only one loud trumpet to which Dr. Carl Etterley would respond again. The corpse was cold. A coroner would say that Dr. Etterley had been dead at least twelve hours, Nat guessed.

But he had touched another cold corpse that afternoon—a corpse which had been a living girl ten seconds earlier! Now his own hands were damp with sudden, chilly sweat as he bent over the doctor, his mind trying for some reasonable diagnosis for this sudden epidemic of corpses.

Cheerfully, liltingly, the musical doorbell of the apartment sounded through the dank, cold air.

THE man at the door looked surprised when he saw the blond detective. Anyone might have been surprised to meet that particularly intent look with no compromise in it, over an ordinary apartment threshold.

He was a polite little man, though, and he peered at Nat almost tenderly over his thick rimless spectacles. He said in a softened voice, "Dr. Etterley—may I start attending to him now?"

It wasn't loud, but it made the little man jump. Nat said, "Who the hell wants to know?" and he kept his fingers tight around the man's lapel when he said it.

"Dear me. I'll be *glad* to go away if you don't want me! We don't usually take these rush calls. We only hurried this time as a favor!"

There was something undeniably genuine about the man's half-fearful indignation, as though he honestly thought Nat a madman, and a boorish one. The detective's hand dropped to his side. "Wait a minute," he said. "I think there's a misunderstanding. Where do you come from, and who sent for you?"

The little man drew a white business card from his neat black suit, and leaned forward on tiptoe to point his name out to Nat. He was Asa Hammer, representing the Douglas James Funeral Parlor. "Someone phoned us this morning, and asked for a man to come for Dr. Etterley. It's all very queer. The doctor—he is dead, isn't he?"

"Yes," said Nat. "Excuse me." His voice was too quiet this time to startle the little undertaker—but he felt anything but quiet. He dashed back to Dr.

Etterley's bedroom, which seemed to be the direction whence that faint sound had come . . . the sound a man stirring in sleep might make.

Whoever had stirred, it was not in sleep. In sleep, no one buries a knife in his own heart. For in the maroon monogram over the doctor's left breast pocket, there quivered the erect hilt of a knife. But the doctor had been dead! Someone had called an undertaker for him that morning! Did two people want him dead? There were three doors in Dr. Etterley's bedroom, with a bathroom beyond one of them. The bathroom was empty, and its other door was locked. Someone had escaped through it; that someone had knifed Dr. Etterly and gone into the adjoining bedroom—

Nat didn't find anyone in the other bedroom. He didn't go there. At the front door, where he had left Asa Hammer, a man shrieked once, and then was still.

The little undertaker was slumped across the threshold, his eyes astonished. There was a little black hole in his forehead.

NAT PERRY got nothing from the smartly-uniformed elevator operator. He had taken a lot of people down, the man stammered; he had seen nothing extraordinary, heard nothing, and didn't want to believe anything. Nothing like murder had ever happened in his neighborhood before. The doormen were equally co-operative.

It wasn't Nat's job to quiz them. The police could find out who had killed Asa Hammer and struck a knife through the corpse of Carl Etterley. Nat's business was with another man, a man who had tried to kill him and who had started him on a trail that was spotted with death.

Aaron Bluff—Nat was convinced he was the man. Behind Aaron Bluff, was the figure of his foster-father as he had seen it last night, stepping out of a hearse.

He was going to Bluff's office again, and this time he knew better what he had to say to the man. Few words would be exchanged, but they would be to the point, and followed by action.

There was no light behind that anonymous elaborate plate glass door on the fortieth floor of the skyscraper. The door itself was locked. Nat laughed dismally. He had found out one thing about Aaron Bluff's business, at any rate—shop was closed before six. He could find out more. Once again the Bleeder picked a lock.

He found himself in an airy waiting room, overlooking the East River. Bluff couldn't be doing badly, he thought. A door marked Private beckoned him further.

Aaron Bluff had salvaged at least his office furniture from the debacle of his nightclub. There was a box of cigars in the top drawer of Bluff's desk and a flat fifty of fancy cigarettes, the kind that women put in long holders and men don't like to be caught with. In the bottom drawer, there was a pinch bottle of Scotch and a quarter-inch thick cardboard folder.

Nothing else in the office, anywhere, suggested that Bluff was a business-man. The waiting-room was upholstered, innocent even of pencils—and except for a fountain pen stand and an empty filing cabinet, the office might have been a sitting-room in a private home.

And in the cardboard folder, there were exactly two receipts, in carbon. One was dated late in February, stating that Aaron Bluff had received two hundred dollars from Henry Burnside. The other, dated last month, acknowledged the same amount from Mrs. Beatrice Etterley.

Things flashed rapidly through Nat's mind. "To Carl, all my love, Bea." A photo—draped in black. Mrs. Beatrice Etterley had known the nature of Aaron Bluff's business, and she was dead, and her husband was dead. A girl had come out of Bluff's office to die within minutes. What kind of business was it, that contact with it was so fatal? What kind of business could keep Bluff going, on a visible intake of four hundred dollars in three months, when four hundred dollars obviously wasn't enough to pay the office rent?

Nat wheeled sharply as he felt the sudden draught. The door behind him was open, and the man on the threshold had his finger on the trigger of an automatic.

PERRY whirled sideways, letting the bullet sing into the desk's mahogany side. He recognized in the short nattily-dressed gunman one Ownie Wing, a bookie who collected in blood if he couldn't collect in coin. Wing had good reason to protect Bluff's secrets. When Bluff went down, Wing would go down with him. It was self-protection, and Wing was taking it seriously.

Nat took the same idea just as seriously. He dove at the bookie's ankles, a measured cadence of bullets rapping out over his head. Wing sprawled forward, over the detective's tense body, and the gun skidded a few inches on the carpet. Nat came to his feet, gracefully as a cat and Wing somersaulted over him, landing on his head beyond the desk. This was Nat's fighting style, this studied co-ordination of every muscle in his body. It wasn't new—it had been used in the East, centuries earlier. Scientific, requiring a minimum of effort in the application, based on exact knowledge of his own and his opponent's anatomy, the technique was a deadly weapon for any man who took the pains to learn it. It was this technique which had made the Bleeder feared in the underworld—it was complemented by simple-looking blows which had killed men Perry dared not leave alive behind him.

Wing moaned. His head was twisted queerly to one side, but he managed to raise himself, holding onto the edge of the desk. He looked at Nat, and in the falling dusk of the curtained room, seemed to realize for the first time whom he had attacked. "Bleeder!" He started to talk, hectically, in a high-pitched voice that had the hysteria of pain running through it. "My God, Bleeder . . . you're making a hell of a mistake! I didn't expect *you* here . . . your old man. . . ." He paused, and his breath came heavy. He looked at Nat with his little eye's like a trapped weasel's.

"Shut up about my old man," Nat commanded.

"Like hell I will! This cinches it. To-morrow anybody who reads the papers is going to know it. Your old man's a wise guy, Bleeder—but he can't play two ways with us! And you don't dare touch me for it, because you know—"

Nat's arm reached out, described a short vicious arc that ended at the side of Wing's throat. The man gasped. His face turned purple, and he crumpled backward like a stack of paper. "You won't talk about him," Nat said, "because your mouth isn't fit to say his name."

Ownie Wing did not answer. There was another reason for his not talking. He would be saying nothing at all from now on. Nat's blow had fractured his jugular.

The detective's hand shook a little as he pocketed those two receipts from the cardboard file, whether from anger or shock, he wasn't sure. He's had no compunctions about killing Wing—it was mere life insurance on his own part. But Harry—Nat had killed a man to keep Harry O'Connor clear. And he wasn't sure himself, that Harry O'Connor belonged in the clear.

He sighed. That wasn't his business. They'd quarreled, and maybe O'Connor had broken faith with his employer, the law. He hadn't quite broken faith with Nat Perry. There was that memory between them, that undeniable fact that the Bleeder had lived to walk the streets only because of O'Connor. There were other things, things that had happened in all the years of their intimacy.

Because of those things. Nat would have silenced any man who threatened what Wing had threatened . . . even a man who hadn't tried to kill him first.

It gave him a queer feeling of instability, to be working on the wrong side of the cloth from Harry. He had a pictured image of the old man before him now, a sawed-off, broad-shouldered old man with tired blue eyes and a gait slower than had been the gait of that man who gave him new life fifteen years ago. It was a long time since he'd taken advice from Harry, or needed it—it was a long time ago that Harry started needing him. Maybe Harry still needed him. He had to think so, anyway. He had to think so, if he wanted to keep going.

Maybe I needed him too, Nat thought. Maybe I always will. He knew where he had to go next, and he knew he had to get there in a hurry, because a man's life depended on it—but somehow, the life of that stranger seemed less important than it would have been if Harry had cared about it, too.

He forced himself to think of the urgency of this trip as he drove southward. Henry Burnside had transacted business with Bluff. It had not been the kind that Ownie Wing transacted with him. Hal Burnside was captain of the undefeated Overbrook Polo Team, and the papers had given him a build-up as one of the hardest-training, cleanest-living athletes in amateur sport. Therefore, Hal Burnside bade fair to be transferred shortly from the sports page to the obituaries.

When he stepped out of the elevator on the fifth floor of the house on Washington Square, Nat suddenly stopped forcing himself to think about the puzzle of Hal Burnside and Aaron Bluff. He didn't

have to force it—it hit him between the eyes. There was a man standing at the door of the Burnside apartment, explaining to someone on the other side that he had to get in.

The man at the door was Harry O'Connor.

CHAPTER THREE

The Bleeder's Destination

NAT couldn't see the man on the other side of the door, but he heard the voice clearly. It was a cool annoyed voice, and it sounded as though its owner were recovering from a slight touch of amusement. "Of course you're a policeman, Inspector," he said. "I've already taken your word for it. But we don't want the police. I take it you're supposed to be a public servant—not a public nuisance. So will you please leave us alone?"

Harry O'Connor's face got the look on it that Nat remembered from crises past. The old plainclothesman started forward. The door slammed in his face, and the lock snapped with a sharp, cutting click. He stood there for a moment, glowering at the door, as though he were of two minds about breaking in.

Then the look faded, leaving nothing but a bitterness that had become almost habitual of late. If Nat had ever seen a man angry, that man was his foster-father. There was a good reason for Harry's wanting to get into that apartment; there was generally a good reason for anything Harry wanted to do badly enough. But it apparently hadn't been good enough for a search warrant!

The old man's eyes met Nat's face, and the ghost of surprise crossed his lined face. His voice had no warmth. "Looking for me?"

"No, Pop, I—" Nat stopped. That wasn't true. He had been looking for O'Connor, all day. He knew that, by the feeling it gave him to listen even to O'Connor's surliness. He felt less alone, and completely confident once more. He didn't know Harry's game. He knew why he was here himself, but he didn't know what had brought Harry here. Even if it were the same thing—he didn't like to think of how Harry had found out. Bluff might have told him, last night in the hearse. . . .

But those questions in his mind—were only questions. The important thing was that O'Connor was here, and whatever trail he'd followed could wait till later.

They stood there for a moment, the young man and the old one, and the old man's bitterness seemed to cover a certain shame. Nat wanted to tell him it didn't matter about that quarrel, but he couldn't—they hadn't quarreled that way before, and consequently, they had no experience in patching up after.

In the next moment, they weren't looking at each other, nor were they standing still. From inside the Burnside apartment, a woman's voice, forgetting all reticence in pain, shrieked, "Oh God, *help* me!"

They didn't have to do anything about the locked door. It opened of itself before them, and a man whose full fair face was twisted and ashen shouted at them, "Inspector—it's my wife! For God's sake, get a doctor!"

The two men rushed past him, into a bedroom where a woman lay taut and still, as though she had stopped moving in the middle of a convulsion. She was stretched across a chaise lounge, her long white fingers biting into the upholstery, her blue dress clinging to her body moistly. When Harry touched her, his mouth went tight, and he showed Nat his hand. It was wet. Nat understood that. There was a cold dampness coming out on his own skin . . . it was something in the very air of the room. They turned her over. The pretty face—it must have been

pretty, before it turned almost the same dark blue as her dress—stared at them in numb, perpetual horror.

Hal Burnside stood at the threshold, his face quivering, his big hands rubbing aimlessly against one another. He looked helpless and a little awed. He said, the way a large child might have said in the face of disaster, "Aren't you going to call a doctor?"

With a practiced hand, Harry O'Connor touched the young woman's wrist, her temples, her heart. He looked at Burnside, and said in a flat, unhappy way, "Of course. I'll call our own medical examiner. But I can tell you all he could. She's dead."

"ISN'T this going to tip your hand, Pop?" Nat asked.

O'Connor's eyes were bright in the darkness. Too bright, Nat thought. "What the hell do you mean?"

"Even if the medical examiner calls it heart failure," the dectective continued slowly, "would you let a hearse call for the lady, and take her away—for good?"

O'Connor didn't answer. He simply stared, numb. To Nat, it seemed almost natural . . . like the other holes he had helped the old man out of. The Bleeder began to feel on familiar territory again.

He'd been playing a close game with the murderer, O'Connor had, and now he had reached a showdown too early. Nat knew it. It was all Bluff's move now. . . Bluff had sent O'Connor to see the Burnsides deliberately, because he knew what was going to happen. Harry had two ways of sinking deeper into the hole, and no clear way out. He could either aid and abet Bluff's scheme by keeping his mouth shut—or he could put his own hand on the table, a hand with no trumps in it. There was evidence, if he didn't let them bury the body. Not startling evidence. Just a young woman whom the police medical examiner would declare dead of heart failure. And heart failure isn't murder.

There was evidence somewhere, Nat thought, something he could pull out of of his memory, something he could slip up the old man's sleeve himself and play for a jackpot. And then he had it. It was a little jagged triangle of glass, that had been broken out of his own windshield.

"Never mind, Pop," he said, "I'll take care of this end. You keep playing the way you started."

O'Connor looked at him, puzzled. Then he shook his head slowly, and left the room. Hal Burnside said flatly to the blond detective, "You don't belong here."

Nat looked again at the young woman who would shortly be pronounced dead of heart failure. "I know I don't," he said. He left.

He found a drug store across the side street from the house that fronted Washington Square. It was eight-thirty, a calm warm evening, and bare-headed girls strolled across the Square, humming as they went.

The Bleeder had a weapon now, one that Aaron Bluff had furnished himself. Nat remembered how oddly chill all those rooms had been for such a warm day. He remembered too, the knife in Dr. Etterley's heart. His fingers felt thick as he fumbled through the telephone directory. A name on a white card . . . and a polite little man, who had looked at him as though he were mad, and who had died shortly after.

Then he found it, the Douglas James Funeral Parlor. They had taken one call in a hurry; they would take another one faster than that.

"I'm sorry," said a man's voice, sounding not at all sorry, into the phone. "Too short notice—we couldn't manage."

"But you managed earlier," Nat stated, "when you sent Asa Hammer to Carl Etterley's." There was a short silence. "This may surprise you, but you're in

line to have a neat series of murders pinned on you. You wouldn't like that, and neither would I—because someone else did it. You can call Inspector Harry O'Connor of the Headquarters for confirmation. Mention my name—Nathaniel Perry. Here's the address again . . . Washington Square South, Fifth floor. Burnside."

There was a pause, and then the voice commented softly, awedly, "We'll check. There'll be someone right over. Will they expect him?"

"Yes," Nat hazarded. He was sure that the first undertaker to arrive would be expected. "There's just one thing; *don't embalm her*. If you do, you'll run into trouble."

Someone exclaimed incredulously at the other end, and Nat replaced the receiver. He loitered just inside the drug store, unaware of the two girls at the counter who stared at him over their sodas, unaware of anything but that entrance on Washington Square.

The grey hearse, with the "Douglas James" on the left door in small script, pulled up in fifteen minutes. In an agony of apprehension, Nat watched the two men enter, waited for their return. If he could have thought for them, hurried for them. . . . But they had no inkling of the nature of this call, and Nat waited, his poised body giving no hint of the nervousness he felt. Suppose the others came before they left? Suppose Burnside—but Burnside wouldn't. Burnside wasn't staunch enough, at this point, to question details. He would accept whatever disposal offered itself.

The men came down. Between them they carried a box. Nat knew that Althea Burnside was in it. The medical examiner would pronounce no verdict over her, and the predatory hearses that had roamed the streets that day, like tumbrils looking for victims, would never hold her. Privately, Nat said a short prayer for the soul of

Asa Hammer, who had been an honest man, sent on a murderer's mission to throw the Bleeder off the trail.

Slowly, the grey hearse lost itself in the shadows of Sixth Avenue. They were safe now—they had gotten away. They were good men, Nat thought in an ecstasy of relief, fine men. If he died tomorrow, he wanted the job of burying him given to the Douglas James Funeral Parlor, and he hoped they would make money on it. He could have pinned a medal on Mr. Douglas James.

And then he saw the second hearse streaming up to the door.

ONCE again, Nat Perry stood a little distance away from the door of the Burnside apartment, and saw someone refused entrance.

"But she's gone!" Hal Burnside was saying. "The undertaker has called for her!"

One of the three liveried callers laughed. It wasn't a friendly laugh. "All right mug," he said. "This is a paid delivery. You asked for it—now you're going to take it." He nodded at the other two, and Nat saw his face. He had seen that face twice before since noon—once while he was trapped in an airless coupe, and once when he tried to stop the chauffeur of a limousine that carried a dying girl.

Burnside was yelping. His big stocky body blocked the doorway, and his face, that had been white when his wife died, was florid and ugly. "Take your damned foot out of that door—this house is mine!"

The liveried driver swung his arm back. There was something round and black in his hand, and it was set for damage. The man swung the blackjack through the crack in the door, which suddenly burst open. The two figures rushed inside, just as Nat started to run, and then the door slammed shut again.

He threw himself against the door, felt something heavy smashing into it from the other side. He tried the knob, and when he looked at the lock, he knew that it had been smashed. There wasn't a key in the world that could unscrew that mangled metal. Inside the apartment, he heard Burnside's muffled, "Don't! Oh God, don't do that! Please. . ." And then there was a crashing sound, as though someone were throwing furniture.

Nat heard his own voice joining the frightened chorus that echoed down the corridor, as one door after another popped open on the fifth floor. "It's a murder!" he shouted at them. "Call the police!" Someone, a very old woman, was tugging at his coat, begging him hysterically to take care of her, and he pulled away, and hurled himself again and again at the unyielding door.

Then, loud as sound itself, he heard an ominous silence from inside—and it drowned out all the other voices, and everything that was echoing frantically in his own brain.

For a second, he stood quite still, damning himself for a fool—the service entrance! Of course, they'd have used that! The silence inside the apartment couldn't have been more than a second's duration when Nat Perry darted past the corridor of excited tenants, through the one door on the floor without an apartment number on it. He was in the service hall, all right, and that grey door on his left had been left ajar—but he knew by the descending spot of light through the crack in the elevator shaft† that he was just that second too late.

He took the staircase, flying down with his finger-tips barely steadying him at the bannisters. He reached the street just in time to see a black hearse disappearing at the far end of Washington Square.

Wherever they were taking Hal Burnside—or what was left of him now—was the Bleeder's destination.

CHAPTER FOUR

Special Funeral Service

THE route was direct. He knew they hadn't suspected pursuit. His hands were steady on the wheel, and his eyes clear, but something was trumpeting in his brain almost dazingly. O'Connor— he'd get O'Connor in the clear once more.

Seventh Avenue South, merging at last with the unpopulated shadows of Varick Street. . . . Broadway at its narrowest, and east on Canal Street. Then, south again . . . and east. . . . Once, at an intersection, a private car gave the hearse right of way after the light changed, but Nat picked the trail again at the entrance to the Brooklyn Bridge.

He followed at a discreet distance, merged in the traffic of Brooklyn's Atlantic Avenue, and then the hearse swerved into a crooked cobblestone sidestreet that ended alongside an elevated line. For two blocks, he followed under the El, the sound of his wheels and the hearse motor in front of him sounding loudly through the dark. Unless they were deaf, he thought uneasily, they knew they were not alone—unless they were less bright than he expected, they could have guessed who was following them.

He'd given them too much credit, he decided, when the hearse pulled to a stop in front of a pale and dingy storefront, unlit, inscribed, "Daniel Ferris, Mortician." They'd given him the show. He stopped, and peered at the street sign on the corner, to find the address. His pencil had made one thin line on a piece of paper when something jolted thunderously into the rear of his car. His hands flew instinctively ahead of him, and he tried to brace himself against injury to his face.

When he looked to one side, it was too late. The long lean face of the chauffeur of the hearse was faintly visible beyond an outstretched arm, and the sick sweetness of anaesthetic was making a blur even of that. . . .

He felt sick before he opened his eyes, and sicker when he opened them. After a while, the dizziness and the sickness passed. He tried to move, and found it impossible. There was a pale overhead light glowing above in the ceiling, and within a few yards of him, there were men talking in low tones. He tried to see them, and couldn't. To either side of him, inches away from his face, were satin surfaces.

Then he knew where he was. He was lying, bound hand and foot, in an undertaker's parlor, flat on his back in a coffin.

He pulled at his arms, but they were stiff against his sides. Stiff—the word was unpleasant. One of the voices in the corner was raised to an audible murmur. "Hey, he's awake."

By the dim overhead light, Nat saw a handsomely preserved man of fifty bending over him. It was Aaron Bluff. He said, "Why, hello, Bleeder."

"Go to hell," Nat told him. His voice sounded faint, a little fuzzy.

"That's where you're going, Bleeder. When you spring the lock on the devil's private office, give him my regards."

Well, it was evidence he'd been after, Nat thought. He'd been sure Bluff was out for him—and he'd gone snooping for evidence so that Harry O'Connor could legally put an end to Aaron Bluff. And now he had his evidence. But it didn't look as though he were going to use it.

"It was nice of you, using chloroform," he said. "A knife seems to suit you better."

BLUFF made a deprecating gesture. "You'd have made a messy corpse that way. Besides, everybody knows you're too careful to tangle up with knives. No, Bleeder, you're going to be

buried on the up and up, and not even
that doddering old Pop of yours is going
to have a come-back. They'll be mighty
surprised when the Bleeder finally dies of
heart failure!"

"You mean," Nat queried quietly,
though the words echoed crazily back
and forth in his own brain, "you're going
to bury me alive?"

For a moment, Bluff looked startled.
Then he said, "Let's not call it that. For
all medical purposes, you'll be dead. And
really, before we bury people, we're con-
scientious enough to embalm them."

"You're no undertaker," Nat went on.
What was he doing? Stalling for time?
That was hopeless. There wasn't a chance
that anyone would trace him to this god-
forsaken corner of Brooklyn before that
chill dampness he had felt so many times
during the day became more acute, and
finally permanent. "You're a salesman.
You sell air-conditioning apparatus for
homes and private cars."

"So what?" said Bluff.

"Listen," Nat told Bluff. "You are
obvious to me—you'll be obvious to someone else, too. You won't drop the game,
either—you're too pressed for cash. That's
why you had to have the girl killed, this
afternoon. You were so eager for business, you had to solicit it. I don't know
who she was, but I'll take even money
she had a rich relative, and was right in
line. You offered to get rid of the relative, for a cut of the inheritance of course.
She was a nice girl—she left you like
she'd have left a cobra. She wasn't going
to the police—not right away. She was
just going to check with someone you'd
given as reference—a satisfied client
who'd been saddled with a wife he didn't
want, and who had conveniently become a
widower, Dr. Carl Etterley."

Nat paused, and Bluff remarked con-
templatively, "Bleeder, how do you do
it? I suppose you know you weren't supposed to get far enough to see Miss Turner in the first place. And now you turn
up with her family history."

"It was a little piece of glass," Nat
said. "I found it in my lap after I smashed
my windshield. That's a funny thing,
Bluff—for a piece of glass to fall *in* when
you bust it. Something must have been
pressing harder than I—say, at fifteen
pounds per square inch. That something
was air. And there wasn't any in the
coupe. You had one of your men install
one of your air conditioners in the car I
rented, which could empty the space of
air in less than a minute's time. Finally, I
remembered how creating a vacuum low-
ers the temperature. You had another
one of your gadgets in the girl's car. A
thing like that must take quite a while to
install and you couldn't have installed it
while her car was parked outside."

Bluff turned up his palms. "As you
say, I am guilty of creating a vacuum.
Several vacuums. In other words, several
nothings. And I'm going to show you the
inside of one of them. That's what I'm
doing to you—nothing."

"So I see," Nat remarked drily. "But
you did more than that to Dr. Etterley,
when your stooge and hearse-driver,
Daniel Ferris, reported that I was about
to call on the doctor. You were afraid I
knew too much—that I'd work on Etterly, bring him to. He'd already paid to
have that air-cooling apparatus installed
in his home—you had killed him with it,
or half-killed him, because being a normal
man, he wasn't likely to keep mum about
what was on his conscience. I got there
too soon, so you had to use the crude
way.

"It's a great set-up, Bluff. In the long
run, you might even have charged the
whole thing up to a technical accident.
Your air-conditioners weren't even capable of killing people. You proved that on
me. Your victims just went to sleep, and
got embalmed before they woke up. But
see where it gets you; somebody else is

going to notice the same thing about a piece of glass. Soon you'll have to solicit more business, and the next customer may get further than the Turner girl did. And Harry—"

"Oh, Harry?" said Bluff. "I'm not bothering about him. I wouldn't waste the effort. I'll just let him break himself. He'll do a better job at it than I could."

Nat felt something snap in him at that. He surged upward, his body straining bitterly against the bonds that held it. Men were holding him down, and it was hopeless. He tried not to think about what was coming, as they closed the lid on the casket. Bluff brandished a screwdriver. . . . The cover shut down.

Then it came. The terrible cold, that ate into him like acid. The feeling of cotton stuffed into his lungs, the mad rhythm of his heart . . . and curtains. . . .

SOMEONE said, "I think he'll be all right now, Inspector." For a second, Nat thought he was very young once more, and that he was getting over a traffic accident which had happened when he was fourteen. It felt the same way— and there was Harry O'Connor's face bending over him, with the marked disgust veiling an elegant pleasure, and he knew his head was in O'Connor's lap.

O'Connor said softly, "You make me sick."

Nat Perry touched his own face gingerly. It felt neither warm nor cold. That was probably because his hands and face were the same low temperature. But at least his hand moved. He flexed his knees, cautiously—they worked too. "Pop," he said, "how do I come to be alive?"

"Beats me," O'Connor admitted. "You were dead as hell when I found you." Nat looked to one side. There was a window, and dark streets were moving past the window. He was riding in an ambulance, he surmised, except that it was

pretty fancy inside for an ambulance. "I'm getting pretty old," O'Connor went on, "to be running out to Brooklyn in the middle of the night to round you up. If you'd kept your nose clean, like I told you, I could have waited till morning."

"But, Pop—" Weakly, Nat tried to raise himself on one elbow, and realized that now he was going too far. "Pop, how did you know where to find me?"

"Couldn't have missed if I tried. There was a message for me when I got back from the Burnside place. It seems some dangerous lunatic called the Douglas James Funeral Parlor and asked them to pick up a corpse they weren't supposed to embalm. In this state, that was fishy. I took three guesses, and who did I suppose it was? Well, I was right. So I tailed you."

"Well," Nat protested, "at least I got you enough evidence to burn Bluff. Althea Burnside—"

"Althea Burnside doesn't remember what happened, except she woke up scared stiff, with a lot of palms and lilies around her. Nobody's going to burn Bluff. He's dead."

"Heart failure?" Nat asked.

"Yah. Heart failure due to mayhem. He was trying to escape an officer."

Nat didn't ask which officer. He felt neither smart nor invulnerable, as he had grown to feel in the past eight years. He said fervently, "They're white people, the Douglas James Funeral Parlor. What did they call me again?"

"A lunatic," Harry repeated. "Old Doug was so excited he drove me out here himself. He's up front now. Want to thank him?"

Nat looked again around the interior of the ambulance—no, it wasn't an ambulance. It was something *else*. "No, Pop," he said a little feebly. "Just wake me up when we get out. I don't want to ride in a hearse again . . . for a long time!"

THE END

By all rights, that should have been the end of
The Bleeder. . . .

*Nat Perry, the inimitable manhunter called "The Bleeder," loses a
five-thousand-dollar retainer, but wins a bloody victory over a crime
monarch who kills at will—by no visible means! Another gripping
story of the world's most vulnerable dick, who this time doesn't even
know what new force he must defeat!*

THEY DIE ON SCHEDULE!

by
EDITH & EJLER JACOBSON

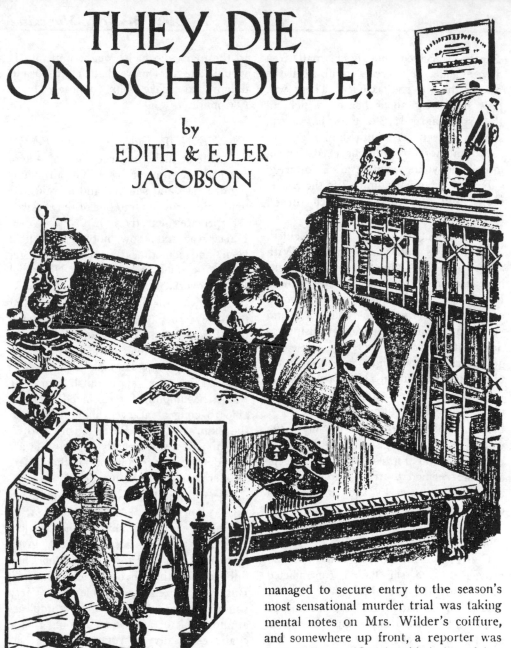

CHAPTER ONE

The Frozen-faced Borgia

IT was hot in the courtroom, but it was hotter outside. In the back, two attendants were laying bets on Virginia Wilder's chances of acquittal. Every one of the fifty-eight women who had managed to secure entry to the season's most sensational murder trial was taking mental notes on Mrs. Wilder's coiffure, and somewhere up front, a reporter was jotting down: "On the third day of her ordeal, the beautiful Borgia remained as impassive as on the first. This woman, against whom the state has built an air-tight case for the murder of her husband, young Doctor Grant Wilder, sits beside her lawyer as calmly as though she were at a tea for the Ladies' Auxiliary of the Clinton Hospital . . ."

She was more looked-at than a visiting cinema star, more talked-of than Hitler.

She had received enough fan mail, free advice, and crank threats to fill a cell the size of the one she occupied. There was only one thing about her on which all the world agreed: She must be smart; she could keep her mouth shut.

All the world, with one exception; a tall, blond young man in a suit of navy gabardine who was admitted to the courtroom after all others had been turned away.

She's a fool, Nathanial Perry decided. Even if she's guilty, she's a fool. With a face like that, almost any alibi might have been meat for a lawyer like Arnold Ruppee. . . . He looked at the woman on trial. She was silent and grave and young, and before the curious transformation that comes over persons accused of grave crimes, she might have been beautiful. Beautiful in an almost professional way, and rather sweet. That, of course, didn't have to preclude murder.

Mrs. Wilder had given the press the worst possible impression. She had given her lawyer no impression at all, except that she seemed to trust him to defend her. Yet, two weeks ago, Ruppee had offered Perry five thousand dollars to unearth any data that might support a reasonable defense for his client.

Guilty? The police had virtually proven it, and she hadn't contradicted them. But Ruppee didn't take hopeless cases, and he had never lost a client, so far, to the chair. Ruppee must have seen some path to freedom for his client; five thousand is a lot to throw away on a futile gesture.

Nat Perry, through having worked with the police, respected their final opinions. His foster-father, plainclothes Inspector Harry O'Connor of Homicide, had helped pile up incriminating evidence in the Wilder case. And now, as Nat leaned against the wall in that hot little chamber of justice, listening to testimony he had already heard, his thoughts drifted to the man who had brought him up. It would take a lot more than five thousand dollars to make him oppose Harry O'Connor.

O'CONNOR had saved Nat Perry's life at their first meeting, years ago. He had given an orphaned kid an example of nerve and stamina and morale that made him grow up into one of the shrewdest private detectives in New York. Harry was sixty now, not the man he'd been, and sometimes he managed to get his work done only because Nathanial Perry covered up for him unfailingly.

That was the debt of a lifetime, and the desire to pay it was Perry's reason for sticking to a career more perilous to him than to any man alive. His life was risked every time he took a case. The simplest violence might finish him — he was a haemophiliac. His blood was unable to congeal at even slight breaks in the skin. No, Nat Perry wasn't throwing his life away merely to substantiate the department's contention that Mrs. Wilder was guilty of murder.

Perry's wandering stare caught a return glance from Mrs. Wilder. She looked unseeingly at him, and then turned. The newspapers, because she'd given them no other peg for a soubriquet, had dubbed her the "Frozen-faced Borgia." But that frozen look made Nat Perry vaguely uneasy. It was definitely unpleasant to think of any woman going to the chair, especially as young a woman as Mrs. Wilder. He had already decided she was not too bright. It was barely possibly she could have another reason for her silence.

The more Nat thought of it, the worse he felt. Police investigation had hinted at no accomplice, but there mightn't be an accomplice. Besides, that was the only human explanation to someone who knew how silent she really was. Ruppee must have guessed at something like that.

He looked up expectantly as a new defense witness was called. The look of worry deepened on his face, and his hands clenched at his sides as he stared at the short, shabby Negro with defective teeth who answered to the call for Johnson Tolliver.

The man was sick, but it wasn't his sickness that brought an ominous silence into the packed courtroom. His wide white rolling eyes had an unseeing terror that made Perry think with startled intuition of death and that fear which is stronger than death. A fear so strong it forced a dying man to stalk into a courtroom to testify—as though he were the victim of Voodoo, come back from a century-old grave to tell a story he had been bewitched into telling.

No one ever heard what Johnson Tolliver was about to say. The little Negro's arm was raised solemnly over the Book, and his lips were parted to repeat an oath, when the invisible thunderbolt struck.

Suddenly, before a silent, shocked courtroom, the Negro's face went the color of grey ash, and his features screwed into a mask of pain. His left hand clutched his abdomen, but that solemn right arm, the arm he had raised to bear witness, stiffened in mid-air, rigid as in catalepsy.

A silent eternity was compressed into a second—and then the silence splintered as Ruppee's witness screamed wordlessly to the invisible power which had stricken him.

Before anyone had time to move toward the fallen man, another shriek echoed again and again through the courtroom, the shriek of a woman.

IT was the Frozen-faced Borgia, breaking her silence at last. Over the heads of the confused attendants, Perry could see her. She wasn't human—she was a fury. It was as though she knew what had died on the witness stand, as though

she had seen all faith, all ideals, withered by a blow from nowhere, and known herself a helpless party to the destruction.

Ruppee was trying frantically to calm her. No one helped. They were no longer citizen-spectators, those people in the court—they were a terrified herd, stampeding away from a brutal miracle.

Perry shouldered his way toward the defense block. He felt that Ruppee needed him. His own mind was as terror-gripped, for the time being, as everyone else's, but some vestige of normalcy reminded him that black magic is impossible. Normalcy gripped him more completely, when he reached Arnold Ruppee.

"Do you see now?" the pudgy little lawyer yelled over the chaotic din. "Not you nor anyone else believed my client innocent. You all had her convicted and condemned before she ever came to trial!" He whirled like a dervish toward the bench, where Judge Ferris was rapping vainly for order. "Johnson Tolliver's testimony alone would have freed my client. I demand a postponement until this murder is investigated!" He turned toward Perry, and his voice dropped. "And in case the police bungle this investigation as they bungled the last, my offer to you still stands."

It was too violent, too unheard-of, Perry thought. Sharply, he realized that if he took the case now, he might be called on to solve a black miracle singlehanded. He might face alone this grisly thunderbolt which had turned a roomful of people into terror-stricken beasts. . . . He wrenched away from Ruppee's grasp. He had to look at Johnson Tolliver. There'll be a reasonableness to it, he felt, an explanation; something a man can understand who's seen death in all its recognizable shapes.

The corpse was ugly. Even in death, the right arm was as incredibly stiff and disjointed as a log attached to a man. A phrase leapt into his head, the only phrase that tallied with that sight. Blasted by lightning. And that was no explanation at all.

The one man who could have saved Virginia Wilder from death, according to Ruppee. . . . Was she *fated* to die? His eyes followed her as she was led from the courtroom to her cell. Turning, he found Ruppee's anxious face close to his own.

He tried to keep his voice cool. "Nice show, Ruppee," he said. He succeeded better than he expected.

The defense lawyer's eyes grew horrified, and once more Perry found his arm gripped tightly. "Show? You mean I— Perry, you're crazy!"

Maybe that was true—Ruppee looked saner than any other man in the vicinity. There was a surprising strength in the pudgy lawyer's manicured fingers, and a surprising lack of emotional upset in the grey intellectual eyes that alone saved his face from grossness. He looked exactly what he was: an attorney who has met his first break in a desperate case, the first incident that might conceivably sway public opinion the other way regarding his client.

"You can't help but understand what this means, Mr. Perry," he continued, more calmly, almost triumphantly. "Virginia Wilder was framed, and we're trying the wrong party. I can get her an acquittal on what we have now. But I want more than that. I want justice. For the last time, will you help us?"

Nat suddenly wanted to say *yes*—but he knew he was feeling more than he was thinking, that he was still infected with a trace of that rabid mass hysteria which hung like a tangible substance over the courtroom.

"Wait until I'm satisfied that what Johnson Tolliver had to say was important," he said slowly, "and until I've spoken to Virginia Wilder. After that— maybe."

The anxiety faded from the lawyer's plump face, and Perry saw beneath it the profound relief of a harried man. "Come with me," he said. "I think we can see her immediately."

THE State's case against her was strong and simple. She had sent for help at four in the morning, and when the police arrived they found her husband dead. The amount of strychnine in his stomach must have been administered four hours previous, or at midnight, to kill when it did—and there had been no one in the Wilder home but Dr. Wilder and his wife. How could a shabby Negro have broken that case?

She was small-boned, delicate, and the most striking thing about her wan, sweet face and her low, quiet voice was fatigue. As though some tremendous burden had fallen at last from her shoulders, Perry thought, and she was finally free to think how weary she was. She apologized to both men for having made a scene in the courtroom.

"It was a ghastly sight. You couldn't help it," Perry said.

She shook her head, and answered with quiet abruptness, "That wasn't it. You see, Grant died like that, exactly like that, on the morning of April tenth."

Ruppee sat down heavily, his mouth wide open, staring at Virginia Wilder in the thin light of the cell block. The Frozen-faced Borgia was breaking her silence. Now she looked neither frozen nor sinister. She looked haggard and troubled. "Until now, it hasn't seemed to matter," she went on. "Nothing seemed to matter after that night when Grant came home to die. I didn't realize then that an innocent man might die because I had stopped caring enough to tell what I knew."

Was it her silence that had killed Johnson Tolliver? Silence on what? "Did you know the witness?" Perry asked.

She nodded. "He was a cab driver who had the stand in front of our home. He drove Grant away that night, and brought him home again at half-past two in the morning. Grant—was very ill. He died soon after. . . . I don't know how Mr. Ruppee found out. It wasn't I who told him."

Ruppee had been right. Tolliver's testimony would have cleared Virginia Wilder. The State's whole case rested on the fact that Grant Wilder had been home alone with his wife the night he died!

Ruppee hopped to his feet, looking like a huge ground bird. "Virginia! Where was your husband that night?"

A deep flush came into her cheeks, spread slowly over her face and throat. Her voice grew very hushed. "I didn't tell you before, because I didn't think I could be convicted of something I hadn't done. I loved Grant too much—I was too proud—to desecrate his memory if I didn't have to. He was with Peggy Anderson, his nurse. I lost everything but that memory—long before he died. But if I'd known another innocent life would be taken, I'd have told."

Ruppee said, with a brusqueness that barely concealed a note of triumph, "You couldn't have saved Johnson Tolliver. I'd have had to call him as a witness in any event. The world, Mrs. Wilder," Ruppee grew oratorical, "does not accept any person's unsupported testimony without corroboration, not even the word of an innocent woman like yourself. . . . Mr. Perry, what are you going to do now?"

Perry said, "I'm taking a stab at that corroboration. Where does this Peggy Anderson live?"

CHAPTER TWO

Death's Perfect Timing

NAT went out into the June sunshine with a sense of startlement greater than he usually felt at the beginning of a case. His own susceptibility had in times past rendered him utterly ruthless with the underworld. In spite of his handicap, he was expert at equalizing the risks between himself and his enemies, yet he felt now that all his old defenses were useless in this particular case. That morbid sense of superhuman intervention he had felt in the courtroom had not died with his excitement. It remained, and grew stronger.

He tried to put it out of his head as he nosed his green sedan steadily through morning traffic, but it couldn't be done. He could think of other things, but only with thought processes. There was something inexplicable about Johnson Tolliver's death, something no amount of cool reasoning could clear up. It was that desperate compulsion which had made the Negro drag himself into court to testify —and to die.

The timing of that death! What earthly agent could have stricken a man down at the last possible moment? Was it some dark unseen power that Johnson Tolliver had defied? And if Grant Wilder had died in the same manner, as his widow said he had, had his death been timed also?

Timed to involve his widow in a skein of murder-guilt?

It wasn't possible. Grant Wilder had died of strychnine poisoning, and no chemist can predict the efficacy of strychnine to the split-second.

He was still groping for a credible solution when he pulled up in front of a cream-and-red facade on Charles Street, in Greenwich Village. It was almost unbearably warm, with the sun reaching its zenith, but there was an instinctive premonitory chill inside. Nat Perry. He looked about. There were few people in sight. A small Italian boy with scuffed shoes and enormous brown eyes asked solemnly, "Watch your car, mister?"

"Sure." He gave the boy a dollar. He

didn't know what he expected, and that was the worst of it, because he knew he could expect something. "Don't stand too near it, and don't let anybody see you watching. If you see anyone trying to monkey around, run for the cops. Understand?" The boy nodded, wide-eyed, and Perry entered the flashy-fronted building.

A thin girl with a white face under pale flaxen hair answered his ring at the third floor rear apartment. She wore a blue silk bathrobe, and she plucked nervously at the folds of it with her left hand, as a dope addict might fidget. Traces of un-removed cosmetic outlined her sharp mouth, looking ghastly in the daylight that filtered through the hall.

"Yes," she said too quickly, "I'm Peggy Anderson." Then she looked at him with an odd combination of terror and pleading, as though she were trying to determine whether he were wolf or shepherd. There was youth under the nerves and the stale lipstick, youth gone haywire and terror-silly as only youth can go. She was twenty at the outside. She was nothing a man in his senses would have preferred to beautiful Virginia Wilder.

But something else about her struck Nat. She was helplessly desperate as a puppet revolting against a puppet-master. Her terror had an un-human quality that made him think of Johnson Tolliver.

Was she afraid of the same thing? Was it visible, was it behind that half-closed door? "I'm a friend of Mrs. Grant Wilder's," he said, as gently as possible. "I want to talk to you. She doesn't mean you any harm."

The gentleness wasn't enough. "No!" the girl exclaimed. "You can't come in— you don't belong here!" Her hand dropped the loose edges of her bathrobe, and darted toward the door. It was a clumsy gesture, with no strength in it, and with comparative minute effort, Perry shoved his way in.

It was a neat little room, with a college banner across the wall above a studio couch, and reprints of good etchings on either side of a maple bureau. There was no sun, but the room could have borne the scrutiny of sunlight. It looked not at all the kind of room where a drunken party-girl would have entertained a drunken philanderer.

He asked. "Was Grant Wilder here the night he died?"

The girl had looked jittery. Now she became utterly panic-stricken. Her voice rose, as though to convince some unseen audience, and she cried out, "He was, he was! And I'm not sorry! He loved me, see! He came here—"

She didn't finish, and Perry saw why she was using that clumsy left hand to hold her robe. A certain stiffness came to her thin immature body, and she jerked like a marionette on strings. Her mouth opened, as though to emit a scream, but the scream was never uttered. One hand clenched at her waist, and she doubled up on it in ghastly pain—but the whole right arm hung like a length of stone from her paralyzed shoulder. She staggered toward him, her face writhing in torment. He caught her as she fell.

When Perry felt for her heart-beat, he found nothing. She was dead. Dead, with the same look of torture on her face that had been on the face of Johnson Tolliver. Dead, with the testimony Johnson Tolliver hadn't had time to utter stifled on her parted lips.

There was a phone in the hall, and in a voice that sounded cool enough to be someone else's, Perry heard himself summoning Homicide.

HARRY O'CONNOR'S eyes narrowed into hard blue slits. "If you were anyone else on God's earth," he said ponderously, "I'd say you were deliberately pulling something pretty bad. Do you think we're trying to convict Mrs.

Wilder for the fun of it? I don't know what she told you, but she didn't tell it to us when we were willing to give her a break.

"She wouldn't do it because she couldn't have told a trained cop a thing that would hold. She waited for a sap like you to come along—"

"Pop!" O'Connor had come into a room where invisible death had taken another witness, and the sight only made the old man more furious.

"—a sap like you," the plainclothesman continued implacably, "who'd run riot for sentiment. But you're not the only sap. Ruppee got your client free on bail. A very high-powered bag of wind, Ruppee. As for that business in the court, there isn't a trick Ruppee wouldn't pull."

Perry's face went as hard as his foster-father's. It had to. There was too much going on inside him. It wasn't what O'Connor thought—that was understandable. O'Connor hadn't heard Virginia Wilder's story. It was the way the man felt.

"Give it up," O'Connor said more softly. "Nat, this isn't your kind of game. You've got half the crooks in town scared stiff of you. They call you the Bleeder—and they don't call it out loud. But the man who roped you into this belongs to the other half. He'll want you either on his side, or—dead!"

"At least," Perry answered, "I'm giving Mrs. Wilder the benefit of the doubt until she's proven guilty. That happens to be the law, but maybe you don't remember the law."

The two men exchanged stares, not in enmity, but in fright. The fright showed on O'Connor's face, and not on Perry's—but Perry felt it. And he knew that O'Connor's fear was for the man some called the Bleeder. As he turned to go, he knew O'Connor had said one undeniably true thing: he wasn't fighting an ordinary crook. The Bleeder had established enough of a reputation for deadliness to guarantee him a modicum of immunity where he was known. But this was different.

This time, he didn't even know from what he needed to be immune. He didn't know who was checkmating him, and more important, he didn't know how it was being done.

What had frightened the Anderson girl? Justice? But she had protested passionately that Wilder was with her on that fatal night, and if she read the papers, she must have known that would put her right in Mrs. Wilder's spot, removed only by hours from trial for first degree murder. Would she have felt safer in a spot like that—than where she was?

Because she would have been safer—and he was almost sure' she had been lying.

Not his game? Not by a long sight. It didn't look like any lone man's game. But what he hadn't bothered to tell O'Connor, what the other man knew already, what had brought the fear into O'Connor's eyes and into Perry's heart, was that he couldn't give up now. He was in it up to the neck. Peggy Anderson's death proved that the killer knew he was working for Virginia Wilder. If Johnson Tolliver had been timed to die, and Peggy Anderson, then it was within the realm of possibility that somewhere, someone was making a memento of the Bleeder's name on the second hand of an incomprehensible clock.

CHAPTER THREE

Mrs. Wilder's Corpse-Guest

THE street was still innocent of people, even of the boy he had engaged to watch his car. Perry's eyes scanned the pavements, and on the diagonal corner, located a small wide-eyed figure, frantically waving him back.

He retreated into the doorway, one hand feeling toward his gun. He didn't understand now, yet he knew there would be trouble. The kid, having assured himself that his temporary employer was standing still for the time being, darted down the block toward Seventh Avenue.

The next ten seconds went livid, as though illuminated with hell-fire. It had barely penetrated Perry's mind that the child was running toward a strolling patrolman a block ahead, when something like a war broke out immediately to the west. A gun crashed, and the pavement erupted into little scars.

Five paces from where he had started, the small Italian child dropped suddenly and horribly. The shooting stopped, and then Perry knew why the child had waited for him to emerge before running for the police.

After that shocking reveille of gunfire, Charles Street woke from its noon siesta to a rocking blast of sound. For almost a minute, fragments of Perry's green sedan continued to drop into the gutter. There had been an explosive under the car—placed there by someone who had foreseen the exact second of Perry's exit.

There was a red haze in his brain, and the vague shape of a certain realization in it. His mind flashed back to the loud, almost shouted protest of the Anderson girl, just before she died, and in that remembered echo, a number of things became clearer.

Another figure took dark shape, far up the block, on the shaded side of Charles Street, emerging from a delivery entrance. A man with a gun. This was understandable language at last, Perry thought savagely. He leapt into the street, started after the killer. His automatic was poised when something about the fleeing figure forced a sharp hoarse cry back into his throat and kept him from firing.

The killer's right arm was swinging like a pendulum at his side, stiff, jointless.

At the corner of Charles and Blecker Streets, Perry's hand reached out to grasp a paralyzed shoulder. The swift moment of reckless rage was dead in him. He was facing — not the puppet-master, but another of his puppets.

PEOPLE were coming down the street, outraged people who from their windows had seen the child killed. The thin elderly man, hollow-chested under his worn respectable suit, struggled feebly in Perry's grasp as he gaped at them. "You've got to let me go," he whispered. "I didn't — any jury would acquit me! But I'll die if I don't get back to him—"

There was a cold certainty inside Perry that the man was telling the truth. Once, this oldster might have belonged to the same order of beings as those people who approached him with hot hatred in their eyes. Once, he might have been subject to judgment by their laws. But that time was gone. He was the maimed projection of another will, outraging the earth he walked on. He had the stamp of terror in his ashen face, the same terror that had marked Johnson Tolliver and Peggy Anderson.

They were dead, but this man was alive. He was Perry's only link to justice in the case of Virginia Wilder.

The crowd was thickening, but the patrolman had arrived, his eyes round and shocked. He recognized Perry, nodded curtly, and then tried to stem the mob from the detective and his captive.

"Please, please!" the man whimpered. "He'll kill me if I don't report to him— he could kill me a thousand miles away. I didn't want to hurt you. I'm not the one . . ."

"Who is he?" Perry asked. "What has he done to your arm?"

"I don't know! I don't know how he did it—" the frightened voice broke off, and for a moment, Perry thought the man was going to die then and there.

In a voice he might have used to soothe a lunatic, Perry persisted, "Tell me where he is."

The answer was a whisper deathly as a last confessional. "I can't be sure. He can be in more than one place at a time. You might find him now with that woman they freed on bail, the Wilder woman."

Behind him, Perry heard a short, shocked laugh with no mirth in it, "A nut," said the patrolman.

Perry said, "Get this man to a prison hospital—I'll report there later." He rammed through the crowd, into a cruising taxi at the curb. He heard himself give an address on upper Riverside Drive, and an order to hurry, but there were other words ·in his brain, and thoughts coming so fast that the words for them were half-formed.

A child had been killed in broad daylight, by a man deathly ill, with no motive. Anyone would call it insanity.

At last the ghastly aura of events shrouding the Wilder case began to assume a pattern. Nat Perry knew he had crossed purposes with the perpetrator of a devilish and brilliant scheme, who had so far enjoyed the added benefit of luck. But luck like that couldn't hold out—it was maniac's luck.

He was no longer surprised at the thought that the man he wanted would be at Mrs. Wilder's. It seemed the most logical place for him to be. A certain detachedness came to Perry, so that he could relegate the blood and the pain he had seen to another part of his mind. Maniac's luck, against the man who refused to die. Nat couldn't afford to doubt the outcome. He had to think as clearly as though he were playing with wooden pawns instead of flesh-and-blood ones, and as though the stake were infinitely less important than life and death. Much later, he would remember what had happened, and in Nathanial Perry's cheerless thoughts, the child who had died on the pavement would die a thousand times again. But not now.

Fifteen minutes later he stood at a sloped curb, with the Hudson sparkling behind him, staring at a barren-looking window with its shades drawn. It still sported a small undusted plaque reading Grant Wilder, M.D. Wilder had been dead two months. But the apartment wasn't empty now.

The shade slapped violently, only once. Wind hadn't caused that, nor were his eyes playing tricks. He was on the verge of an encounter with the power that reached out of nowhere to kill.

THE door to the apartment on the first floor was locked. There was a length of steel wire in Perry's pocket, and the Bleeder's fingers were dextrous. But time was limited. Whatever had slapped that shade had been moving quickly, and this was an unfamiliar lock. He pried the ends of the curved wire into the keyhole, and let them tremble among the tumblers, delicately, surely. The second time he tried it, there was a dull click.

Very quietly, he shut the apartment door behind him. He was in a dark hall, musty-odored, as though nothing had breathed in it for weeks. The darkness concentrated into the solid hurtling mass of a human body, flying into him, and the impact knocked the revolver from his fingers. The attack was sooner than he had expected. He glimpsed a fair-skinned face, lean and pale as his own, angry and intent, as he braced himself.

A hundred thoughts wrote themselves on his brain during the next third of a second. No terror-stamp of slavery on that glimpsed face. This was the man, not one of his underlings. This might be a trap, this might be the end of the Bleeder, but—his thoughts ended abruptly as the brief combat itself, as the dim· apartment re-echoed to a shrill and soulless shriek.

Perry broke away from his antagonist, ran through the darkness, down the long hall. Virginia Wilder had shrieked like that, that morning in court. By the pencil-line of light that came through a crack in the shade, he saw her. She was crouched in an overstuffed chair in the carpetless living-room, her mouth a frozen oval. She was unharmed. It took strength to shriek like that.

He wheeled about, expecting to face his recent opponent. There was no one. No one in the hall, no one in the living-room where Virginia Wilder had grown suddenly silent. Nathanial Perry had been close enough to put a bullet into his quarry's heart—and the man was gone.

He looked at his client with a kind of numb fury. There was still terror in her face. And then he saw that they were not alone. He followed her glance across a threshold into another room, where another woman was seated on a couch.

The woman wore a hat and coat, wrapped surprisingly close for the heat. There was a thick, sick-sweet odor in the heavy air about her couch. She did not speak as Perry approached, nor turn her head, and when he touched her, she fell abruptly on her side.

She was dead. He knew, from the odor, and the swollen look of decay on her face, that she had been dead for many days. Even in the coat, even after all that time, he knew by the right arm of the corpse that he had found all that was left of another crippled puppet.

The detective sought for the shreds of detachment in his brain, and did rapid mental arithmetic. The police had closed the apartment a month ago, and this body must have been here for almost half that time. It was the link he needed—the proof that the murder-series which began with the death of Grant Wilder had not been interrupted, merely to resume today.

He heard Virginia Wilder's gasps lengthen into sobs. He did not speak to her as he crossed the room and picked a dust-covered telephone from a side-table. He kept his voice low and distinct; Harry O'Connor's voice at the other end was neither. It was high-pitched, as an old man's voice often grows in excitement. "Nat? We've got the report on Tolliver. Ever heard of jake-leg?"

"Not lately."

"You wouldn't have, lately. It went out of circulation a good fifteen years ago, before they even repealed prohibition. It's a distilled ginger drink, a hell-brew that the old-time hi-jackers used to sell at eight dollars a quart. It crippled some people, blinded others, and killed or paralyzed about two thousand kids whose parents thought they needed something for a cold. That's what Johnson Tolliver had in his stomach. There was something else, too, but we won't know about that till the examiner's finished with the corpse. Where are you?"

"I'm uptown," Nat said, "with Mrs. Wilder and a corpse. It's not such a fresh corpse, but keep that under your hat. You can use it as a peg to re-arrest her. She's guilty as sin, but I'll need a little time to make it stick."

CHAPTER FOUR

"Two Places at Once. . . ."

HE heard a startled gasp behind him as he replaced the phone. Virginia Wilder's face was no longer merely white —it was livid.

She clutched at the back of a chair, and her knuckles were pale with the effort. Her cheeks blazed and she was beautiful. Beautiful enough to make a man lie and cheat and murder . . . beautiful and evil as the first sin. "You're insane," she said.

"Maybe," he admitted. "I'll grant you that—until I've cleared up the details. Though I'll have a hard time proving what I've just said. Obviously, the corpse in this apartment met death while you were in jail, which would seem to exonerate you. But even so, I'm not as insane as the man who conceived this hellish scheme."

Triumph crossed her face, fleet, desperate triumph, with fear and guilt beneath it. "So you see—" she began.

"You probably banked on that," he went on. "You and the man you've been working with. You expected that if anyone did get wind of your scheme, it would seem fantastic beyond belief. But Johnson Tolliver's death in the courtroom served as well as his testimony would have to indicate a frame against you— which made that spectacular timing seem useless to whoever wanted him dead.

"Then it occurred to me that it couldn't matter, from the murderer's point of view, whether Tolliver testified or not. The important thing was for him to die, so that his death could add weight to your innocence and point at someone else's guilt. Exactly the same logic applies to Peggy Anderson's death, except that she lied, and she spoke louder than necessary. She wasn't the actress you are.

"She spoke loudly—and yet there were only the two of us in the apartment. If it was true your husband was out most of the night he died she had undoubtedly seen him. That was why she was drawn into the case and terrorized. Adding those two things together, I would say he had been in the house, probably in the apartment next door to hers. That's where I'm going to look for your accomplice— and while you're back in police custody, nobody's going to stop me from finding the man or woman you and your co-worker must have planned for a frame."

There was a fiery quality about her that he had not seen before. *"Can't I stop you!"* she cried. "I'll show you! You won't dare go through with this! I'll tell the police you're assaulting a decent man—"

"And suppose the police find your decent man has assaulted me—fatally? Then they'll have a certain murder case. There isn't a chance of that, of course. But you think there may be."

Her face went grey again; the fire had died to an ash. Still, she held herself erect, her hands tight on the chair back. "You don't know what you're saying," she whispered. "I could show you that. And I could show you a great deal about love. . . ."

He laughed, a sharp ugly laugh, and her eyes went wild with fright. Like a small trapped animal, she turned and bolted for the door. He stepped into her path, caught her wrists in his strong hands. She went limp without struggle. He could feel her body pressed close against him. Her eyes were shut, and she did not move, but her heart was beating furiously. She was playing her last desperate card.

For a moment, he knew how it must have felt to risk everything for her. Then he pushed her away from him. "Sit down," he said, "and don't bother trying that again."

She knew it was hopeless. She could neither lie nor flirt her way past him. Her hands reached out like a cat's claws. "You filthy Judas!" she cried. "You—"

As he seized her shoulders and held her forcibly away from him, Nat Perry's heart was somersaulting at last. She may not have realized it in her fury, but her fingernails were far from being futile weapons; they were capable of killing him.

That was how O'Connor found them. Perry turned to the older man, who stared at him bewilderedly. "You can make her talk now, Pop. I'll see you later and explain."

A PATROLMAN was walking up and down in front of the cream-and-red facade on Charles Street. He looked hot and intent, and at the sight of Nathanial Perry, surprised. "Coming back for more?" he asked. "The old man's ready to give you hell when he catches up to you."

"The old man's busy elsewhere," Perry said. He went into the dark hall again, up the three flights of stairs. Two apartments on that floor, and he had been in one of them already. The neat white plaque on the door of the other read *Dr. Ralph White.* He might have expected to find another doctor, he thought. The lock was easier than Virginia Wilder's.

He was in a short foyer opening into what seemed an office. A lean, pale man sat in a tall chair behind a big desk, and his cold blue eyes met Perry's stare unflinchingly. It was the man who'd escaped him, the man whom Virginia Wilder's scream had saved from justice in that dark little hall uptown. This time, there would be no scream, and no intervention. Perry kicked the door shut behind him, bolted the chain with his left hand. The gun felt stern and steady in his grasp.

Dr. White did not rise, nor flinch, nor blink. There was a revolver on the desk, and a welling dark circle of ooze on the side of his head. He was dead.

Perry's hands went hot and wet, and he sheathed his gun. It wasn't suicide. Dr. White's arms were clasped on the arms of his chair. He had not died by those hands. Murder had forestalled justice once more.

Behind him, a voice said quietly, "Don't move now, or you'll never move again."

Very slowly, his hands held visibly at some distance from his hips, Perry turned round. Then he thought he was either crazy, or in another world.

If the man behind the desk, with a hole in his head, was the man he had tangled with before—so was the man with the gun!

"I told you not to move," the new-comer repeated. His voice was not cool—it was harsh, sibilant. "If you'd come ten minutes later, you would never have known that the dead man was my brother. You would have had a perfectly satisfactory scapegoat, and the eminent Dr. Ralph White would have succeeded in death, as he did in life, in denying the existence of his criminal twin."

"It had to be like that," Perry said very quietly. "Of course. . . . Peggy Anderson, who lived next door, was obviously speaking for your ears when she raised her voice to talk to me. I'd have been here much earlier if your poor murderous dupe hadn't told me you were at Mrs. Wilder's.

"There's nothing miraculous about a man's being in two places at once, White. Any normal mind, under ordinary circumstances, would immediately leap to the explanation of twins. But those weren't normal circumstances. You took that old man's mind and visited the living fear of death on it. You persuaded him that only you could save him from the slow, sure effects of the poison you had given him. You made him a monster who would shoot down a child.

"You knew I would go to Mrs. Wilder's—and so did she. You both knew that I would meet your brother there, because she had sent for him. You even hoped I'd kill him."

White grinned. "Fine, Mr. Perry. That's all I wanted to know. If Peggy Anderson's words led you here, then I don't have to worry about anyone else arriving immediately. How much else have you guessed?"

PERRY said wryly, "Enough to tell you that there's an excellent reason why you oughtn't to shoot me on the spot. But I'll let you do the guessing on that for a while. As for Grant Wilder's murder: He found out that you knew his wife rather too well. Taking you for your brother, he came here that night two months ago and met you, posing as Dr. Ralph White. You poisoned him that night, and sent him home."

White's face was growing pale, but his voice was still steady. He kept the gun trained on Perry, and the defiance in his voice indicated some inner struggle about using it at once. "Yes, and the scheme's going to work! Virginia's been vindicated. The police are going to find a confession among my brother's effects. I've built a small fortune out of my private business, enough to support Virginia and me some place where we'll never be found. We've got more than Grant Wilder's insurance; we've got the insurance on all the people whose beneficiaries I obliged."

"I see," said Perry. "That accounts for the old man and the woman whose corpse I found in Grant Wilder's apartment. Posing as Dr. White, you administered slow poison to your chosen victims for a cut in the fortunes of their heirs. It was a two-edged weapon; before the victims died, they went through a period of sheer terror. You used distilled ginger with some drug that enabled you to control the paralysis that precedes death from jake-leg . . . and in the inexplicable uniformity of that paralysis, lay your hold over your victims.

"I'll wager you first met Virginia Wilder when she contacted you to do away with her husband. And that his death was the first. You accomplished it by ordinary means—deliberately—so that police might think they had a case. After that, you saw your chance to let your brother take the blame, with you and your exonerated woman friend free. Then, none of your other murders would have seemed unsolved. I have only Virginia Wilder's word that her husband died as your other victims died—the word of a murderess trying to frame an innocent man."

White's face went livid. "You've told them about Virginia," he said.

By all rights, that should have been the end of the Bleeder. But Nat Perry was no longer in front of the desk when the bullet landed. He was on his stomach, skidding across the floor toward White. His powerful trained fingers twisted around the man's ankles, and jerked. White grunted—it happened too quickly for a louder protest—and fell backwards. Then Perry was on him.

"John!" It was a woman's voice at the doorway, and there were men's fists rapping against the door Perry had chained shut. "John, don't try any more—"

Virginia Wilder's voice. A voice utterly hopeless, lost beyond redemption, but to the man Perry was fighting it was like a command. He went limp. As Perry stood away from him, he came shakily to his feet. "You win," he said, in a ghost-tone. "Better open the door."

O'Connor was there, and his prisoner, the prisoner who would not escape again. She lifted her hands to John White, and he took her in his arms. . . . Perry didn't stay to see what happened after that.

It was cooler on Charles Street when he went out. A child had been killed on that corner; the red stain was still visible. As he remembered the child, all those waves of revulsion he had fought down earlier rose in Perry.

"Caught 'em, didn't they?" said the patrolman, with satisfaction.

"Yes," said Perry. "Yes, they caught 'em." Caught what? Virginia Wilder's poignant and evil beauty, that would leave this world a darker place for having existed in it? Would anything they did to those two people in the apartment upstairs bring back the life of a dead child?

"Hell," he said to the cop. "I ought to be sorry. It's costing me five thousand dollars."

THE END

BUBBLES OF MURDER

A Full-Length Peter Quest Novel

Horribly, gruesomely, they died. And all that remained of each of those wealthy victims was a blackened, bubbling mass! This was the terrifying mystery Peter Quest resolved to break before the tide of death could reach lovely Lucy Hallam—even though Peter's secret ambition was to die victoriously battling against just such heinous crime as this!

The gun chopped down on
Smokey Joe's head.

CHAPTER ONE

The Frightened Bankrupt

THE sharp urgency of that voice, dinning on Peter Quest's eardrums like needling rain on a tin roof, was an almost physical thing that filled the spacious office. He smashed out his cigarette in a metal dish and pressed the receiver more tightly against his ear.

"You're misinformed," he broke in. "I take but only few cases these days."

The man on the other end of the wire persisted desperately. "I know all about you, Quest. You've broken scores of cases the police couldn't touch. You're the only man who can handle this, if you only will, and you've got to do it. Quest, you've got to! I'm no longer a wealthy man, but I'll manage to pay you somehow."

"It isn't that, Hallam. Matter of fact, I ask no fee ever." He could appreciate

By JOHN KOBLER

One of the most baffling, thrill-packed murder mysteries we have ever had the pleasure of presenting!

the man's financial difficulties. Arnold Hallam, his brother Grover and half a dozen other directors of the Gotham Trust had forfeited their shirts when that famous banking institution had closed its doors forever.

"Quest, listen to me!" The harrowed voice sank suddenly to a hoarse whisper as if in terror of being overheard. Peter Quest could feel the man hesitate, stare about him to make certain he was alone. "A horrible thing is about to happen, a thing that will plunge this entire city into a nightmare. It must be stopped. It—I dare not talk about it here. I must see you."

The man's gnawing terror was not to be denied. Peter Quest realized that and pity stirred within him, even as his old lust for the chase quickened his pulse. He said, "I'll wait for you."

"Thank God! I'll come at once—at once."

It was then ten minutes after six of a bleak, wind-lashed September evening.

Quest cradled the receiver thoughtfully

and wandered over to the high windows overlooking the deep canyon of Fifth Avenue. He stood thus bemused, his thoughts turned inward upon himself.

A strange creature, this Peter Quest, a strangely reckless creature. They said of him that he knew no fear of death. They were right. It was living he feared, or at least living after the doom doctors had predicted came to pass. For slowly but inevitably, Peter Quest was losing his eyesight. Glaucoma, the diagnosticians called it, a gradually increasing fluid-pressure within his eyeballs. Attacks of blindness burst on him more and more frequently now, blindness that could be relieved temporarily only by whitish drops from the tiny phial he carried in his vest pocket. One day the drops would be of no avail; he would become totally blind forever, helpless, dependent.

Peter Quest didn't want to be around when that happened. And so he plunged himself time and again into insanely dangerous undertakings, hoping ultimately to go out fighting, fighting what he loathed with all his being—crime.

HALLAM had mentioned Quest's numerous triumphs. That was not what Quest called them. His files bulged with newspaper clippings, recording the sensational cases in which he had figured, but across each he had scrawled the word "failure." For him there could be only one success, the adventure that terminated with his own existence.

His vision was dimming now, as it did sometimes in moments of tension and excitement. He uncorked the tiny phial, tipped back his great, leonine head and let some of the precious liquid trickle into his pupils. In a moment his vision cleared again.

A clock was chiming the half-hour when Quest heard the faint wheezing noise which warned him that his private elevator was in motion. He stepped out into the hallway to receive his caller.

The regular elevator service for the forty-story office building stopped at the thirty-seventh floor. The remaining three floors were connected by a small self-operating elevator, and these Quest, who enjoyed a sizable private income, leased as his home, office, crime laboratory and crime library.

The indicator over the frosted glass doors was swinging around with the ascent of the elevator from the thirty-seventh floor. Then it stopped on 38. Quest was puzzled. Surely the doorman had told Hallam to go to the top story.

When, after a minute or two, the elevator climbed no higher, Quest started for the service stairs. Two curious sounds restrained him. First, the elevator door sliding back, some one getting out. Next a faint sound, so faint that it would have been lost to ears less keen than Quest's: A moist plop like the bursting of a soap bubble.

Where was Hallam? What was the man waiting for?

Quest thumbed the button which would bring the elevator up to 40. Slowly, smoothly it rose, its shadow showing finally behind the glass door. It shivered to a stop, but the door remained closed. Within the car nothing stirred.

Quest called, "Hallam!"

Silence.

He stiffened with sudden, chilling foreboding, gripped the door and slid it open. Instantly a pungent, overpowering odor, acrid fumes, assailed his nostrils. He could scarcely breathe or see for it. He crushed a handkerchief to his nose, stepped into the car. He saw it then, and the ghastly horror of it sent his heart crashing against his ribs.

Weltering in a corner, was a thing blackened and charred and heaving wetly like hot bubbling tar. It bore a grotesque resemblance to a human body. The outline of a hand showed, a head half eaten away, and all boiling and writhing as if it were alive. It was as though an immense pillar of flame had licked the body, searing off flesh and clothes in one hellish caress.

The stinging fumes, Quest knew, were of some corrosive acid. It was even now eating through the floor of the car. Perceiving the danger, he dashed back into his office, returned with a rope which he wound around the fetid remains and lugged them out into the hallway, and none too soon.

The next instant the flooring collapsed, dropped down four stories.

AT A sign from old Si Todd, the medical examiner, two police sergeants carted off the shriveled remains in a canvas hamper. As they closed the door behind them, the doctor turned a baffled, worried countenance toward Detective-Inspector Haverill, enormous, paunchy chief of New York's homicide squad.

"They must have sprayed him with some corrosive acid, I'll stake my reputation on that. But it's like no acid I ever saw. Might conceivably have been a highly concentrated form of cyanic, except cyanic isn't known in the free state."

"Maybe cyanic gas," Quest put in.

"Yes, that's barely possible, though I fail to see how either could accomplish such destruction in a few minutes. How the thing was done—that's something else again."

The office was hot and heavy with smoke that the three men had made with an endless chain of cigarettes as, for the last two hours, they had tried to fathom the circumstances of Arnold Hallam's fearful death. In the adjoining room a young girl waited, Hallam's daughter, sobbing brokenly while her uncle, pale and distraught tried to comfort her.

It was late. The fingerprint men had gone, the police photographers had finished their jobs. Only Haverill and Todd

and Quest remained, confronted by the most infernal problem of their respective careers.

"By my reckoning," Quest said, "the killer waited for Hallam on the thirty-seventh floor. It must have been some one he knew and trusted. He got into the elevator with him and murdered him. Must have knocked him out first or he would have screamed with pain. He could then have walked down a few floors, mingled with the crowd and slipped into one of the regular elevators without attracting attention. Remember I heard some one getting out of my private elevator just before I found Hallam."

Haverill cleared his throat. "I don't suppose there's any doubt it was Hallam. We'll never be able to tell from fingerprints. There weren't any fingers left."

"All I can tell you is that Hallam called me about twenty minutes before he was murdered. He wanted to tell me of some plan, some threat to him and others, I gathered. It's reasonable to suppose that he was murdered so that he couldn't tell. We have the testimony of the doorman who recognized Hallam from newspaper photographs and the elevator boy who took him up to thirty-seven. That seems fairly conclusive."

Haverill jerked his head toward the adjoining room. "Let's have a word with the Hallam girl."

He swung open the door, revealing a slim, lovely girl, her body graceful for all the grief and horror that wracked it. A tall man, of high coloring and silvery hair, bluff and forthright, stood at her bowed shoulders, clumsily stroking them. At sight of the three men he made a pleading gesture not to distress the girl further in her sorrow. But she caught the gesture and mastered herself with a strength which commanded Quest's instant respect.

"I'm all right now, Uncle Grover," she said weakly. "These gentlemen need my help and I'm ready to tell whatever I

know to help find whoever—whoever—"
She couldn't finish.

HAVERILL advanced into the room.
"I appreciate that, Miss Hallam.
You're very game." But it was to Grover
Hallam that he addressed himself first.
"Mr. Hallam," he began, "do you know
of anything in your brother's life that
would explain this?"

"Certainly not!" the silvery-haired man
barked gruffly. "Arnold was the kindest
of men. So far as I know he had no
enemies, at least none capable of—" He
moved over to the window, out of the
girl's hearing, drawing Haverill after him.
"—none capable of killing him so atro-
ciously."

"Many of your depositors must have
suffered when the Gotham failed."

"Are you suggesting— That's absurd!
I think the public knows that the failure
was due to circumstances over which
neither myself nor my brother had any
control."

Under cover of their vibrant voices
Quest gently approached Lucy Hallam.
It was in the spirit of the man to feel a
moral obligation toward her. Her father
had enlisted his sympathy. Death, he felt,
did not relieve him from the obligations
that sympathy imposed.

"Miss Hallam," he whispered, "have
you any inkling of what your father wanted to tell me? I'd like to help you. I believe he would have wanted me to."

She glanced up. The ghost of a smile
flickered through her tears. "I'm glad,"
she murmured. "I'd like that." Then, revolving his question in her mind, she answered, "No, none whatever. Dad was
terribly upset over something lately. I
thought for a time . . . money . . . those
terrible losses. But somehow this seemed
to go deeper. I never knew. He never
told me. Fear, I think it was, deathly fear
of something or some one."

She interrupted herself suddenly as

a recollection troubled her memory.
"What is it?" Quest urged her.

"Nothing . . . nothing that could have
anything to do with this."

"One never knows, Miss Hallam."

"Perhaps you're right. It happened
only this morning. I burst into Dad's
library quite unexpectedly and he was
there talking with the strangest man who
ever came to our house. He was awful,
filthy, in rags, and I thought he was
drunk. He was the sort of miserable, un-
shaven derelict you see sometimes down
on the Bowery. Naturally I asked Dad
about it afterwards. He told me the man
was a former employee, a poor wretch
who hadn't had a job in years. He'd come
to Dad for help. That's all, really. It
isn't much, is it?"

"I don't know. What's the man's name?
Where did he go?"

She shrugged. "I haven't the slightest
idea. I didn't see him when he came. I
didn't see him when he left."

"Miss Hallam," Quest said with sudden, hard resolution, "that man must be
found. You must help me find him."

She looked at him with wide, staring
eyes. "Certainly, Mr. Quest. I'll be glad
to. Only I . . ."

CHAPTER TWO

First Night

OWING to his defective eyesight, Peter
Quest rarely attended the theater.
But a nagging curiosity had moved him
to purchase an orchestra seat for the opening performance of the new musical com-
edy, "Words and Music," featuring Asa
Dorn and secretly backed, so it was whispered, by her husband, Carl. Quest wanted
to observe those two strange birds in their
natural habitat.

Asa Dorn was one of the most remarkable women in that vivid sector of New
York society which is neither cheap and

nouveau riche, nor grandiose, aristocratic and dull. Beautiful in the exotic manner, clever and mysteriously elusive, she had pursued many talents before she married the eminent corporation lawyer. At various times she had been a painter, author, musician, singer, and social welfare worker.

Carl Dorn was a no less colorful figure. A slim, cold, fastidious man, he was as famous for his taste in food, wine and lovely women as for his legal victories. He lived expensively, although as counsel for the Hallam brothers and large stockholder in the defunct Gotham Trust, he had suffered a terrific financial set-back. It was this latter, perhaps, Peter Quest reflected, which had persuaded Asa Dorn to try her luck on the stage.

Quest sat in the mellow-lit pit of the Palace Theater, casually examining the ermine-swathed women and swallow-tailed men, disciples of the new café society, who had emerged *en masse* to applaud one of their most brilliant members. But a bitter disappointment awaited them, and Peter Quest.

The stage manager appeared suddenly before the silvery curtain and held up his hand for silence.

"Ladies and gentlemen," he announced almost tearfully, "the management deeply regrets this, but our leading lady was taken suddenly ill less than an hour ago and will not be able to appear in tonight's performance. Her part will be played by—"

The name of the understudy was drowned out by disappointed groans, murmurs of sympathy.

Peter Quest swore softly to himself and reached under his seat for his hat. A woman behind him, hissing at her companion, "There's Carl!" stayed him. He glanced up at a mezzanine box in time to see a lean, elegant figure slip through the claret-red velvet curtains and take his place in the rear of the box. He glanced

rather coldly at the audience, permitted himself a faint, sardonic smile and, dismissing them from his attention, consulted his program.

The woman behind Quest muttered, "Fancy Carl showing up when Asa is ill, or supposed to be ill. She's a very temperamental woman, you know. I wonder—"

WHATEVER she wondered was lost to posterity in the dimming of the house lights. A deep, rich flush spread along the hem of the curtain. Music burst gaily from the orchestra, invisible in its sunken pit.

Quest had not removed his eyes from the box, which was now pitch black but for the gleam of its occupant's snowy shirt-front and white tie. The music, sprightly, tuneful, held its listeners so that Peter Quest, alone of all those men and women, caught the tiny pin-point of light that danced suddenly over Dorn's head. It was infinitesimal and gone in an instant —no more than the refraction of light on the sides of a glass bowl. Yet to Quest it was oddly troubling, so much so that he half rose in his seat.

Too late. . . .

A scream ripped from the black depths of that box, ripped, echoing and re-echoing through the theater like a thousand tortured souls in hell. One short, knife-sharp scream soared high above the blare of cornets, and died on the ultimate note. Then deathly stillness that for a timeless instant held every human being there paralyzed in its icy grip.

So suddenly had it exploded that Quest froze as he was, half sitting, half standing. With the flaring up of the house lights he straightened. All eyes shifted to the box, shifted away again in unbelieving, nightmarish horror of what they had beheld.

Murdered Arnold Hallam's words rang in Quest's memory. ". . . a thing that will plunge this entire city into a nightmare."

WHAT a moment before had been an elegant, immaculately clad human figure was now a distorted, writhing grotesquerie, a black, liquifying, jelly-like mass. Its jerky, heaving movements lasted less time than it takes to record it. The whole flaccid hideousness toppled, poured rather, over the railing of the box, fell sickeningly into the aisle beneath.

The vacuum of utter silence, utter-lifelessness stretched to a seeming eternity before it erupted into chaos, madness. Half the spectators surged forward, drawn to that nauseating horror that diffused its acrid fumes through the theater. The others tore for the exits, trampling each other in their fury to escape.

Quest retained his senses sufficiently to work his way methodically into the lobby and find a telephone booth. Shortly he was talking to Haverill. "Better get down to the Palace Theater quick," he managed unnaturally calm. "It's happened again. You'll need the riot squad. This time it's—it's—" But words eluded him.

He could serve no useful purpose, he told himself, by returning to the raging inferno inside. But a speculation, a question that had been lurking at the back of his brain all evening, now swelled to vital importance. He leafed through a telephone directory, seeking the address of the Carl Dorn residence.

The wind had freshened. Peter Quest, waiting before the four-story Sutton Place mansion, lashed up his coat collar against the cold. In the chaotic frenzy of the last minutes he had left his hat in the theater so that he may well have looked like a homeless tramp, for the butler, opening the door a fraction of an inch, declared loftily, "I told you this morning to come around to the rear entrance. We do not admit beggars at the front door." Before the words were fairly out of his mouth he realized his error. He flung open the door wide. "Oh, I beg your pardon, sir! I—I thought—"

"Yes," Quest said, instantly alert, "what did you think? Who did you take me for?"

"Dear me, this is terrible! Madam will never forgive me. You see, sir, a wretched tramp, a derelict, sir, came begging this morning. Mrs. Dorn, out of the great kindness of her heart, gave him some money and I thought, I truly did, sir, that he'd come back for more. Your shadow, sir, misled me. I'm frightfully sorry."

"Forget it." It was odd—the thought raced furiously through Quest's mind— that Arnold Hallam's death, too, had been prefaced by the appearance of a tramp; odd that both men were involved in the Gotham Trust debacle, that both died in the same appalling manner. Aloud he said, "Kindly inform Mrs. Dorn that Peter Quest would like a word with her."

"Mrs. Dorn is ill, sir. I'm afraid she couldn't possibly see you now."

"I think she will receive me. Tell her—" He faltered, reluctant to break the news so brutally, but he knew the value of surprise tactics. "Tell her Mr. Dorn died at the Palace Theater a few minutes ago."

The butler went grey, winced as if he had been struck by a physical blow. "Mr. Dorn—died! I—"

"Tell her, please. I'll wait in there."

He strode past the butler and entered a simple, but richly appointed drawing-room, commanding a view of a spiraling, wrought-iron staircase. The butler gawked at him a moment longer, then padded unsteadily up the staircase.

Quest had not long to wait. Within thirty seconds Asa Dorn appeared at the top of the staircase, clad in a black negligée that sleekly sheathed her magnificent body. Had she planned it, her entrance could not have been more breath-takingly dramatic. Her long, pale face, framed in raven black hair, the tapering shadow cast by her body, produced an effect of almost sinister beauty.

SOFT rays from wall-brackets high-lighted her slow descent, spraying eerie shadows around her. Her eyes were narrow, Oriental, her face impassive.

She went directly to Quest, murmured in a flat, dead voice, "What is this nonsense? There's nothing the matter with my husband. He left me this evening in perfectly good health."

Quest sensed that this icily composed woman could sustain any shock, however violent. He said flatly, "Your husband was murdered." Briefly, concisely, he related the events of that evening.

As he spoke she averted her head, moved off to the far end of the room. Her shoulders seemed to heave a little, in the manner of an actress, Quest thought, who wanted to show restraint in grief. When she turned back to him, she wore again that impenetrable, frigid mask. Either the woman felt no sorrow whatever or her control was such as Quest had never in his life witnessed.

"Why have you come here to tell me thus?" she demanded. "Who are you?"

He explained that, too, outlining his activities since Arnold Hallam had frantically appealed to him—too late.

"I see," she said, sublimely unperturbed. "and you think I may be able to supply you with useful information."

"I had some such hope," he admitted. "For example, I have learned, quite inadvertently, that a beggar called at this house—"

She cut him off sharply. "My dear Mr. Quest, any acts of charity I care to perform are entirely my business."

"I imagine you're right. Then perhaps you won't mind telling me this: You failed to appear at the theater tonight. It seems you were ill. Frankly, Mrs. Dorn you seem to be in remarkably good health, considering—"

This time she made no reply, but moved toward a bell-rope. She pulled it lightly. Almost instantly the butler appeared.

"Mr. Quest is leaving, Dodge."

Peter Quest grinned, flicked his hand impudently. "Don't trouble, my man. I'll find my way out." He bowed mockingly. "Good evening, Mrs. Dorn. I trust I shall have the pleasure of pursuing this conversation further at a later date."

"I'm sorry, Mr. Quest. Whatever I have to say will be said to the proper authorities—including the fact that a severe attack of sinus kept me from the theater tonight."

"Well, thanks for that scrap of information anyway."

He left the house unable to suppress a surge of admiration for this superbly controlled woman to whom sudden, violent happenings were no cause for loss of poise. He would far rather, he admitted to himself, have every thug in gangsterdom for an opponent than Asa Dorn, widow of Carl Dorn. He had an idea she could sting as sharply as a scorpion.

He walked briskly west, heading for his home on Fifth Avenue. The strain of that hectic evening was taking its toll on his failing eyesight; he badly needed rest and sleep. Yet he preferred walking as a stimulant to his harried brain and nerves.

He swung through a dark, squalid side-street between First and Second, crossed the El-shadowed avenue and plunged into the gloomy half-light of the next. Midway down the block the small hairs at the nape of his neck began prickling. He saw nothing, heard nothing, yet an unmistakable increase of tension in the atmosphere about him told him he was being tailed. He knew it, sensed it infallibly with his super-keen instincts that were almost animal-like.

Too familiar with the technique of tailing and being tailed, he didn't turn, but listened instead, heard behind him, distant but definite, brittle tap-tap of heels on the cold, hard pavement. Some one was watching. 'Some one was following.

There was no fear in Peter Quest, but the instinct to fight back, to smash the forces of evil was as strong in him as his preparedness to die fighting when the hour came.

He quickened his pace, careful not to betray his knowledge. At the corner he turned swiftly, ran ten or twenty feet, ducked into a railed-off basement. Then, and only then, did he venture to look back.

As he looked, a lean, muscular man, similiar in build to himself, emerged from the side street. Quest shrank back, merging his shadow with the twisting, jagged shadows around him. Presently the man passed so close that Quest could have extended his arm and touched him. The ancient ruse had worked, worked too easily. Quest found it difficult to believe—

A winking mote of light, two motes— minute, dancing slivers, hovered suddenly over the man's head. With the shattering realization that he had saved his own life at the expense of another's, Quest straightened.

He burst from his hiding-place, lurched forward, knowing in his shrinking heart he could never reach the man in time. He yelled a warning.

The man wheeled. His mouth dropped agape in surprise and then from it issued a hyena-like ululation that cut off dead with the blow of instant destruction. It was as though a great black cloud blotted out the lean figure. . . .

When Quest reached the spot, a viscid, seething mass was befouling the sidewalk. Little remained of a human being beyond the man's hat.

Bitter, sickened, Quest knew his instincts had not failed him. He had indeed been followed. But not by this poor devil. They had mistaken the lean man for Quest.

H E SLIPPED warily into his duplex apartment on the thirty-seventh floor of the Acme Building, filled with an infinite sense of defeat, feeling small, ineffectual, crushed. Never had he pitted himself against evil so powerfully malignant, so omnipresent—just how thoroughly omnipresent he realized at once when he moved deeper into the darkened room.

The tiny points of light, the fateful yellow specks that twice that night had heralded ghastly death, were there, dancing four feet above his own head!

Then they were everywhere, the killers! There was no escaping their venom!

The specks danced closer and now a familiar, acrid odor pervaded the room, Split seconds he stood motionless, staggered by the closeness of doom. The next instant he was calm, icily calm. He watched the thing, whatever it was, approach and dip lower, lower. . . . He streaked across the room, his hand clutching for the light-switch. He flipped it, drenching the room with light.

The nature of the creeping death was all at once made hideously clear. A huge bubble, such as children blow with pipes, floated lightly in mid-air, wafted by unseen air-currents. A cloudy vapor, grey and dense, swirled within its iridescent chamber. In the precious instants left to him for thinking, Quest knew the hand which had released the floating death must have been lurking in the apartment seconds before his arrival.

The thing rotated gently, floated closer, began descending. It would burst, he knew, on contact, spraying whatever it touched with its deadly, consuming fumes.

He dared not make a dash for the door lest he explode the bubble with violent movement. It hung squarely in the center of the room, barring his path. He was trapped, cut off. He could only stare at it incredulously, shrinking back against the wall, geared to spring aside the moment it burst. So long as he could watch it, follow the slightest shift of its direction he was safe.

So long as he could watch it!

In that moment of all moments his cursed weakness attacked him. His head pounded with dizzying throbs, his vision misted over. Then the black, impenetrable curtain dropped before his eyes, imprisoning him more effectively than steel bars.

He fumbled for the sight-restoring drops. There was no time. The bubble hovered too close.

The one frail chance remaining to him was to grope his way to the door before the bubble burst. He dropped to his knees, flattened out on his belly and began inching forward, reasoning that the descending globule of death would take longer to reach him in that position.

HE had negotiated perhaps half the length of the room when his already taut nerves were jolted to the snapping point by a shrill gasping.

"Mr. Quest, let me in! It's Lucy Hallam. I had to—"

He reared on one elbow. "Stay out! There's danger in here . . . death!"

But he heard her advancing into the room. "Mr. Quest, your eyes!"

She must have seen it then, because she screamed. For one frightful second Quest thought the bubble had burst upon her, reducing her lovely young body to liquefying foulness. But she spoke again. "That thing, what in God's name is it?"

"What part of the room?" Quest demanded. "I can't see."

"Over by the window."

When she said that he knew he was safe, beyond the immediate path of peril. "Would you mind," he asked her, "giving me a hand? My eyes go back on me every now and then."

He felt her soft, warm hand close tenderly over his, guiding him to his feet. He lost no time now in producing the phial with its whitish drops, introducing them into his sightless eyes.

"My God—look!"

He stepped in front of her, shielding her from possible danger. But for the moment there was none. Through a thinning mist he saw the bubble fall rapidly, strike the edge of a table at the far end of the room and, with a fuming, spluttering hiss, shatter, scattering its liquid fire, leaving a blackened cavity in the center of the room.

The girl was sobbing against his shoulder. "That's how they killed my father!"

"I'm afraid so. And how they nearly killed me twice tonight. I owe you a great debt. You saved my life coming when you did."

Her voice took on an undertone of hysteria. "Oh, God, that's funny! That's really funny. I came here because I was half insane with fright!"

"All right. You're safe now and you're going to stay that way. Pull yourself together and tell me about it."

HE GRIPPED her elbow firmly and propelled her into the next room.

"What are you afraid of, Lucy Hallam?"

"They're watching me, I know they are," she sobbed, white and quivering. "Wherever I go I can feel them watching, and it's—it's as if they were waiting to—"

"No, you mustn't think that."

"But it's true—ever since Dad died. Last night when I left the house I saw a car standing across the street. The moment I appeared, the shades shot down and I could see shining, greedy little eyes peering at me through a slit. Then the car raced off. Why?"

Quest had a shrewd idea, but he restrained himself from answering. They had killed Arnold Hallam to silence him. How could the killers be sure Hallam hadn't confided in his daughter? How dangerous was she to their plans? For the first time Quest realized the unimaginable peril of Lucy Hallam's position.

"You're not living alone?" he asked.

"Yes, except for the servants."

"I'm not sure that's wise. Isn't there a friend or relative you could live with temporarily?"

"Uncle Grover wants me to go with him, but I don't want to be a bother."

"It's the best thing, believe me. I'll take you there myself—now. I assure you I'll be far more easy in my mind, if I know—"

She looked up at him, smiling. "You're very sweet."

It was in the taxi that Peter Quest remarked casually, "By the way, Asa Dorn is an interesting personality, isn't she?"

"I suppose she is." But she sensed an ulterior purpose behind the observation. "Why?"

"Do you know her well?"

"I don't imagine any one really knows her well. She's too withdrawn, too—well, cold, though I'm sure many people think she's a saint."

"How's that?"

"Her social welfare work. She's done an enormous amount of private charity work. Surely, you've heard of the Eternal Light Mission down in the Bowery."

"Of course, but I didn't realize that the Dorns—"

"Not the Dorns. Only Asa Dorn. It's her baby. She supports it, operates it, visits the men herself. She gives them food, money sometimes and in several cases has found good jobs for them. It's just another one of her hobbies. Like her acting and music and painting—Why, Mr. Quest, what's the matter? You look almost scared."

And, indeed, Quest's face had become pale and drawn as the girl talked.

"An odd thought struck me, that's all."

He turned abruptly, facing her, and took her slender wrists between his strong, tensile hands. "You'll have to know sooner or later." he said. "You may as well know now. Lucy, Carl Dorn was murdered at the Palace Theater tonight—just as your father was murdered."

She stared blankly a moment, doubting her senses. She shook her head slowly from side to side. "No . . . no . . . where will it end?"

CHAPTER THREE

Fate of a Genius

THE windows of the grey, weathered Amalgam Chemical Research Laboratories, fronting on the East River, gleamed balefully in the deepening dusk. In the main laboratory, a green-shaded droplight eerily highlighted the strongly contrasting faces of two men.

Young Bill Foster, assistant to the great Gabriel Denker, searched his employer's face with troubled eyes. There was something strange and unfamiliar in the look of the gaunt, haggard inventor, almost as though a stranger had taken possession of his body.

"We've done enough today," he said. "I—I'm tired."

Quick sympathy animated the younger man. "You're not ill, are you, Mr. Denker?"

"Of course I'm not ill," Denker snapped. "Why should I be?" But his eyes failed to meet the youth's. "Lock up after me, will you? See you in the morning." He took a step toward the door.

"Mr. Denker?"

"Well, what is it?"

Bill Foster hesitated before he blurted out, "Is it true, the rumor I've been hearing, that Amalgam's on the rocks, that we'll have to close the labs?"

"Close the labs?" Denker floundered. His face seemed to lengthen. "Certainly not! Ridiculous! Goodnight, Bill."

Foster glanced at the clock above the door. It said six-thirty. He yawned and automatically began tidying up the laboratory. As he did so, he came upon a brown leather brief-case, Denker's brief-case, without which the inventor had never before he left the laboratory. The simple presence of that brief-case told Bill Foster something was radically amiss.

He snatched it up and dashed coatless into the night. The waterfront street was empty, desolate. Denker, he knew, customarily took the subway on Park Row to his home uptown.

He legged it fast over the cobblestone side street, his breath issuing white plumes in the freezing air. He dove into the mouth of the subway.

The home-bound crowd was denser than usual, denser than usual.

He glimpsed Denker's thin, almost emaciated figure swinging through the turnstile and called to him, flourishing the brief-case. "Mr. Denker, you forgot—"

The roar of the approaching express drowned him out.

He never knew afterward the exact sequence of events. It was too confusing, too abrupt. He noted a jostling, violent upheaval in the thick of the mob, a spearhead that seemed to thrust at Denker. The next moment he saw his employer totter on the lip of the platform, spin around, an expression of amazement stamped on his intelligent face, and pitch full-length on to the tracks. The wheels smashed over his frail body.

A high, thin sound tore at Bill Foster's ears, a sound that must have been his own voice screaming. He saw a rainfall of crimson spurt up over the platform. The cars mercifully concealed the horror beneath.

He was running like a madman, vaulting the turn-stiles, still gripping the brief-case in a spasm of revulsion and pity and anger.

A voice in the crowd screeched, "Suicide!"

A momentary hush, broken by another quavering voice. "No, not suicide. No train could possibly do that to a man."

As he followed the direction of the speaker's glance, Bill Foster thought he would faint. Neither blood nor mangled flash marked the spot where Gabriel Denker had fallen—only a dark, liquid smear, defying the possibility of identification.

M^R. BALLARD CRAIGIE, of the brokerage firm of Craigie and Smythe, courteously waved his partner into the sleek Hispano-Suiza that waited at the corner of John and Dey Streets. He climbed in beside him and gave an address to the uniformed chauffeur.

"I had no idea it was so bad," he said loudly enough for the chauffeur to overhear. "They should have told us."

"They—yes," the other man agreed. "The firm's ruined, washed up, Phil."

The car met the sluggish stream of theater traffic and nosed toward Sixth Avenue to avoid it. The two portly, worried men in back had relapsed into silence. The chauffeur drove on. Traffic was thin. The car entered the comparative quiet and freedom of Central Park.

The suddenness of it caught the chauffeur totally unprepared. What appeared to be a small delivery truck rocketed out of a side road, semingly from nowhere. The chauffeur wrenched his wheel, swerving out crazily to the right, but not soon enough. The truck struck broadside. His arms shot up instinctively, shielding his face against flying glass.

When the moment of shock had passed, he knew no serious damage had been done. The truck sprawled at an angle, more badly smashed than the Hispano. An oppressive, ghastly stillness lay over the park. The truck was empty. There was no one inside it or around it.

The chauffeur twisted slowly around in his seat. . . .

When a traffic cop arrived he found the chauffeur laughing maniacally.

"What the hell! What goes on here?"

"Inside . . . Mr. Craigie . . . Smythe . . . they . . . they've melted away!"

He was still laughing when a white-faced, badly shaken policeman took him to the psychiatric ward at Bellevue.

COATLESS, his shirt open at the throat, exposing a red, leathery skin, Detective-Inspector Haverill paced his cramped, littered office, champing on a cold cigar. Two days and nights of sleeplessness had left him bleary-eyed.

"Man and boy," he raged, "I've fought criminals, all kinds; killers, thieves, dope peddlers. I thought I knew all the tricks, but this thing stymies me. If I was superstitious, I'd say the Devil was at work."

"Maybe he is," Peter Quest put in coolly, his neat, immaculate presence contrasting sharply with the harassed detective's. "A devil of sorts."

"All I can figure is that these killers have gotten hold of a new set-up, something we've had no experience with, and for the moment we're licked."

"For the moment, perhaps. But there's a very definite pattern running through the whole business, Haverill. If we can read it's meaning, we've got them."

"What do you mean, pattern?"

"Surely, it's obvious. Five prominent men have been murdered. All of them had one thing in common, besides their prominence. Money trouble. Hallam and Dorn lost plenty when the Gotham crashed Denker's firm is known to have been flirting with ruin. Ballard and Craigie guessed wrong once too often. And somebody killed them all, always in the same way.

"Another point of similarity in the pattern. Three times some bum or tramp has appeared in the homes or offices of the dead man a few hours before they were murdered. That kid Foster, you tell me, reported that a bum was seen hanging around the Amalgam labs this morning."

"So what does it add up to?"

"Incidentally, did you know that Gabriel Denker was known to be experimenting with corrosive gases for military purposes? I have even heard that he succeeded in producing cyanic acid in the free state. Odd, isn't it, that he and the others were killed by some such corrosive acid or gas?"

"Odd? I'll— Say, are you suggesting that Denker croaked all those guys, did the Dutch, and came back a couple of hours later as a ghost to kill Ballard and Cragie?"

"Not exactly. But I've got a hunch, Dan. I want you to let me follow it without interference."

"Right now I'd be grateful for a straw to grab at. What have you got in mind?"

"A visit to the Eternal Light Mission," said Peter Quest, smiling oddly.

CHAPTER FOUR

Lady Bountiful

LOLLING against the El-train window, his mouth hanging open loosely like an imbecile's, he made a pitiable picture. A greasy stubble smeared unclean shadows over his swarthy face. Frayed, filthy rags clung to his thin body. He wore no hat or coat or tie and his flesh gaped through holes in his muddy, cracked shoes. But behind his sordid masquerade Peter Quest's mind was alert and clear.

The train jerked to a stop in the heart of the Bowery and he shuffled disconsolately out onto the platform spanning Second Avenue. As he started down the corrugated iron stairs, the rags flapping grotesquely about his stooped figure, his eyes, avid behind their half-closed lids, found an objective. A streamlined, gunmetal roadster, fantastically out of place in that dreary section, waited with motor purring before the mission house two blocks south.

His arrival was nicely timed. Even as he looked, a woman, haughty and regal in a modishly tailored suit hurried across the sidewalk between the car and the building, slipped into the driver's seat and moved off.

Quest waited until she was out of sight before he descended the short flight of stone steps leading into the mission.

He entered a broad, long room in which thirty or forty men, oldsters mostly, milled about aimlessly.

A beefy citizen, less wretched looking than the others and younger, conned him narrowly as he came in. Quest greeted him with a solemn nod. "Free grub?" he asked. "I ain't eaten since breakfast."

The beefy man pointed his jaw at the refectory. "Straight on through, brother. There's enough for everybody, praise be."

"You don't say." He rubbed his stubbled cheek reflectively. "Say, that was some classy dame I seen driving away from here. What would she be doing in a dump like this?"

The beefy man shifted his cigarette stub to the other corner of his trap-like mouth. "Her? That's Mis' Dorn. I'll say she's classy. If it weren't for her, brother, we'd be out in the cold, all of us. She's Lady Bountiful, she is, in the flesh, not a motion picture. You must be a stranger around here not to know about her."

"That's right. I just hit town from the West."

THE beefy man leaned closer confidentially. "Yes, sir, ain't no one goes in for charity like her. Know what? Every month she picks one of us, yanks him out of here and tries to put him on his feet. A kind of soshul experiment she calls it. Gives him money, clothes, a job. It must work too, 'cause they never come back."

"They never—" Quest caught himself up. "Every month, hey?" he pursued evenly. "Well, well, who's the lucky guy this month?"

"Smokey Joe. You know Smokey?"

"I told you I just hit town."

The beefy man searched the room until he located a scrawny, weasel-like creature sitting by himself in a corner, smugly picking his teeth with a match-cover. "That's him. Yes, sir. Smokey'll be leaving us after today."

"Well," said Quest, feigning sudden disinterest. "Me for some grub."

He wandered off, careful not to attract too much attention to himself. An hour passed before he could jockey himself into a position where conversation with Smokey Joe would appear natural.

"They tell me you won the Lady Bountiful sweepstake?" he put in when an opportunity presented itself.

"Hunh? . . . Oh, yeah, yeah."

"Who do you have to kill?"

"Nobody. All I do is show up at this here house and I get staked out to a new lease on life."

Oh, but she's a cool one, is Asa Dorn, Quest thought grimly. No secrecy. Everything open and aboveboard. Sweet charity and no questions asked. Who worries about a bum anyway?

"What house?" he asked aloud.

Smokey Joe's nicotine-stained fingers fumbled among his tatters, produced a scrap of paper speckled with writing. He studied it. "Way the hell and gone out in the country, up Hudson River way."

Quest took a metal breath, like one bracing himself before taking an irrevocable step and said startlingly, "I've got a proposition."

The other eyed him contemptuously, as much to say: what kind of a proposition could you make? "I don't follow you, stranger."

"Where can we talk—alone?"

Curiosity and suspicion quarreled in the bum's mind. The former won and he beckoned Quest over to a small alcove.

Without speaking, Quest removed from an inner pocket a roll of bills and peeled off five one-hundred dollar notes. Smokey Joe's eyes widened until the pupils nearly vanished into his skull. "Holy Mike, did you crack a bank?"

Quest abandoned his pose with an abruptness that left Smokey Joe gasping. "I'll have to lay my cards on the table. I'm a detective. There's something distinctly phony about your Lady Bountiful. Here's five hundred for letting me take your place."

Smokey Joe dug his knuckles into his eyes, as though to dispel a dream. "How do I know— It's beyond me! What—"

"No time for explanations. Whatever happens you're in the clear. Is it a deal?"

But he had to argue persuasively and cunningly for a long time.

"Five hundred," Quest repeated, "for that address and your silence. You keep your mouth shut, that's understood. Because tonight I'm going to be you." He studied the sorry outcast a moment. "We bums look pretty much alike, don't we? I imagine Mrs. Dorn will be deceived— for a while anyway."

THE October hurricane came howling like a banshee up the Atlantic seaboard, blasting $100,000,000 worth of property and drawing in its wake a monster tidal wave that piled up hundreds of corpses like so many drowned insects.

The lofty, exposed table-land overlooking the Hudson River on the New Jersey side and had not yet felt its full destructive force, although even here the drive of the wind was powerful enough to slow a sixteen cylinder car.

Through immense box hedges Peter Quest glimpsed the sprawling, gabled house. It was perhaps a hundred yards ahead and he dared proceed no farther in the car lest he give the show away. He nosed it into a clump of bushes, doused the lights. The gale leaned all its weight on the door and Quest had to exert every ounce of strength to get it open.

His tramp's rags whipped his face and neck like steel thongs. His breath was snatched away from him, his eyelids blown shut. He knew it would be no simple matter to reach the house. Only a hundred yards distance, but every inch was a gruelling, punishing fight.

Lowering his head like a battering ram, he forged ahead. He battled his way closer, closer to the ghostly house. After what seemed eternities, battered and tossed about so that every muscle ached and trobbed, he reached the winding gravel drive. Another twenty feet or so would bring him to the comparative shelter of the portico.

The ponderous oak door swung open noiselessly before he had barely touched his numbed fingers to the bell. They must have been watching, waiting for him, and he shivered a little in spite of himself.

How dim was the interior. The carpet masking the long, arched hallway was thick and soft and it was this that muffled the approach of the lumbering, scarred creature who had opened the door.

"Mrs. Dorn told me to come," Quest announced, mimicking Smokey Joe.

He showed the creature the slip of paper. The former took it, nodded solemnly and motioned Quest to follow him. Quest shuffled after him down the hallway and through rooms so shadowy that the furniture assumed weirdly contorted shapes.

They halted before a heavy door situated somewhere deep within the bowels of the house. The hulking creature neither knocked nor called out, but shoved the door open and gave Quest a slight nudge which sent him over the threshold. The door thudded shut.

A FIRE smouldered in a Gothic stone fireplace large enough to admit a man. But for the faintest indirect lighting the source of which was invisible, this was the only illumination. A burnished deal table occupied the center of the room and around it sat four rigid black figures, casting on the wall behind them looming shadows.

They were swathed in some dark material so that the outlines of their bodies were diffused and uncertain. They appeared to be amorphous masses rather than clearly defined human beings. A strip of black velvet, broken by two narrow slits at the eyes, masked each face, and the reddish glints which the smouldering fire struck from these slits were the only evidence of human life.

Fervently Peter Quest prayed that one of those masks did not cover the face of Asa Dorn. Otherwise his imposture must be discovered sooner than he had planned. But the obscurity protected him a little.

How long he stood near the door, exposed to the icy scrutiny of those lifeless figures he didn't know.

But at length one of them spoke, the tall, lean one, in a voice low and muted. "Sit down—over there."

A white hand, rising from the shapeless figure, indicated an empty chair at the head of the table. Quest shuffled over to it, playing for all he was worth the part of a befuddled, bewildered bum. He sat down heavily.

The somber voice spoke again. "You needn't be afraid. These masks, this secluded house, are for our protection and yours. They need not alarm you."

"I—I don't like it just the same," Quest mumbled as Smokey Joe might have done.

"You're probably troubled as to why we've sent for you, why so much trouble has been taken over an insignificant man such as yourself."

"Mis' Dorn, she said, she—" He whined in a shaky voice.

"Forget about that. She is not with us just now, but you will receive everything she promised you and more. This is not entirely a philanthropic undertaking. It goes somewhat deeper than that." He paused to glance at his mute companions. They nodded approvingly. He went on in

that even, deadly tone. "It is not necessary for you to know too much. I may say that we are engaged in an experiment, a sociological experiment if you like. Call it a whim, a rich man's fancy. It doesn't matter.

"Wait, please. Hear me out. All of us here are prominent men, important men. You will know us when the proper time comes. It happens that for reasons of our own it is convenient for us to withdraw occasionally from the public eye, to retire, to work behind the scenes. What we require—well, in a word, is a stand-in, a double."

"It's crazy," Quest flung at him, pretending not to understand, but across his mind flashed the complete, fearful picture of what these men planned. Almost from the beginning he had guessed at something of the sort. Now he knew, knew positively, and the utter, vile ruthlessness of it staggered him. Aloud, he shouted, feigning panic, "I want to get out of here!"

"I AM NOT finished. You will hear what I have to say, if you please. We are prepared to pay you handsomely. You will have a comfortable home, an office, a business even, secretly directed by ourselves, of course. You will take the place, professional and social, which one of us has temporarily abandoned. We require only that you impersonate one of us and follow instructions. There will be nothing illegal or dangerous in those instructions."

"But, if even I was willing, how—" Quest began.

"I anticipate your question. You are wondering how you will be able to pose successfully as another man. We have arranged for that. Indeed, it is the crux of our whole plan. No doubt you have never heard of synthetic flesh? No, I thought not. It is a little secret invention to which only we hold the key. With this substance we can literally mold the features of another man upon your face and body, yes, even to the fingerprints of that man! The disguise will be complete, impenetrable. You think we are mad? Then know that at this moment a number of men such as yourself are walking about the city accepted as others. I repeat, there is nothing to fear from the law or from us. Every detail has been carefully worked out. This is all you need trouble yourself with, for the present. Well?"

Quest delivered a star performance of a man torn between two desires. He could feel the four men edge forward imperceptibly, hanging on his answer. Finally he started to speak. "How much would—"

He never concluded. At that instant occurred the one incalculable, fatal thing. The door behind him thundered open and a familiar voice shrilled, "I'm tellin' you I changed my mind. I figured I was being chiseled out of something. That guy ain't Smokey Joe. I'm—"

Quest spun around in his seat. "Shut up, you fool!"

Too late, Smokey Joe realized his error. Panic flecked his eyes as he saw the four masked men, saw them rise menacingly. He wheeled, started to run back the way he had come. The big creature who had come with him to the door reached out, pinned his arm in a grip of iron. One of the masked men lifted his hand in a silent command. A gun, gripped by the muzzle, showed in the creature's hand. He chopped down on Smokey Joe's skull. The derelict crumpled like an accordian, sinking to the floor with a wheezing, sobbing noise.

"Take him to the laboratory," the tallest of the masked men said.

The muscular creature slung Smokey Joe over his shoulder like an empty sack of meal and carted him away.

Quest, too, had risen, but the four men formed a menacing ring around him and each held an automatic trained on his head. One of them implanted furious hands in his hair, jerked back his head and peered searchingly into his face.

"Well, well, well," he said at length, "Mr. Quest, as I live and breathe!"

QUEST wrenched himself free of that fevered grasp. "Yes, but you're through, licked. You'll never get away with another."

The man laughed softly. "Did you hear that, gentlemen? Our detective friend here says we're through. He must mean that he's going to walk out of here and tell the police all about us. Now we couldn't allow that, could we?"

"You wouldn't dare—" Quest broke in, but he knew they would.

"I think," murmured another voice, that of the tall, lean man, "that there is no longer any need of these masks. Mr. Quest, permit me to introduce the members of our little fraternity, our—er—suicide club."

He indicated the first man. A hand pulled away the velvet strip.

"No," said Carl Dorn, "I'm not a ghost."

One by one the masks came away and Quest gazed in turn into the murderous eyes of Ballard Craigie and Philip Smythe and lastly, saturine, gaunt old Gabriel Denker. They were all there—all except Arnold Hallam.

Dorn, as though anticipating Quest's thoughts, explained airily, "Hallam is not with us, unfortunately. You see, we really did have to dispose of him. I fear his conscience started bothering him and became a general nuisance to all of us. Oh, we don't mind telling you about it, Mr. Quest. Our only regret has been that no one could appreciate the true brilliance of our organization. Such a neat scheme, don't you think?"

"Suppose I tell you," Quest said. "I think I've got the whole picture now. Every one of you are facing bankruptcy, complete financial ruin. You saw a way out by murdering a lot of poor bums made up to look like you—congratulations, Denker, that synthetic flesh is probably your most remarkable invention—and arranging with your wives or brothers to collect the insurance. Then, a meeting perhaps in another country. Hallam, I imagine, got cold feet when he realized his daughter would be involved."

"That's a pretty good analysis," Denker conceded.

"You are also to be congratulated, Denker," Quest resumed, "on your cyanic gas bubble. It is cyanic, isn't it?"

"It is and shortly you will have the opportunity of watching it work at first hand. After that, with Miss Hallam disposed of—"

A pang of agony shot through Quest's heart at the thought of Lucy Hallam in the hands of these inhumanists. "I'm not dead yet, gentlemen. I'll live. I'll live to destroy you all. As for Lucy Hallam, she's out of your reach, thank God. You'll never be able to touch her so long as she remains where she is."

A low-pitched chuckle filled the room, turned Quest's heart to stone.

"With Grover Hallam, eh? Oh, yes, the young lady will be safe with him. Very safe indeed."

Quest's stomach somersaulted and he felt an icy breath blowing on his neck. "What—what," he stuttered hoarsely, "are you driving at?"

"Why, nothing, my dear Quest, nothing at all," murmured Carl Dorn, *"except that Grover Hallam happens to be the originator of our society!"*

CHAPTER FIVE

Murder in the Air

BEYOND a certain degree of terror, human emotions mercifully can no longer function. The mind either ceases to register, becomes stultified or loses its sanity altogether. Peter Quest had long passed that limit.

Harrowed on the one hand by Lucy Hallam's imminent peril and his inability to reach her in time, on the other by the forced spectacle of pitiful Smokey Joe prepared for devilish butchery; his emotions were numbed, his reasoning powers temporarily atrophied.

He could only stare dully through the slot of the dungeon-like cubicle into which they had thrust him—stare at the obscene frightfulness about to occur in the adjoining cell.

Greenish pale under a flickering overhead lamp, Smokey Joe held the center of the tiny, barren stone chamber, paralyzed as a rabbit is paralyzed by a stoat. His mouth worked open and shut soundlessly. His body twitched. Otherwise he was incapable of movement or flight.

Smokey Joe knew he must die. That was patent in his abject, cowering terror. But he did not realize the source and nature of the destruction about to descend upon him, and Quest was thankful for that. Only he understood the significance of the small, circular grate directly above Smokey Joe's head. Only he knew that at any moment it would disgorge its silent, floating death.

He knew all there was to know now about the hellish death-globules of Gabriel Denker, bubbles spun of thin, fragile glass and filled with cyanic gas. Glass fashioned to shatter at the slightest touch and easily directed from a powerful blow-pipe.

And they had placed Peter Quest where he must witness this atrocity and savor in advance his own liquidation. For his own life he cared nothing, but to stand by helplessly while another human being cringed, defenseless, exposed to brutal murder—that was an intolerable ordeal for a man of Quest's spirit. . . .

Oh, God, it was coming now! Oilily the glistening bubble swelled in the opening of the grate, blown to immense size by unseen hands. At first only a segment of its curved surface showed in the grate and within it swirling, cloudly vapors. It grew, rounded out to its full globular shape and all at once broke free from its source. Two fire-spitting eyes seemed to glow for a moment in the grate, then vanish.

It skirted the ceiling a while, bouyed by air currents. And Smokey Joe saw it. Its meaning was alien to him, yet he sensed it carried danger for him. His neck craned back at a hideous, unnatural angle and his eyes followed the thing.

Now, from behind the grate, some one was directing its course, wafting it down, down, down until it floated within inches of Smokey Joe's head.

Quest fought an impulse to shout, warn him to run. Of what use? The end would only be prolonged, the final kiss of death more horrible. Let it come quickly. Let the poor devil's sufferings be finished.

Smokey Joe managed to shake himself out of his torpor of fear enough to twist away from the approaching bubble. It pursued him with uncanny accuracy as though it had a volition of its own. It was near, so near now. . . .

SMOKEY JOE flung himself across the room and, for the first time, saw Quest through the glass slot.

His hands clawed at the opening and his voice soared in a final scream of panic and pleading.

"Quest, for God's sake, do something! Save me, save me!"

Those eyes, those bulging, glazed eyes that tore at Quest's heart—they were more than even he could face. He turned away and, as he did so, knew it had happened. He heard the familiar moist plop, the insidious hiss and Smokey Joe's scream choked off in his throat. At last it was over. Thank God it was over!

The desire to look into that death-chamber was too strong to resist. He looked and black nausea, revulsion, swept over him in wave after wave.

What was left of Smokey Joe festered in a black, viscid jelly on the bare, stone floor.

Quest lost track of time, lost awareness of himself. All sensibility, all emotion receded into black, suffocating nothingness.

He didn't know how long a period had elapsed when steps outside the steel door recalled him to alertness. They had come for him. His turn now.

The door opened and they loomed in the doorway, their cruel, rapacious faces slashed with sharp, dancing shadows—Denker and Dorn and Ballard and Craigie and the massive, gorilla-like creature who did their bidding. Behind them the lights flickered as they had ever since Quest had come to that house.

Denker crooked his claw-like finger beckoningly. Quest made no attempt to resist. His pride restrained him from giving them that satisfaction. He walked boldly up to them without flinching.

"We have decided," Denker purred, "that you will do nicely as a substitute for Grover Hallam. Hallam dies tonight or, should I say, dies by proxy? This way, Mr. Quest."

So that was it! The synthetic flesh would be applied to his own body and he would die as Grover Hallam.

The increased flickering of the lights stirred up a curious idea in Quest's mind. The violence of that flickering was comparable now with the violence of the gale howling through the night. The lights threatened to go out!

Denker realized this, too, and a slight twinge of annoyance crossed his features. He spoke over his shoulders to the others.

"Those damn lights! Must be a wire down."

"Better fetch some candles," Ballard suggested. "We don't want to be caught without lights, not if we're going to clean things up tonight."

Darkness! To Quest that word so casually dropped whispered a faint hope. For the first time since he had been afflicted, his weakness placed him at momentary advantage. Accustomed as he was to long spells of blindness, he had developed the blind man's extra-sensory gifts. If the lights failed, he would be able to feel, if not to see, while the others would be helpless and confused. They had guns, yes, but it's not easy to find your target in the dark.

If only the lights would fail—now at once! His once chance to crush this sinister murder ring—and save Lucy Hallam, if there were time.

But even that hope receded as Denker turned to the huge creature. "Do you hear? Get candles. Quickly. Before— Damn!"

At that instant the entire house was plunged into pitch blackness. And into Peter Quest's mind came a mental picture of the lanes of escape he had charted. . . .

LUCY HALLAM met her uncle's gaze and shrank from its intensity. He was smiling and holding the tips of his spatulate fingers lightly together. But there was neither warmth nor humanity in his smile.

"Uncle Grover!" the girl sobbed, "You're—you're joking!"

"I fear not, my dear. You've become a great nuisance to your old uncle. So much so that we shall have to—"

The girl's hands fluttered to her temples. "Am I going mad? You, my own uncle—my father's brother—*you're going to kill me!*"

Another voice spoke, a sound as thin

and venomous as the flickering of an adder' tongue.

"I've had enough of this. Let's get rid of the little fool."

Asa Dorn shot a cigarette stub from her jade holder into the wastepaper basket. Her long, pale, beautiful face betrayed an urgency stronger than mere expediency. She was relishing this crime, perversely, sadistically, for its own sake.

Lucy Hallam edged away from them. "Keep away! Don't touch me!"

"Let her go," the older woman laughed mirthlessly. "That's just where we want her."

As Lucy looked behind her and saw the tall open windows twenty stories above Park Avenue, Asa Dorn's meaning dawned on her. They meant to force her through that window, send her body hurtling to horrible destruction on the pavement below.

And there was no help for her in her uncle's apartment. She was imprisoned in that thick-walled, soundproof study. She could scream. No one would hear her. She knew this and made no effort to scream. Instead a cold, grim desperation steadied her.

"You murdered my father," she accused them, "and now you're going to murder me. You miserable swine! Do you really think you'll get away with this?"

"I'm sure I don't know why not," Hallam rejoined, stepping nearer to her, blocking off the space between her and the door. "You've been upset by your father's death. You have no money, nowhere to go, and so you're taking the easiest way out. You're committing suicide, my pet. It won't be the first in this city."

"He'll get you," she hissed between clenched teeth.

Asa Dorn laughed that terrible mirthless laugh of hers. "The child must be

Getting Up Nights
Often Caused By Kidney Strain

Bubbles of Murder

talking about that man Quest. Shall we tell her?"

"Mr. Quest won't get us, my dear Lucy," Hallam said, "because we've taken care of him."

He stood barely an inch from her, his vast chest and stomach blotting out her frail figure. The window-frame pressed into her spine and he came on, forcing her back, back. . . .

Fear swamped her now and she pleaded with him piteously. "Uncle, please, please don't! I don't want to die. I won't talk. I'll go away. I won't bother you—"

"Now!" Asa Dorn's voice cut across hers. "Don't let her talk you out of it, Grover. Do it—now!"

She had seen a subtle weakening of his determination. The brutality of it seemed too much for even him. He realized this and, as if he feared to weaken altogether, sprang—drove his powerful shoulders against the girl.

With a shrill cry she toppled backwards, shot through the open window and, in her swift descent, hooked her arms through the grille beneath the window. She clung there, twenty stories above death, praying some one below would see her.

"You idiot!" Asa Dorn rasped. "If

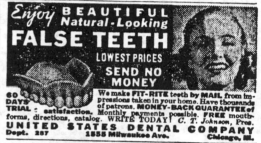

Classified Advertising

any one saw— Stamp on her hands, quickly !"

Hallam retreated from the window, beaten. "No, I can't do that, I can't."

"Then I'll do it."

She strode to the window, holding in her hand a heavy crystal paper-weight. She raised it, brought it down with crushing force on the girl's knuckles. Lucy Hallam bit her lips. But her hold on the grille tightened.

"Damn you, damn you, you little—"

Again she swung the weapon.

But it never landed. Hallam's choked cry jerked her around. She caught a swift glimpse of Peter Quest, pale as death, his clothes in rags, standing in the doorway, holding an automatic. It was her last glimpse of anything.

The gun spat. She spun around, dropping the paper-weight and pitched forward.

Hallam, with the courage of desperation, fumbled for his own gun. Death barked in Peter Quest's hands again and Hallam crashed over a' chair, came to rest a foot from his accomplice.

A moment later Quest was hauling Lucy Hallam up to safety, cradling her bruised hand between his own, murmuring tenderly to her. "Are you all right, Lucy? Are you all right?"

"Oh, yes . . . Thank God, Peter, you came. The others. . ."

"I escaped. They can't get far. Haverill's got every officer and trooper in the state out for them. Don't worry, Lucy. It's finished, finished!"

And Peter Quest smiled tenderly at this girl who, as he himself, had gone through hell. . . .

THE END

CLINICS FOR KILLERS
A Peter Quest Novel
by JOHN KOBLER

What was happening to the injured patients admitted honestly to New York's leading hospitals—that sent them home to slay and ravish their unsuspecting loved ones?

From somewhere far away she heard a dull report. . . .

CHAPTER ONE

Blood Will Tell

(3:45 a.m. Thursday, January 12th, 1939)

THE narrow, macadam road coiled thinly under an arcade of stripped, gaunt trees. The night was moonless, hazy. On the distant hillsides a few mist-veiled lights shone feebly.

A lone car splashed over the road's rain-washed spine. It was long and low-slung, and its unrelieved blackness suggested a coffin. The hunched, massive figure at the wheel seemed an integral part of the car. His greenish-white hands, making two gleaming smears on the wheel, were the only contrasting spots of color.

He swayed from side to side with the careening of the car, making a humming noise in his gullet. His bullet-shaped head, bald and hatless, was set low in his upswept collar like a turtle's. His was the face of a battered ex-prizefighter, one would have thought, with its flat, smashed nose and scarred cheeks. Black holes gaped between the fang-like teeth that jutted from lips thick as fat worms. His skin had the sickly-white hue of a dead fish's belly; eyes and mouth held intense ferocity.

His head was cocked to one side in a harking attitude, for within that immense, domed cranium there sounded forever the 'roar and screech of cars on a dirt race-track, metal smashing against metal, and the crackling of flames. Those hellish sounds inside his brain had tormented him since one spill too many had finished him as an auto racing champion, leaving him a crash-drunk, revenge-lusting maniac. One thing only could alleviate the relentless pounding in his head. One thing . . . Craving for it brought a hideous, twisted grin to his lips.

He croaked hoarsely, "Yeah, boss, I'm doin' like you said. I'm obeyin', boss. Then you gotta give it to me. You gotta stop the noises. You gotta, boss. . . ."

Terror clouded his burning eyes, terror of his consuming need, and what would happen to him if he failed to quench it. His greenish-white hands crisped around the wheel.

For the moaning old man who lay in the rear of the car, Krock, the driver, felt little concern. Too spent to scream for help or lift the shades, the old man could only claw ineffectually at the leather upholstery. Suddenly the speeding car struck a bump, jolting him to the floor. The impact winded him, but he managed to roll up against the front window. With all his ebbing strength he reached up, tapped against the pane and fell back, swooning from the effort.

The feeble tap intruded itself upon the roaring in Krock's head. He glowered, glanced briefly behind him and moistened his lips in anticipation, for there was fierce pleasure in the thing that lay ahead of him—next to the little needle that brought oblivion, it was the highest pleasure.

Presently his darting eyes spied a deep roadside ditch; the appointed spot. The car slid to a halt.

Recovering consciousness, the old man pleaded, "Water . . . water. . . ."

KROCK lumbered out of the driver's seat, walked around to the back and yanked open the door. His loose-jawed, ape's face thrust itself into the black interior, came within an inch of the old man.

The latter's eyes widened in horror. He tried to wriggle out of reach. "My God, what are you going to do to me?"

Alert for the sound of intruders, Krock placed his ham-like hands under the old man's arms and dragged him brutally from the car, letting his knees bang the running-board. The old man groaned in pain.

"Let me go. For God's sake, no more! I can't stand any more. I'll pay you anything, do anything."

But no amount of money could bring Krock deeper ecstasy than this . . .this torture, this killing. His breath issuing in quick gasps, making clouds in the cold air, he lugged the old man around to the front of the car, dropped him directly beneath the wheels. Understanding froze his victim. His mouth worked wordlessly. He could no longer speak nor stir. But Krock took no chances. He aimed his foot, smashed it full into the old man's face. A high, shuddering sigh . . . a spurt of blood that stained Krock's trouser-leg. Then Krock smiled his slow smile.

The humming in his throat deepened as he climbed back into the car and shifted into low gear. The wheels bumped softly over the inert body. Ribs and sternum cracked. The hideous noise of it brought a shiver of maniacal glee to Krock.

He jumped out again, went to the body, bent down, felt the heart. His hand came away red with blood. He consulted his wrist-watch, nodded, satisfied. He toed the body over toward the ditch. It vanished from sight.

He was about to return to the car when he noticed that in being dragged out the old man had lost his heavy camel's hair coat. A cunning expression entered Krock's eyes as he retrieved it, lowered himself into the ditch and slipped the coat about the lifeless body.

He surveyed his handiwork, then dashed back into the car. None too soon. Headlights showed beyond the crest of the hill behind him. A motor purred. He meshed his gears and lurched off into the night, muttering wildly, "It's done, boss. A sweet job. You'll be satisfied, boss. You'll give it to me now, quick, quick, 'cause I gotta have it. . . ."

The second car passed the spot. The driver noticed nothing unusual for his eyes were trained on the wooden road-sign that said: HIGHLAND ROAD.

(6 p. m. Wednesday, January 11th, 1939)

PETER QUEST lolled back against his bed in Hutchinson Memorial Hospital, Westchester County, his restless hands plucking at the white coverlet. He heard Nurse Kovac unhooking his fever-chart. He couldn't see her for the bandage that covered his eyes.

He cursed himself for a fool. Why had he submitted to the operation? He knew in his heart, no matter what Dr. Halmey told him, that it would be useless, worse than useless. Long ago doctors had warned him that nothing could save his eyesight. Chronic glaucoma, they called it. Increasing spells of blindness that only drops from the little phial he carried could relieve—for the moment. Then one day total, irrecoverable loss of vision. He had lost precious weeks, letting his old friend, Lester Halmey, talk him into an operation.

A strange man, Peter Quest. In the annals of crime-detection no criminologist had ever been more reckless, more foolhardy. Yet from Quest's point of view it wasn't foolhardiness that moved him to take insane risks. It went deeper than that. Peter Quest didn't want to be around when the fatal day of blindness came, reducing him to helpless dependence. He wanted deeply, with all his being, to die in action, die fighting crime as he had fought it all his life. But a mocking Fate decreed otherwise. Again and again he had escaped from what seemed inevitable destruction. These escapes he termed failures. Bitterly he felt that he had not yet fulfilled the curious destiny he had conceived for himself.

Nurse Kovac's throaty voice broke in upon his reflections. "Good evening, Dr. Halmey."

Quest heard Halmey's footsteps pad briskly across the linoleum-carpeted floor. "Hello, butcher," he jeered.

He felt Halmey's firm, yet sensitive grip on his arm, heard his voice. "Feel pretty frisky this evening, don't you? Well, I guess we'll have you out of here soon. Let's have a look."

His fingers deftly unfastened the bandage, while Nurse Kovac lowered the blinds. Quest batted his eyelids hard, trying to pierce the darkness. Halmey snapped on a tiny pencil flash and probed the pupils.

"See anything?" he asked.

"Sure, I can see that light and your finger."

"Hmmmmm," said Halmey, the way doctors will.

Quest grasped his wrists. "Look, I want the truth. No tripe. Give it to me straight, Les, or I'll wring your neck."

Halmey remained silent. He backed away from the bed and gestured at Nurse Kovac. She made light and Quest could see for the first time in three weeks: Kovac, brawny, hatchet-faced; Halmey, lean, tall, elegant. Neither of them spoke.

"Well?" he snapped savagely.

Halmey shrugged helplessly. "If it were any one else—but, no, I can't lie to you, Peter. Perhaps I was unwise to give you the slightest hope, but it's no go. At least not permanent recovery."

Quest stuck a cigarette between his thin lips, flicked a match on his thumb-nail. "Forget it. I never expected anything else. How long before I—"

"Ah, I can give you some encouragement there. A year anyway. Maybe longer. That depends entirely on how well you take care of yourself. Excitement, of course, will inevitably bring on temporary attacks of blindness. You've got to avoid it." He broke off to smile impatiently at Quest's wry expression. "I know, I know. But no more adventures for you. If you should get a spell or two, use those drops. They'll clear your vision at once."

"Thanks, Les. I know you've done everything possible. I—now what the hell was that?"

THE door stood ajar, commanding a view of the corridor. A strange trio had burst from the room directly opposite Quest's. A young girl, slim and red-lipped and lovely, was struggling in the grip of a nurse and an elderly man, black-bearded, glittering-eyed, whom Quest recognized as Dr. Emil Kranz, the famous brain surgeon. The girl's face was as white as the corridor walls.

"You think I'm insane," she wailed hysterically, "but I tell you the man in there is not my father! He's not the man I brought to this hospital."

Kranz murmured in syrupy, soothing tones, "My dear Miss Barton, isn't this a trifle fantastic?"

"Oh, I know he looks like dad," she went on wildly. "That's what's so—so horrible. Because he's not, he's not! What have you done with dad? Where is he?"

Halmey rose from Quest's bedside, snapped, "Excuse me a moment." He stepped into the corridor. Nurse Kovac made a motion to shut the door, but Quest restrained her, sudden interest tingling his spine. "No," he commanded, "leave it open."

He heard Halmey addressing the girl, "What seems to be wrong, Miss Barton?"

The girl told her story in staccato, incoherent gasps. Two months before, her father, Van Cleve Barton, had been injured in a motor accident, sustaining a nasty concussion. She had driven him to Hutchinson Memorial Hospital where Dr. Kranz had performed a successful brain operation. Then gradually she had come to feel, within the last few days, that her father had undergone some subtle change. Now, on the eve of taking him home she felt certain that the man lying in Room 112 was not Van Cleve Barton.

Quest watched Kranz and Halmey exchange significant glances as the girl unfolded her incredible story. When she paused for breath Kranz let his hand fall lightly on her shoulder. "My dear lady, believe me, your nerves have been strained. You are suffering from—er—from slight delusions." He glanced at Halmey for approval, got it and resumed: "I would strongly suggest, before taking your father home, that you have a little chat with Dr. Upham, our chief psychiatrist. . . ."

Brutal, Quest reflected. Too crude. The suggestion brought a violent change to the girl. To Quest it was patent that she was making a masterful effort to disguise her fears, to pretend she had suffered a momentary collapse. She said with forced calm, passing her hand across her brow, "I—I, dear me. What have I been saying?" She shoved the door of Room 112 open, looked in. A querulous voice drifted to Quest's ears. "What's going on here, Grace? What's the matter? Why don't we get started? Kranz says I can go tonight."

"Yes, Dad, we'll leave at once."

She turned back to the doctors, submerging her fears which Quest sensed had not been dispelled. "I've made an absurd mistake. Forgive me, please."

Kranz rubbed his hands together, beaming. "There, you see. I told you. Now, whenever you're ready, you and your father—"

"I know. We'll be leaving shortly. Thank you, doctor."

Quest leaned back wearily against his pillow. "You can close the door now," he told Nurse Kovac. She obeyed. "Funny thing," he mused aloud. "I thought I knew a thing or two about nerves and mental aberrations, but that young lady didn't look neurotic to me."

"No," the nurse agreed. "Still, overtired nerves play strange tricks on a body."

"No doubt." Quest lit another cigarette. "Who are they, the Bartons I mean?" he asked with deceptive casualness.

"Oh, they've lived in Rye a long time. Miss Barton had her tonsils taken out in this hospital five years ago. Mr. Barton retired from the oil business several years ago, after his wife died. He's a very wealthy man, I understand. And Miss Barton—well, I dare say you've seen her picture in the papers plenty of times."

"I never read society news."

It annoyed Quest not to be able to rid his mind of the ridiculous incident in the corridor. Later that evening, as he sat on the pavillon, star-gazing, he heard the girl's familiar melodic voice and turned to see her guiding a silvery-haired, tall old gentleman toward the elevator. She seemed calm, reassured. Her arm was linked affectionately through his. Yet, as the elevator-door opened to receive them, Quest experienced a crazy impulse to call out, to stop them. It passed instantly. The elevator sank out of view.

* * *

The ape-faced man rocked back and forth in his rat-hole under the eaves. . . . "It'll be time soon, boss. Ah, it's gonna be good, good. . . ."

* * *

LATER that evening Quest's nagging thoughts crystallized into action. When Halmey came in for his last visit of the day, saying cheerfully, "You'll be leaving us tomorrow, Peter," Quest beckoned him closer.

"Meanwhile," he said, "I'm bored, restless. How about fixing it so I can visit the lab? I'm always interested in what your bug-men are doing."

"Well, we don't usually let patients go in there, but seeing as it's the famous Peter Quest—Just for a minute, mind you."

A few minutes later Halmey took him down to the immaculate, white-tiled room on the first floor where three white-coated youths were busy over test-tubes and microscope slides. He introduced Quest to a stocky, tow-headed worker named Browning.

"He wants to kibitz," he explained.

"It will be a privilege to have him," Browning replied courteously.

Halmey smiled, left the laboratory.

"Is there any special phase of our work you're interested in?" Browning asked.

Quest said something about tubercules, stalled for an opening. When he saw his opportunity, he put in off-handedly. "Ever make a blood-test of old Barton?"

"Why, yes. Matter of fact, we gave him a transfusion when they brought him here and had to determine his blood-group."

"Which one?"

"Which blood-group you mean? Let's see." He thumbed through a row of glass slides behind him. "Barton, Van Cleve Barton. Here it is. Group A . . . Say, why are you interested? You're not a doctor."

Quest grinned mischievously. "Oh, I've always been curious about the composition of blue blood. You hear so much about it. Now, since Grace Barton had a tonsilectomy in this hospital, I suppose you had to test her blood, too. What would her group be?"

"We didn't check for group. General characteristics, that's all."

"Oh, I see. May I have a look at her card?"

Puzzled, Browning returned to the card index, began searching. Without knowing exactly why, Quest sensed an ominousness, a foreboding, through that super-keen sixth sense of his.

Browning drew out a card. "Here you are," he said.

Quest looked at the card, stiffened. "My word," he said.

The young technician said, "What's that?"

Peter Quest said, "Oh, nothing. I was thinking of something else." His mind was whirling. He knew enough about blood properties to know that the data he read disproved paternity in the case of the Barton girl and the man just released as her father! The unique detective dashed from the laboratory, ran up the two flights to his room. Nurse Kovac was turning down his bed. Quest barked, "Never mind that! Get my clothes. I'm leaving."

"Why, Mr. Quest, you can't do that. You're not supposed to be discharged until morning."

"The hell with that! This won't wait." He added in a prayerful whisper, "Please God, it isn't too late already!"

As he hurried into his clothes, despite Nurse Kovac's dismayed protests, he glimpsed Kranz passing his door. The surgeon halted, fixed him with his beady, gimlet-like eyes, faced-about and went back in the direction whence he had come.

CHAPTER TWO

Vanishing Millionaire

DISTANT church-chimes boomed eleven times as Quest's roadster slid smoothly into the bluestone drive, rolled to a halt before the white, colonial mansion, ghostly in the cold moonlight. Its facade was blank, lightless. Nothing stirred on the vast, thickly-treed estate. The small hairs at the back of Quest's neck prickled warningly.

Cautiously he mounted the broad stoop. His hand moved toward the bell, faltered. He tried the door-handle. It yielded. He crossed the threshold. Moonbeams feebly illuminated a lofty, paneled vestibule. He made out a winding oak staircase, stout oak doors on either side of a long, high hallway.

He frowned. The door unlatched . . . no one about . . . servants either asleep or absent. His pulse quickened with nameless fears. He took a step or two along the hallway, froze as a groaning cry drifted up from some place far below. It was sepulchral, that groan, ghastly. It sounded again, more faintly. Quest's keen hearing, compensating for his debilitated vision, traced it to a spot directly under his feet.

He swung around, headed for a small arched entrance-way that apparently gave into a pantry or kitchen. It was too dark to determine the nature of the room, but he could make out two or three doors. He tried each. The third opened on a steep staircase leading down.

At the base of the stairs his groping hand found a light-switch. He flipped it up, flooding the bare, stone room with blazing light. His wild hunch had been right—he had arrived too late!

A girl's nude body sprawled on the cold stone; the soft, swelling curve of thigh and breast was still warm. The once pretty face was contorted in a mask of unutterable horror. The head—Quest, who had seen many corpses, momentarily averted his eyes—the head hung by a shred of flesh. A knife had slashed through to the spine.

That eerie cry—it meant that the horrible thing had been done but an instant before, while he stood uncertain in the hallway above!

He approached the lifeless, nude body, forced himself to study it, knew that not death alone had visited Grace Barton. She had been brutally ravished.

A COLD cigar traveled slowly from one corner to the other of District Attorney Hanson Harding's tight, hard mouth. He paced his well-worn carpet, hands clasped behind his back, red hair stiff as a porcupine's quills. Occasionally he shot piercing glances at the three men seated against the wall.

Peter Quest returned the glance blandly.

Dr. Kranz plucked nervously at the tips of his black gloves.

Dr. Lester Halmey shook his head dazedly.

Harding wheeled abruptly on Kranz, rapped out, "Doctor, as chairman of the hospital board, I hold you partly responsible for what's happened. Grace Barton knew the man she was taking home was not her father. She told you that. You inferred she was insane, as much as threatened her with one of your psychiatrists. That seems to have scared her into keeping quiet. She went home—to her death!"

"One moment, Mr. Harding. No one could possibly have guessed the man was an imposter. The resemblance was perfect. I think Mr. Quest will agree with me."

"I do," Quest said quietly. "Since seeing photographs of the real Van Cleve Barton, I would say only a person who had known him intimately for a long time could have detected the difference. The blood test was the only thing that tipped me off."

"All right," Harding said. "Then the assumption is that somehow the real Van Cleve Barton was smuggled out of the hospital after his arrival and this imposter substituted."

Halmey broke his long silence. "Not necessarily. The substitution may have occurred before the Bartons ever arrived, and it took the girl some time to realize the subtle difference. As a matter of fact, I may say that no other explanation holds water. Your men have questioned Nurse Smythe. You have her statements that either she or Nurse Jones were in the room during Barton's entire stay. Both have been on the hospital staff for more than six years and have unimpeachable records."

Harding grunted, ruffled his red hair. "So how does it shape up?" He shook his head furiously. "The damnedest thing I've come up against in twenty years' experience. The Barton girl takes him home. Either she planned to shake him after she left the hospital, or had convinced herself that maybe she was suffering from delusions. Anyway, according to this butler—" he glanced at the papers on his desk—"Jennings, Barton announces he's going for a little stroll. Seems he was always a great walker, fair weather or foul. This is about two hours after they get home. Jennings doesn't see the girl and assumes she's gone to bed. He watches Barton walk out of the house, goes to bed himself. We can only guess what happened. The fake Barton comes back, drags the girl down to the cellar, attacks her, slits her throat. Why, what in blazes is behind it all? Frankly, gentlemen, I don't know. But, by God, I'll find out! And the Hutchinson Memorial Hospital had better have clean hands or I'll close it up quicker than you can say Van Cleve Barton."

"And meanwhile," Quest put in, "you've got not one, but two missing men —the fake Barton and the real one."

Harding bit on his cigar savagely. "Do you think I've forgotten that? Hell, it's the damnedest part of the whole business! I've got every cop in the state on the lookout!"

*   *   *

A smile of obscene ecstasy transformed the ape-man's face. He stirred on the cot, clenching and unclenching his murderous hands. Idiot babbling drooled from his worm-like lips. "The noise, it's stopped . . . and the pounding . . . That's better, boss, better. . . ."

THE telephone on Harding's desk burred urgently. He pounced on it like a ravenous tiger, hugged the receiver to his ear. "Yes," he said tensely, almost in a whisper. He listened. A raucous, machine-gun voice, shaky with excitement, rattled over the wires.

The color drained from Harding's face. His cheek-muscles clenched. He said, "At once," hung up, turned slowly to the three men. "Gentlemen," he announced in a dead voice, "Van Cleve Barton has been found."

The three men leaped to their feet. Kranz gasped, "Where—how?"

"In a ditch off Highland Road. Dead. Run over."

Halmey expelled his breath in a long, sibilant hiss. "God!"

"You, Dr. Halmey, and Dr. Kranz, I must ask you not to leave the county. Care to come with me, Quest?"

When they reached the drear, wind-lashed spot, police had completed their routine investigation under the direction of Captain of Detectives Greer. Resor, the Medical Examiner, kneeled beside the crushed, mangled corpse. He glanced up as Harding and Quest lowered themselves into the ditch.

"What's the story?" Harding said laconically.

"It's a pretty familiar set-up. He seems to have been hit by a heavy car going fairly slow. The contact with the car must have rolled him over into the ditch. Look at those wheel-marks."

He pointed to muddy, circular bands across the chest where car-wheels had bitten deep.

"How long would you say he's been dead?"

"Well, in this weather a body would keep in pretty fair shape for twelve hours or more. I'd say it happened some time last night."

Greer strode over, flicked his hand at the District Attorney. "Hell of a thing, Harding," he commented. "I can't figure it out. We're satisfied that this is the real Barton all right, though we'll check with fingerprints right away. But if the real Barton disappeared from the hospital, he must have been wandering around alive and well until last night."

"Unless," Quest remarked, "he was held prisoner until last night and released only to be murdered."

"Hold on, Quest," Harding interrupted. "This may have no connection with the other business. It may be just what it looks like, a hit-and-run case."

"No," contradicted Quest flatly. "This man was murdered."

Greer, Harding and the doctor jerked toward him.

Harding asked quietly, "How do you figure that?"

Quest said, "You'll notice that the wheel-marks circle his suit. But there are no wheel-marks on his coat. That coat was put on Barton after he was deliberately run down."

CHAPTER THREE

Lightning Strikes Twice

PETER QUEST'S one-room cubbyhole of an office high over Fifth Avenue had the severe simplicity of a monk's cell —a scarred, pine desk, two shaky chairs, a rush mat, and a bulky green filing cabinet stuffed with newspaper clippings. Those clippings held the secret of Quest's driving force.

QUEST SOLVES MASON KIDNAPING . . . FAMOUS SLEUTH GIVES EVIDENCE IN BURNHAM TRIAL . . . DOPE RING SMASHED BY PETER QUEST . . . QUEST REVEALS . . . .

Scores of them, attesting to the man's unique flair for tracking down criminals, for cracking the toughest criminological nuts. Yet across each one he had scrawled in his bold hand, "failure". For him there could be only one success—that crime-hunt that would culminate in his own death.

A pile of newspapers, accumulation of the recent hectic days when he had no opportunity to read them, towered on the desk. His eyes ached from scanning them. He shut them and leaned back, fingering the tiny bottle of whitish drops in his vest-pocket. In this mood he let his mind play over the baffling circumstances of Van Cleve Barton's death, for the fingerprint experts had definitely established the mangled body on Highland Road as the aged millionaire's.

The telephone shrilled, scattering his thoughts. Wearily he uncradled the receiver. "Yes?"

"Peter, this is Les Halmey." The doctor's normally resonant voice was thin and sharp.

"Hello, Les. You sound worried."

"Worried? Of course I'm worried. Those dumb cops haven't learned a thing. We're exactly where we started."

"True, but at least the hospital's in the clear. That's something."

"No, Peter, that's just the point. We'll be under a cloud until we can prove definitely that the hospital was in no way responsible for what happened. That's why I called you. You see, I'm the new chairman and—"

"Oh? Congratulations. What happened to Kranz?"

"Resigned. He couldn't stand the gaff. The thing got on his nerves. I think he's confining himself to private practice. Look, Peter, the directors authorized me to ask you to investigate the case on your own. Discreetly, you understand. You don't have to say anything to the police, not that they're getting anywhere."

Quest was silent a moment.

"Hey, are you still there, Peter?"

"Yes. I was just thinking it over. I'll take the case, but I must have a free hand. Is that understood?"

"Of course. We'll discuss your fee later."

"There won't be any fee."

He hung up. He stared a while out the window, tried to recapture his train of thought and fell again to studying the newspapers of the last three or four days. A tiny paragraph tucked away in a second section caught his attention:

Homer Mangrave, millionaire broker and socialite, was injured today when a speeding taxi driven by Eric Bensen leaped the curb at Park Avenue and 46th Street, knocking him down. Mangrave was accompanied by his debutante daughter, Lita, when the accident occurred. Suffering from shock and bruises, he was taken to the Harvey Sanitarium in an ambulance that happened to be passing.

Dr. Emil Kranz, who attended the aged financier, stated that the injuries were slight. Bensen was arrested and . . . .

Quest sat bolt upright. Kranz! For the second time in a few days Dr. Kranz had acquired a wealthy patient, an old man injured in a motor accident. The coincidence was slight, probably meant nothing. Still. . . .

HALF an hour later Peter Quest stood in the gleaming white reception room of swanky Harvey Sanitorium off Park Avenue. He spoke to a dark, pert girl seated behind a mahogony table. "I beg your pardon," he murmured, "is Mr. Mangrave, Mr. Homer Mangrave, permitted to receive visitors just yet?"

The girl smiled freshly. "I'm sure he is, but not here."

"How's that again?"

"Miss Mangrave took her father home this morning."

Quest clucked self-accusingly. Of course. How stupid of him. Those newspapers had been nearly a week old.

"In that case," he resumed, "I wonder if I might inquire after his health from the physician who attended him. My name is Quest, Peter Quest."

"Dr. Kranz is a very busy man. I really doubt—"

A harsh voice cut in. "Not too busy to receive an old friend. Good evening, Mr. Quest."

Quest turned to see the sour-jowled, bearded surgeon. He sensed at once that beneath that surface suavity lurked a gnawing anxiety.

Kranz said, "I had no idea you were a friend of the Mangraves."

"I'm not. But my curiosity was stimulated by a curious similarity of events. Surely, Doctor, they have not escaped you. Your very connection with this case is—well—interesting."

Kranz's face darkened like a thundercloud. "I think I understand what you are driving at. Disabuse yourself. The notion is too fantastic." But his tone lacked conviction, and Kranz must have realized

it. He gripped Quest's elbow and led him down a corridor beyond hearing of the dark-haired girl. He glanced about him uneasily, his voice dropped to a shaky whisper. "Listen to me, Mr. Quest. I left the Hutchinson Hospital because the entire place had come under a cloud of ill favor. I have my career to consider. I was fortunate enough to secure a valuable post on this staff. You see, I am being frank with you. Nothing shall interfere with my work here. Nothing, do you understand, Mr. Quest?"

"And what should interfere?"

Kranz seemed flustered. "Ach, I don't know what I'm saying. Seriously, Mr. Quest, you would do better not to meddle in affairs that don't concern you."

"As it happens this may concern me vitally. I'll be frank, too. The Hutchinson people have retained me to get to the bottom of the whole business. Now, I feel strongly that you're keeping something to yourself. I have no authority to compel the truth, but I mean to learn a lot more about the Mangraves. I may as well start in the director's office."

Kranz looked desperately alarmed. His fingers quivered. "No, no, you must not do that. There is something. . . ."

"Well?"

Kranz's voice dropped so low Quest had to lean closer to hear. "The same insane thing, Quest. She—Miss Mangrave —for a moment she seemed to think that her father was not—"

Quest balled his fists, uttering a choked cry of fury. "God, you mean to tell me she suspected another substitution?"

"Only for a moment before she took him home. After I talked to her, she saw it was ridiculous. The news stories about the other—they—they must have weighed on my mind."

"You damned idiot! You, the great Kranz! She told you that and you let her go after what happened before?"

"I have my career to think of," Kranz

said feebly. "I did not want this hospital involved in a scandal. Besides, the whole thing was too absurd, too impossible. There is a limit to coincidence."

"By God, if anything's happened to them, you'll sweat for it! The address, the Mangraves' address—quick!"

White around the gills, Kranz gasped out a number on Riverside Drive. "Quest, for God's sake, don't be too hasty! It isn't possible—"

But Quest had whipped ·around and headed for the revolving door. Swinging down the stone steps on the side street he signaled a taxi from the far corner. It turned around, started for him, but not quickly enough. A second taxi, appearing as from nowhere, cut in front of the first and braked smoothly to a halt before the hospital. The cabbie held open the door for Quest, ignoring the first cabbie's explosive curses.

"Where to, mister?"

"Eight-ten Riverside Drive. Better shoot through the Park."

* * *

You don't need to worry, boss. Everything's under control. I ain't never let you down yet, have I? I ain't starting now. It'll be done, done sweet and smooth . . . just wait.

A S THE taxi neared the heart of Central Park, its headlights winking like giant glow-worms in the black, misty night, Quest noticed a curious thing. His racing thoughts, his taut nerves had dulled his normally keen perceptions. He had paid no specific attention either to the cabbie or the taxi. But now his eyes chanced to fall on the metal holder in which the law requires every taxi-driver to keep his photograph. It was empty.

Strangely uneasy—he was not yet certain why—he studied the broad, muscled, hunched back of the cabbie, noted the way his bald, hatless head was set down in his upswept collar. Only the man's hands were visible, glistening oily and greenish-white. His uneasiness swelled, sharpened his alertness. Suspicion became certainty. He must see the man's face. He called out suddenly, "Hey there, can't you go any faster?"

It didn't work. The cabbie muttered darkly without turning around, "Not in this fog, mister. Just sit still. We'll get there."

Less and less did Quest relish the situation, although the cabbie's purpose was not yet apparent. Could it be an ordinary after dark hold-up? Or perhaps a new racket? He doubted it. He smelled the trap into which he, in his desperate urgency to reach the Mangraves, had blindly stumbled.

Knowing this, he grew icily calm. His hand instinctively found the small, light automatic he carried in his inner overcoat pocket. What would be the man's first move? He waited, tensely, his eyes riveted on that powerful, menacing back. Far ahead a thousand lights outlined the delicate tracery of Central Park West. Presently they would emerge from the park. Surely nothing could happen then with thousands of cars streaming along the avenue and a traffic cop on the corner. . . .

The engine sputtered. Their speed lessened.

"Why are you stopping?" Quest asked tightly.

"Something wrong with the engine."

The car stopped suddenly, throwing Quest forward. His grip tightened on the gun. For a timeless instant the two men sat frozen like figures in a grotesque drama. Then slowly the cabbie's head lifted, came in line with his mirror. His voice, violently changed, charged with venom, rasped, "Keep your hands in sight, mister."

Instead Quest whipped out his gun, held it steadily in full view. "Okay. Whatever your game is, forget it. Keep driving and don't lift your hands from that wheel."

The cabbie twisted around and for the first time Quest beheld the monstrous, inhuman face with its heavy, blood-hungry lips, the projecting, fang-like teeth and the venomous eyes. The mouth widened in a mirthless grin. He calmly reached into his own pocket, began drawing forth a gun.

Quest had no choice. He aimed for the man's shoulder, jerked the trigger. A sharp, metallic click sounded. Nothing happened. His finger pressed again and again. The hammer stuttered harmlessly.

The monster croaked, "Don't waste your time, mister. We took care of that little toy. Sure, we visited that hide-out of yours. Can't have folks going around with loaded rods. It's against the law. Now hop out—double time!"

Quest swore impotently. His stinger was drawn. He was momentarily helpless. A motor humming behind them brought him a surge of hope. A sedan hove into view. He turned toward the side-window. The monster shoved his gun closer, stabbed it at him.

"You haven't got a prayer," Quest said. "Too many cars will be coming along."

"You don't say? Well, you better let 'em keep coming. One peep and I nail you where you sit. Now I don't want to spoil that upholstery so suppose you get out nice and quiet-like."

There could be no question but that the monster was in deadly earnest. Quest shrugged philosophically and started to climb out. "Don't make any slips," he remarked coolly. "If you do, you won't survive them."

ANOTHER car whizzed by. Quest took a step forward. His belly came up hard against the cold gun muzzle.

The monster jeered. "You're a nervy bird, but don't get too ambitious. There ain't gonna be no slips. Start walking."

The gun dug brutally into Quest's spine. He staggered forward, entering the pool of light cast by the taxi's headlights. He tried to understand what the monster wanted of him.

Then, understanding burst upon him with paralyzing clarity as the monster, with incredible agility, leaped back into the taxi and gunned the motor. The heavy wheels started rolling.

Quest understood, then. God, yes, he understood! So it had come. His old enemy—his friend rather—Death. For himself he was content to go this way. But the Mangraves and others yet to be enmeshed in this fiendish, far-flung plot whose taproots he only dimly perceived—what of them?

One hand on the wheel, the other flushing Quest with a gun, the flat-faced man snarled above the roar of the motor, "Keep walking and walk straight. If you leave the road, you get the whole dose between the shoulders. It's up to you which way you want it."

The pattern was to be repeated. In the daylight they would recover his body where it had been tossed amongst the roadside bushes. Another hit-and-run victim.

His eyes probed the engulfing darkness. Shrubbery lined both sides of the road. An exit yawned perhaps two hundred yards ahead. He would never reach it alive. The few passing motorists, his only salvation, eyed him indifferently, concluding he was either drunk or an eccentric midnight stroller. They flashed past, their tail-lights streaking the night like low-flying comets, so many hopes fading one by one. To make a wild dash for the bushes—one chance in a million. His back offered an unmissable target.

The taxi picked up speed, forcing him to quicken his pace. The race was pitifully unequal, a man pitted against an eight-cylinder car. The wheels gained on him foot by foot. He could hear the monster chuckling in enjoyment of this ghastly game of hare and hounds. He threw a glance over his shoulder as he ran and saw the contorted, kill-crazy visage, gloat-ing and slobbering obscenely. He felt the headlights hot on his neck. The glare dazzled him. He averted his eyes, thrust his knuckles deep into his eye-sockets to dispel the dizzying light. But his vision failed to clear. He was blind!

It had happened, the ultimate catastrophe. Excitement had aroused his old weakness. Now he could scarcely maintain a straight path even if he wanted to. He floundered, unseeing, helpless, his legs pumping madly in an effort to keep ahead of the taxi. The monster shifted into third. The wheels whined and sang with increased speed.

The car roared close behind him. The road must be clear, the monster ready to plow him under. If only there were time to use his sight-restoring drops!

With a final sprint of energy he lurched blindly to the right, half ran, half dove into what he hoped were tall bushes. A volley of shots rang out. Pain needled his shoulder, blood gushed warmly down his arm. He thrashed forward. Thorny branches lashed his face. Suddenly he crashed into a tree. The impact hurled him backward, spun him around and he pitched forward on his belly. For a moment he could hear nothing but the furious throbbing of his own heart. Then, a slamming taxi door echoed in his ears. The monster was gunning for him. To be found this way, blind, incapable of further flight meant instant annihilation. As he lay on the cold, damp earth he managed to extract the small bottle. He freed the eye-dropper, tilted his head, let the precious drops fall on his sightless pupils.

His vision cleared just as the monster came crashing through the bushes. He saw Quest's prone body, advanced to within three feet, raised his gun, took careful aim. Simultaneously with the shot Quest sprang, hurled himself against the monster's legs with a fury that tumbled him to the earth. The bullet whistled past his head. The monster grunted, tried to free his right arm. Quest kicked at his wrist and sent the gun flying five feet out of reach. The monster dove for it. Quest deftly hooked his foot around the monster's ankle and jerked him backward. The heavy fall winded him. Quest scrambled forward on all fours, retrieved the gun.

As he wheeled to fire it, the monster, mingled fear and cunning flecking his eyes, raced back through the bushes. Quest fired twice. A howl of pain told him he had found his target. But before he could fire a third time the monster had the taxi rolling. It swept around the curve as Quest reached the roadside.

Spent, chilled to the core, his shoulder burning like fire, Quest stared after it dully. Then he brushed off his dirt-stained clothes and staggered forward.

UNIQUE among New York's private residences, the Mangrave house stood in a plot of paper-smooth lawn, ringed by a high, wrought-iron fence. Velvet-curtained French windows opened on a flower garden at the side.

As Quest approached, he saw a pencil of light streaming thinly under the curtains. He skirted around to the side of the house and peered through the slightly parted curtains.

To an observer lacking his special knowledge there would seem nothing untoward in the domestic tableau within. A slender, proudly handsome old gentleman clad in a silk dressing-gown sat at a teakwood desk amid simple but rich surroundings. Pen in hand, he wrote in what appeared to be a check-book. A young girl stood at his shoulder, her arm lightly resting on his. Despite his tenseness, Quest was seized with the girl's beauty. Soft masses of blue-black hair framed a delicate face that had the texture of ivory. Its soft whiteness emphasized the moist redness of her full lips. Hard, firm, little breasts strained at the tight, apple-green negligee that sheathed her perfect body.

Quest watched the man rip a check from the book and hand it to the girl. Despite her apparent affection for the man, conflict, a faint puzzlement, shadowed her eyes. The man seemed unaware of it. He continued to fill out another check, tore it out, placed it in his pocket. Then he rose and gestured the girl toward the door. Her puzzlement deepening, she started for it and the man, not realizing his every movement was watched, betrayed himself. His handsome features suddenly twisted into a mask of lustful rapacity. His gaze licked the girl's exquisite body, mentally stripping her. He started after her, his long, slim fingers trembling in anticipation.

Quest dared not wait another instant. He tried the handles of the French windows. They held fast. The lights in the room went out. He heard the heavy door open and shut, the footsteps of the man and the girl pad away. He lost precious seconds, as he swathed his hand in a handkerchief and smashed it through a pane of glass. Reaching inside he unlocked the windows, stepped through. He headed unhesitatingly for the door, softening his footsteps as he emerged into a hallway. He listened, holding his breath.

The vast house was dark and still. Where had they gone? Which way to turn? The answer ripped through the house, echoing and re-echoing, a piercing scream of pain and terror. A violent struggle, a dull thud, sounded overhead. He took the stairs at a bound. A second scream drew him to a thick door, locked, impassable. He heard the girl's voice:

"You're not my father. Oh, I knew it! I knew it! Don't touch me—don't come near me! No . . . oh, please, pl—" Deathly silence, broken only by harsh, animal breathing.

Quest jammed the monster's gun against the lock, blasted it open with a thunderous shot. It gave the man warning and, as Quest entered, he crouched behind a chair, his gun spitting death. In that split second Quest saw the girl, nude, lying unconscious on the bed, her sweet body splotched and red where the man had mauled her. A knife had tumbled to the floor, but her body bore no wound. Quest had not come too late.

A slug split the door panel behind him. Indifferent to his danger, he loosed a spate of bullets that ripped through the chair. The man screamed hoarsely, sideslipped, his face mushrooming into crimson horror. He toppled backward, lay still.

QUEST strode over to the body and saw the man was dead. He cursed bitterly. He hadn't wanted it this way. Now, whatever the man's foul secret, it was sealed forever in his lifeless brain.

The girl was breathing faintly. Quest covered her naked body with his overcoat and carried her tenderly out of the room. As he lowered her to a sofa in the living-room downstairs she opened her eyes, shrinking back in alarm the moment she saw him.

He whispered reassuringly, "You're safe now. Please trust me. The danger's over."

Gradually she regained composure. "Who are you? What—what's happened?"

Gently, he sketched the events since Van Cleve Barton's body had been recovered, interrupting himself to ask, "You suspected that man wasn't your father, didn't you?"

"Yes, I did. But it was too fantastic. I convinced myself I was imagining things. I couldn't entirely believe anybody could look so much like Dad and be somebody else. Somehow it's still hard to believe."

"Dr. Kranz helped to convince you?"

"Why, that's true. So he did. But surely you're not suggesting that Dr. Kranz—"

"I'm suggesting nothing. What I do know is that a cunning and brilliant mind is behind these crimes, a man who has devised an extraordinarily method of impersonation. He has succeeded in substituting for wealthy hospital patients creatures who obey him implicitly. How he is able to manipulate these creatures, what is the secret of his frightful power, I don't know—yet."

A low cry burst from the girl's lips. "He was planning to open the safe! He told me he had a chance to sell our valuables, hundreds of thousands of dollars worth, at a good price. He was going to kill me and then—" She shook her head bewilderedly.

"Yes."

The full significance of what had occurred penetrated her fear-numbed brain. She leaped to her feet. "My father! What has become of him?, I've got to find him."

She added almost hysterically, "My real father!"

Quest's eyes darkened with pity. He forced Lita Mangrave gently back to the sofa and took her hands in his. "My dear, I'm afraid you're going to have to be brave. There is no way of knowing where or under what circumstances your father will be found. We can only wait and hope."

Sobbing wracked her and she covered her face with her hands.

Quest announced, "I'm going to call the police. Wait for me here, please."

He found a telephone in the hallway and a moment later was talking to his old friend and friendly enemy, Inspector Chasen. "Bill," he said, "you'd better get up here to the Mangrave place on Riverside. It's another hospital case."

"Like that Hutchinson business? Holy God!" He whistled. "Right away."

While they were waiting, Quest spoke to the girl almost shyly. "Miss Mangrave, I don't want to upset you unduly, but you'll be exposed to a certain amount of danger until this gang or whatever they are is smashed. I'd like to watch over you, if I can. My idea would be to live in this house until the danger is completely passed."

Her head came up and she managed to smile through her tears. "You saved my life. I wouldn't want it any other way."

* * *

Not that, boss, not that, for God's sake! I couldn't stand it. Gimme another

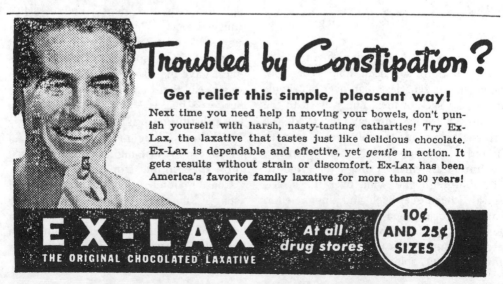

*chance. Just one. I never muffed it be-
fore. It won't happen again. Another
chance, boss, please, please . . . Ah, thanks,
thanks . . . I'll get 'em both next time.*

IN a shabby hotel bedroom twenty stories
above Broadway, twilight shadows
swathed two men. One old, but slim and
aristocratically handsome, lay stiff as a log
on the coverless bed. His skin was grey,
his breathing heavy.

The second man, barrel-chested as a
gorilla, with a domed, hairless, glistening
head, watched eagerly from the foot of the
bed.

From time to time his obscenely red,
long tongue flicked out like an ant-eater's,
licking at his thick lips. Otherwise he was
motionless and silent as a corpse.

The man on the bed shifted and began
moaning. The monster sprang to his side,
balled his great fists and battered him into
unconsciousness.

Wind wafted the din of evening crowds
below into the cramped, stuffy room. The
monster glanced toward the open window,
his eyes seeking the *Times* clock. Quarter
of ten. His brow furrowed.

The bedside telephone rang. He swept
it up, unhooking the receiver in the same
motion, hissed into the mouthpiece, "Yeah,
boss."

The caller uttered a single word.
"Now."

The monster hung up. Moving as if
every motion had been long rehearsed,
he slung the senseless man over his shoulder like a sack of meal and walked to the
window. For a moment he eyed the
crowds below, his terrible eyes fiery with
hatred. Then, unslinging his limp burden,
he hurled the man through the window.
He shot high and wide over the street,
spiraled head over heels and plummeted to
earth. Krock leaned far out, hungrily followed the swift, downward flight, shivered pleasurably as the inert mass smote
the pavement, splattering blood and bone

and flesh. Horror tore from a thousand
throats, soared upward, flowing like balm
into Krock's ears.

He shut the window. He fished in his
pockets for a sheet of paper covered with
scraggly writing and deposited it on the
bed. He tiptoed to the door and, listening for sounds in the corridor, sneaked out
of the bedroom.

CHAPTER FOUR

When Is a Suicide Not a Suicide?

THE evening papers blazoned forth the
details of Homer Mangrave's strange
and terrible death. A suicide note had
been found in room 1010 of the Broadway Hotel. It read:

*"I cannot face old age as a permanent
invalid. I have discovered that I have can-
cer. This was the best way out."*

Another letter had been posted to Lita
Mangrave, begging her forgiveness. If
the handwriting was a forgery, it was the
cleverest Quest had ever studied.

Yet even the newspapers reported Mangrave's death with reservations. There
were too many unaccountable elements.
For one thing, no one in the hotel had
seen Mangrave arrive. They recalled an
ugly, powerfully built man registering the
night before with a huge trunk. He had
vanished since. That trunk—to Quest it
suggested sinister possibilities.

Seated in Inspector Chasen's office
Quest gave his suspicions free play. "I'm
convinced that Homer Mangrave was
murdered just as Van Cleve Barton was.
The substitution was made at the Harvey
Sanitorium. They must have held him
prisoner until last night, then taken him
to the hotel in that trunk."

Chasen pounded the desk with clenched
fists. "I know you're right, Quest, and, by
thunder, I'm going to get Kranz down
here and sweat the truth out of him. He's
the only guy who forms a link between
the two jobs.

"True. And while you're about it you might grill him on these." Quest produced a handful of clips, reports, papers covered with notations.

"What are those?"

"Maybe just a collection of coincidences. But I doubt it. Would you be surprised to know that in the last two years, seven wealthy men have died in circumstances strikingly like the deaths of Mangrave and Barton? The details vary slightly in each case, but the essentials are the same. Sometimes an accident, sometimes an emergency operation. After they got home, they would disappear for a while. Their bodies would show up a few days later, victims of motor accidents, suicides or what-not. Meanwhile they had cashed large checks and sold a good portion of their holdings. I'll stake my reputation that the men who left those hospitals were not the same ones who went in."

"Judas, are you trying to tell me—"

"I'm not trying—I *am* telling you. For years a criminal gang has been operating in this city in an unparalleled wave of murders."

"Unparalleled! I'll say. Look, Quest, there's no use kidding myself. We're not equipped to handle this sort of thing. I'd appreciate it if you'd supplement our work with your own investigations."

"Of course," Quest said, rising. "I never intended to do otherwise."

* * *

Oh, this is slick, boss, slick. It takes a brain like yours to think 'em up and me to carry 'em out. I'll be seeing you, boss, this time tomorrow. I'll have news, great news. . . .

THE Acme Building towered into the black sky, its forty stories dwarfing surrounding masonry. Scattered here and there amid its honeycomb of office windows blinked rectangles of light. Otherwise the white concrete facade was bleakly dark, for it was long past business hours.

The smartly uniformed operator saluted as Quest entered the elevator. They shot up twenty stories. The chromium-plated door slid back noiselessly and Quest emerged into the dim corridor.

"Shall I wait?" the operator offered amiably.

"Thanks, son. I won't be a minute. I've got to pick up some papers."

"Right. I'm not apt to get a buzz at this hour."

Rounding a corner, Quest noted that his own frosted-glass office door was ablaze with light and a human figure moved behind it, though he couldn't remember having left it unlocked. He hugged the wall, tense with caution. The next moment he was laughing at himself for a nervous old maid. If any one was gunning for him, he would hardly advertise his presence by leaving the lights on. Still. . . .

He approached the door on tip-toe, jerked it open without warning. Lita Mangrave was lighting a cigarette from the glowing butt of another. She started violently.

"Who—oh, Peter! Hello. I see you don't mind keeping a lady waiting. It's an ungodly hour for a rendezvous in an office building, but you said it was important so—"

She was clad in a dark dress with a dark, close-fitting hat to match. The simplicity threw her vibrant loveliness into sharp relief. Quest experienced a surging thrill at her presence until its significance swept over him.

"Just what," he faltered, sensing the truth in advance, "are you doing here?"

"Doing? Look, this isn't April Fool's Day by any chance, is it? Because you ask me to hurry over and then you want to know what I'm doing here."

"I asked you to come over? Tell me— when? How? What did I say?"

"You're feeling quite well, aren't you? You telephoned me at home, got me out of bed as a matter-of-fact. Peter, there's nothing wrong, is there?"

Without further discussion he grasped her wrist, dragging her after him through the door. "Come on, we're leaving!"

She pattered along at his side, plying him with questions. "What's going on, Peter? I no sooner get here than you—"

"It's a trap! I never sent for you. God knows who did. But the sooner you're home, the better."

What troubled him deeply, more than he dared say, was the fact that whoever had decoyed Lita here had not yet shown his hand. The man or men must be lurking nearby, waiting, watching . . . *for both of them!*

Some of his tenseness communicated itself to her. He felt her trembling and gave her arm a reassuring pressure. "A trap," she echoed, "so that was it!"

Quest had never seen a more welcome sight than the elevator still waiting, casting its cheerful oblong of bright yellow on the corridor floor. He whirled Lita into it. They started down. She wanted to speak, to voice her fears, but Quest cautioned her silently against involving the operator.

THEY dropped five stories. Quest began congratulating himself that the omnipresent killers had somehow miscalculated. At that instant the elevator shuddered violently, halted with an abruptness that hurled them all to the floor. The drone of the motor had ceased. Only the wind screeching in the elevator shaft broke the sinister stillness.

The operator, frowning, jiggled the hand-control. Nothing happened. Quest glanced at the floor indicator, helping the girl to her feet. The needle rested between nine and ten. Submerging a foreboding of danger, Quest said calmly, "Swell spot to be stuck."

"Yeah. The current seems to be off. Can't figure it out—unless there's been a short circuit. Couldn't be, though. Lights are still on."

Lita bit her lip. Her face was ghastly white. "How are we going to get down?"

"Don't worry about that, lady. There's a hand cable we can use if necessary. It takes long and it's tough hauling, but it'll get us down." He slid open a small panel, exposing two wire cables of the sort used in old-fashioned elevators. Gripping it with both hands; he pulled downward. A wheel whirred and creaked overhead and they jogged and jolted a few feet lower. Presently the motion grew more erratic, shaking them from side to side.

"Now what?" Quest demanded.

Tiny globules of sweat had started to gather on the operator's forehead. "Gosh, Mr. Quest, I don't know. It's like somebody was fooling around in the wheelhouse up above."

Quest craned his head back. Through vents in the elevator roof he could dimly perceive the termination of the shaft. Great slots were cut in the steel plates for the wheels and cables. Then Quest saw them—two long, bony hands reaching down through the slots, wielding a file. They began sawing at the cable. The man's body was invisible. Only those terrible hands showed and with each attack on the cables the elevator shook from ceiling to the floor.

Twang! A strand snapped. The elevator lurched sideways.

Lita and the operator followed Quest's paralyzed gaze. Lita screamed, swayed weakly, but managed to keep to her feet. The operator paled and swore. "Somebody—somebody's trying to cut the cables on us. God, we'll be smashed to a jelly!"

Quest dug his fingers into the operator's biceps. "We've got just one chance. Keep hauling on that cable. We must drop lower before the whole thing goes. I'll help you."

Both men pulled lustily. The car rocked wildly, but they succeeded in bringing it two stories nearer to earth. Quest wondered how hard a fall they could survive. Another strand snapped.

"Wait," Quest yelled. "Maybe I can delay him a bit." He whipped out his gun; aimed through the vents and fired. The bullet sizzled up the shaft, whanged resoundingly against the steel shaft-head. One hand pulled back and they all heard a roar of rage. But the hand, unscratched, soon returned to its murderous task. Another strand parted—and another.

STRAINING every muscle, they hauled themselves two stories lower, as Lita cried over and over, "Hurry—hurry!"

As they passed the fourth story, three strands snapped. The car swerved, banging against the shaft, hanging by a shred. All three now tackled the other cable, dragging on it until the veins stood out on their temples like whipcord. Third floor.

Quest had held his gunfire because he knew only one cartridge remained. He fired that now, but it did no damage.

The fiend in the wheelhouse was laughing, roaring in maniacal glee and cutting through the last strands. Second floor. No, they might be injured now, but not fatally. The killer, too, seemed to realize this. His laughter stopped short. He was howling with frustration and attacking the final strand with sadistic savagery.

Twang! The cable rattled against the shaft in its descent. The killer howled. . . . Quest was thrown off his feet, ramming against the operator as he fell. He heard Lita gasp, felt her hands clutching at him. She cried, "Peter—Peter!" Her safety meant everything to him then.

They say a man's whole life passes in review in swift, critical instants like these. But Quests' mind was filled with only one thought, one concern—Lita. He flung himself toward her to break her fall.

They struck with a horrible, sickening crash. The lights went out in a deafening explosion. Lita's soft body struck his back. Then silence. No motion. No life. The killer was still. The wind whined a little in the shaft.

Rolling over on his side he felt something warm and sticky. The operator was groaning, "My head—my head. . . ."

Panicky, Quest called out. "Lita, are you hurt?"

She answered in a very weak, very small voice. "No, Peter, I'm all right." Thank God!

Then, unexpectededly, the elevator door opened, spraying them with light. They were in the basement. A man looked down. "Hey, there, what's happened? Are you all right? I'm the night watchman."

Silently Quest offered up a prayer of thanks. He knew the killer would have ample time to escape. But at least Lita was alive and within reach of safety.

Half an hour later they were riding side by side in a taxi.

"Do you think," Lita asked, "the elevator boy will live?"

"I don't know. He was pretty badly hurt."

Impetuously, she flung her arms around him. "Oh, Peter, if it had been you, I couldn't have borne it."

"Lita, dearest!"

CHAPTER FIVE

Murder Mimic

THEY sat closely together in the shadow-haunted living-room, Peter Quest and this warmly young, exciting girl who had come to mean so much to him. For all their rapt interest in each other, neither could dispel the cold, penetrating atmosphere of menace that hovered in the vast, old house where death had struck so hideously—and might strike again if they relaxed their vigilance for an instant. But

Lita Mangrave had drawn strength from Quest. Outwardly she remained calm, controlled.

"It's late," Quest said at length. "Why don't you go to bed?"

She sighed. "I could use some sleep. But what about you, Peter? You've worked hard enough to exhaust ten men."

"I'll be along in a minute. I've got a couple of calls to make."

She rose, looked down at Quest. "How can I thank you for all you've done? Without you I think I would have gone mad."

He wagged his head self-depreciatingly and lifted himself from the depths of the sofa. The movement brought him close to her. Her head was tilted back, her lips parted, moist and inviting. Without knowing quite how it happened, he found her in his arms, her mouth seeking his. Recklessly, for he had tried to guard against this, he gave himself over to the intoxication of her kiss. He could feel her warm body throbbing against his through her sheer dress. After eternities, it seemed, they parted, and with returning calm he reproached himself. What could he offer her? What sort of life could they have together with himself doomed to blindness?

He hooked his arm through hers and led her to the stair-well. "Good night, my dear."

She kissed him again lightly. "I love you, Peter Quest. I'll always love you."

He found the strength to tell her, "No, Lita, I'm not the man for you. It wouldn't work. It couldn't."

She silenced him by holding her fingers to his lips. "Don't say that. There couldn't be any other." .

"Lita, I must tell you—"

He never finished. The telephone shrilled suddenly through the silent house. They both started. He smiled ruefully. "I'm afraid we're both jumpy. I'll answer it."

Shortly he was talking to Inspector Chasen. "What's up, Bill?"

The Inspector's voice was expressionless. "Plenty. They've found another."

"Another? Great—" Quest lowered his voice, hoping Lita couldn't hear. "Where? When?"

"Half an hour ago—in the park. I'd like you to be in on this. Do you mind?"

"Of course not. I'm on my way."

"Good man. I'll be waiting for you at the Seventy-ninth Street entrance."

Quest cradled the receiver and knew, even before turning around, that Lita had heard and was standing behind him. He spoke to her with a light-heartedness he didn't feel. "Nerves in good shape?"

"Oh, Peter, I heard everything. When is it going to end, this—this horror?"

"Look here, young lady, you march right up to bed. I'll tell you all about it when I return."

"I hate to be alone in this house."

"There's a cop on the corner, courtesy of Inspector Chasen, and a night watchman. There's nothing to be afraid of. Mind if I use your car? It's parked right out in front."

"Of course not. Be careful, Peter. I'm sure I shan't be able to sleep until you come back."

This time her lips were cold.

Emerging from the house, Quest spied the burly patrolman pacing up and down before the wrought-iron fence. He hailed him. "Keep your eyes peeled, won't you?"

"Yes, sir, Mr. Quest. Don't you worry."

The quickest route to the Park was to turn into the east-bound street paralleling the Mangrave house. Quest climbed into Lita Mangrave's roadster and started the engine. Shifting into first, he swerved sharply to the left, gunned the car up the steeply sloping street toward West End Avenue.

Midway up the hill, he had to slow almost to a halt. A huge steel crane projecting from its wooden shed, which he did not recall seeing there earlier in the day, blocked three quarters of the street. He inched toward it in first. As the car nosed into the narrow space, a crackling, metallic rasp, as of chain-links snapping one by one, chilled his spine. *The crane was dropping on the roof of the roadster!*

He knew at once that the wooden shed was not unoccupied. He slammed the accelerator to the floorboard, trying to escape the path of the down-rushing crane. The car leaped forward, its engine straining—but it was not enough. Metal dinned resoundingly on metal. A rending of canvas, wooden supports buckling with a noise like pistol shots. Blazing lights exploded inside Quest's brain, flared, receded as a wave of engulfing blackness swept over him. His whole body was suddenly a single great pain. He felt himself sinking deeper and deeper into whirling, spinning blackness.

From a vast distance a clanging bell filtered down to his drowning senses. The thought stirred feebly in him: an ambulance . . . funny . . . getting here so soon . . .

Then oblivion.

H E KNEW his eyes were open, but he could see nothing. His head pounded like a piston, pumping up fresh geysers of agony. Sheets grated against his body. Wearily he extended his hand. It came into contact with cool, smooth, metal bars.

A voice murmured softly in his ear. "Great Scot, Quest, you get yourself in some of the damnedest messes! Hey—it's Les, Les Halmey. Don't you know me?"

"Sure I do. Glad it's you, Les. Where am I?"

"Harvey Sanitorium. One of the ambulances picked you up."

Quest struggled to recapture a nagging idea. But it eluded him.

"Old Kranz told me what had happened and, of course, I hurried down

from the country," the other continued.

All at once Quest tried to sit upright. Firm hands forced him back to the pillow. "But Lita, Miss Mangrave—must talk to her."

"Stop worrying about that. She's not. She knows all about it and I assured her, as I can assure you, that you're not badly hurt, though Lord knows why you're not. You ought to see the car."

It struck Quest as odd that Lita was not present. "How long before I can leave?"

"A day or two. You got a nasty crack on the head, but nothing broken inside or out."

"My eyes—"

"I know. But they'll mend, too. I've given you those drops. They should clear up soon. By the way, I brought Nurse Kovac with me. She's taken care of you before. Remember? Now I'm going to give you a light shot of morphine because I want you to sleep. Tomorrow you'll be as right as rain."

"No drugs," Quest objected. He wasn't certain why.

"Come, come, Peter, you're not going to make a fuss about a little thing like this."

He realized the futility of protesting and passively extended his arm. He twitched slightly as the needle broke through his flesh. He wanted to give voice to the certainty growing within him: it had been no accident, it had been planned for him to be here like this. But he was too weak to say much.

"See you when you wake up," Halmey exclaimed.

"So much to do," Quest muttered fretfully. "Les, you've got to get me out of here tomorrow."

"Now, now, just relax."

The last thing Peter Quest remembered before unconsciousness overcame him was Nurse Kovac smoothing out his cover and the ghastly knowledge that he was being manipulated like a pawn in a chess game and that he lacked the strength to resist.

* * *

I'm ready, boss. Just leave everything to me. There ain't gonna be no slip-ups. I'm looking forward to it, boss. It's gonna be a real treat.

THE morphine wore off with unusual speed. His subconscious mind, hitting on all cylinders, had given him little repose. Nor had his vision been restored.

He heard low, urgent whisperings around him. He thought they existed only in his fagged brain. But presently he grew aware of several people circling around the room, watching him. The drift of their words made no sense—at first. He listened.

". . . that's better. That line, under the left eye, a trifle deeper. And notice how those nostrils flare. That's it. You've got it. It must be exact, you understand, so exact his own mother wouldn't know. We can't afford to make mistakes this time."

Comprehension slowly grew in Quest's mind and it was like fingers of ice reaching up, clawing and clutching, through his entrails. He felt cold, so cold he had to clench his teeth to keep from trembling visibly. The voice droned on:

"Is the stretcher table ready?"

A woman's voice now. "Yes. Just outside the door."

"Got your instructions straight? I'll repeat. He's to be wheeled down to the post-mortem room. No one's there but Freemont and I've taken care of him. Be sure to keep that sheet on his face. He's supposed to be the patient who died in one-twenty a few minutes ago. Is that clear?"

"Perfectly. How about Krock?"

"He'll transfer him to the ambulance. He's got it backed up against the side-entrance now. The important thing is to make sure the post-mortem room remains empty for at least two minutes. It'll take about that long."

"Suppose he wakes up?"

No reply, but Quest sensed the brutal gesture. The nurse said, "I see."

"Besides we'll gag him," the man added aloud. "No use running unnecessary risks. Morphine's a tricky drug. Can't tell when it'll wear off. . . . Ah, it's finished. I'll slip into the bed as soon as he's gone. Well, what do you think of it? Could any one detect the slightest difference?"

"It's miraculous."

"Thank you, nurse. I'm rather proud of it, myself. You never knew I was a research man as well as a physician, did you? You see, I learned a great deal about plastic surgery during the war. Since then many men have tried to invent synthetic flesh, human flesh. Only I have discovered the secret."

Quest's heart shriveled within him. It was clear, hideously clear, what would happen after he had been disposed of. The other, the owner of that deadly voice, would assume his individuality, his appearance. Lita would welcome him, take him into her arms, submit to his obscene caress.

He wrenched the soul-searing image from his mind. If he dwelt on it, he would lose his reason, shout, try to fight. And they must go on believing he was still unconscious. It was his only weapon.

Again the woman's voice. "When will you leave?"

"After the internes make their final rounds. Say, in two or three hours. But I don't want our friend, here, found until morning. Impress that on Krock. Van Courtlandt Park might be a good spot.

"We'd better wheel in the table."

"Do so."

Quest heard the creaking of rubber-tired wheels. Two men, one on each side of the bed, approached so stealthily that he nearly betrayed himself with a cry of surprise as stout rope tightened suddenly around his body and a gag was thrust deep into his throat. He choked a little, then made his body go limp as powerful hands inserted themselves under his shoulder-blades and knees and shifted him deftly to the table.

NOTHING further was said. Each man knew his part. Quest felt the flowing motion of the table under him, a soft bump-bump as the wheels crossed the threshold. They were in the corridor. There was no possibility of outcry or movement. He was too securely pinioned and gagged for that. Maddeningly, hospital attendants, doctors, internes, nurses strode up and down the corridor within inches of him and he was powerless to call for help.

"Evening. Is that old Solomon? Too bad. I thought he had a chance after the operation."

"So did we, Dr. Martel. But his heart couldn't hold out. We've got the family's permission to do a post-mortem."

The deadly procession rolled on, stopped, entered an elevator. With a sinking sensation in the pit of his stomach, Quest felt himself being lowered to the basement. The elevator gate clanged open. Out they went, down another corridor. It was still here, still as the tomb. For a shuddering moment, Quest feared they might actually vivisect him. Then he remembered their leader's instructions about Van Courtlandt Park and knew they planned cruder destruction.

As they wheeled him into another room, a rusty, grating voice rasped like a needle on a worn gramaphone disc. "That him? Okay. I'll take over. The ambulance is outside." The monster! Krock!

"Is the coast clear?"

"Sure. Grab his feet."

The powerful hands went under him again and he was lifted clear of the table. A blast of cold air fluttered the sheets enveloping him. Shortly he came to rest on a hard, flat surface. Ambulance doors banged shut. The engine hummed, jog-

ging him roughly from side to side.

How long they rode Quest had little idea. Traffic noises faded. They must be nearing the outskirts of the city. Van Courtlandt Park!

In his desperation he was barely aware of his returning vision. He batted his eye-lids hard together. He could see—what little there was to see. He lay imprisoned in the coffin-like interior. Black walls, black floor, black roof.

The ambulance ground to a halt. He slid helplessly toward the door. His feet thudded against it with shattering force. He shut his eyes quickly, tipping his head back so that he could watch the door from beneath his eye-lids. It swung back. In the opening appeared the hulking monster, grinning lasciviously.

One hand gripped a saw-toothed knife. The other tested its keenness. Satisfied, his loathesome head protruded into the ambulance.

"This ain't in the program, brother," he gloated. "But Krock's gonna have a little fun on his own hook. He's gonna carve you slowly, carefully. I ain't forgot, see, about last time. Nobody makes a monkey of Krock."

He crawled closer, so close his hot, fetid breath fanned Quest's cheeks. Quest's flesh anticipated the kiss of steel.

Krock fumbled with his gag and pinions. "First we gotta untie you so we can get at you."

In the end he severed the ropes. Quest's blood began to circulate again. Krock lovingly fondled his knife. Quest knew that the monster could rip him from crotch to jaw before he could protect himself. As for an attack, he had no space in which to move, to brace himself.

Krock raised the knife, moonlight striking glittering highlights from the polished blade.

Tensing every muscle, Quest drew up his legs. The knife flashed. Hot agony seared his flesh . . .

PATROLMAN CUMMINGS stifled a yawn. Soon dawn would break. He would be free to go home and sleep.

Leather heels tapping on the pavement jolted him out of his musings. He spun around, flicking on his flashlight. It showed a tall, loose-limbed man. Relieved, Patrolman Cummings smiled. "Good morning, Mr. Quest. Things have been real quiet since you stepped out."

"Good. And thanks, officer. There's really no need for you—"

Patrolman Cummings brandished an admonitory hand. "Orders is orders. I got to stick another five minutes."

"Well, don't freeze."

He let himself into the house with a latch-key. Instantly, before he had removed his overcoat, Lita appeared on the stair landing, clad in satin pajamas.

"Peter, thank Heaven you're back! I dozed off for a moment and had the most horrible dreams that something had happened to you."

"Not a thing, my dear, as you see. Don't come down."

She waited for him and when he came within reach, brushed her lips against his cheeks, whispering anxiously, "What happened?"

His arm circled her narrow waist and propelled her toward her own lamp-lit bedroom. "That's what I want to talk to you about. May I come in here?"

"Peter, my bedroom! I don't think—"

"Tut, tut, we're practically married, aren't we?"

"Married?" Peter Quest had never broached marriage before. She looked at the man studiously. "Married? Just like that? It's a bit unexpected. You ought to give a girl a chance."

They crossed the threshold. He backed against the door, closing it.

"Really, Peter, must we have the door shut?"

He smiled a slow, cold half-smile, such a smile as Lita had never seen on Peter Quest's face before. Her forehead creased. "I'm so tired, Peter. Couldn't we postpone this talk until morning?"

"Kiss me!"

The abruptness of his tone startled her. Suddenly his hungry, half-open mouth was mashed against her, his body pressing her with a violence that hurt. A few wild seconds she struggled in his grasp, then wrenched free. She knew then.

"You're not Peter Quest!"

He snarled. He stared past and beyond her into a full-length looking-glass. "Why not? Can't you see? Of course, I'm Peter Quest—to the life."

"No, no, Peter Quest never kissed me like that!"

The man advanced on her menacingly, edging her over to the bed. "Very well, my dear. I didn't figure on feminine instinct. You may as well know everything. Quest is dead! No one can help you."

"What have you done to him? Who are you?"

"Done, my dear? Why, liquidated him—quietly, just as I shall do with you. But first—you're very beautiful, very exciting."

She shrank back, but his fingers fastened in her pajamas. With a single savage gesture he ripped them from her. She thrashed about, her arms flailing the air, her nude body quivering with revulsion and mortal fear. Then she saw the thin, sharp blade in his hand and her eyes rolled upward, almost vanishing in their sockets.

THEY fought hotly, she to shake that iron grip, he to reach her slim, white throat for the death-kiss. She was strong, but under that fierce, maniacal assault her strength weakened, her struggles diminished. She lay back, panting, pinned to the bed. His face came nearer, so near his features fused into a whitish mist.

It was over. Her resistance slackened

entirely. A long, shivering sigh flowed from her . . .

From somewhere far away she heard a dull report. Weirdly, the misted features retreated, went back into focus. She saw the man swaying in front of her, unutterable malignancy blackening his face. His arm swept upward with the knife, started down, then, crazily, he corkscrewed sideways and crashed to the floor.

Lita grew aware of a smoking gun and behind it, pale and haggard, barely able to hold his feet, a second Peter Quest. There could be no confusion this time. She threw herself into his arms, sobbing.

Then both gazed down at the man lying on his face, his back drilled by a bullet. Quest rolled him over and, to Lita's baffled horror, took up the knife and deliberately worked it under the point of the man's jaw.

As he manoeuvred the knife's point under the dead man's skin, it sloughed off, a waxy, paraffin-like mass. Beneath lay the features of Dr. Lester Halmey.

"IT WAS," said Peter Quest in recollection, "the maddest, most ruthless criminal scheme ever conceived. Halmey had an enviable reputation in his profession. I had known him for years without once suspecting the foul, terrible thing that was his brain. He had a Napoleonic complex, wanted power, money. Already

a rich man, he succeeded in organizing a gang within the profession, nurses, internes, attendants, ambulance drivers. Some he paid. Others he enslaved with drugs like the maniac, Krock, who did most of his killing.

"Once sure of his henchmen, the rest was comparatively simple. He would select some wealthy man as victim, stage an accident and have one of his ambulances near the scene. When he got him safely into the hospital, nurses and internes working for him would substitute a killer disguised with synthetic flesh to resemble the patient. This enabled him to gain control of the patient's money, bonds, checkbook or what-not. He always delayed discovery of the body long enough to cash in. In several cases it was necessary to murder the patient's wife or daughter, for no disguise could be perfect enough to deceive them entirely. That was the only weakness in his scheme."

Lita clutched his hand. "It's monstrous, unbelievable!"

"If only I could have acted sooner! So many horrors might have been avoided. But at least you're safe, dearest."

"Peter." She drew him close to her, covered him with kisses.

He did not wish to destroy the beauty of that moment by telling her that he must presently leave her forever—to await his blindness, alone.

THE END

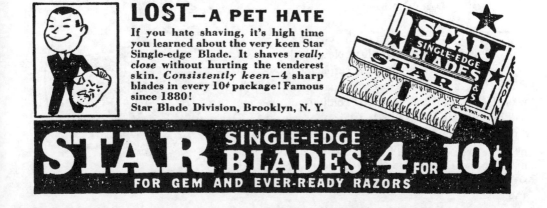

SOCIETY of the SINGING DEATH

A Mystery Novelette by Leon Byrne

In this thrill-a-minute mystery, deluxe Detective Dan Holden labors under a deadly serious handicap. For every weirdly inexplicable death is presaged by an eerie, singing sound which only Holden cannot hear. Yet the very cause of his stone-deafness marks him as the killer's most vulnerable, unescapable target!

Dan could have put a bullet through the python's head, but . . . the death convulsions of the reptile would crush the life from the girl. . . .

CHAPTER ONE

Death's Debate

THE grand ballroom of the ultra exclusive Hotel Perrault in New York was aglitter to the last resplendent chandelier. It was not just a big party—it was *the* party of the year, the coming-out ball of Patricia Farnsworth. Claire Farnsworth, the pretty young debutante's mother, was very happy, for this night marked the end of many bitter years of striving. It meant that at last Claire

Would a group of aging women seek to buy back their fleeting beauty, if the price were--MURDER?

Farnsworth—Mrs. Tom Farnsworth—had arrived socially.

Claire Farnsworth's beauty and charm, and her husband's millions, had never been able to gain for her what her daughter had gained tonight—recognition by New York's Four Hundred. Claire had committed the unpardonable social error in her younger days of going on the stage —a thing which simply "wasn't being done" twenty-five years ago.

The doughty dowagers who ruled the top layer of the upper crust, however, ap-

parently didn't believe in visiting the sins of the elders upon the younger generation, so Patricia's palpitant mother had gone into ecstasies as acceptance after acceptance rolled in, signifying that Patricia's debut would bear the stamp of approval of those who "belonged."

Claire Farnsworth's triumph began at eight o'clock in the evening—and it ended abruptly and disastrously exactly two hours later.

The orchestra had just finished a dreamy waltz. The crowd had strolled leisurely from the dance floor, and Mrs. Tom Farnsworth, still strikingly handsome despite the fact that the curves that had made her a favorite of pre-war

Broadway were a bit more pronounced than they had been, was hurrying across the dance floor to speak to her daughter.

Witnesses disagreed later as to just what happened then, but there were those who insisted that they had heard a queer, droning sound, of uncertain origin, that rose quickly in whining acceleration until it was pitched so high it actually hurt their eardrums—then the sound seemed to vanish.

Mrs. Farnsworth, alone on the dance floor suddenly stopped as though rooted to the floor. A look of pain twisted her startled face. She trembled violently, emitted one scream, and clutched at her chest.

She writhed there in indescribable agony an instant, clawing at the bodice of her evening gown. Her tremulous scream had brought the crowd up short, focused all eyes on her, and several of the men started running toward her to offer assistance.

They didn't reach her—while she was alive—and the manner of her death was utterly horrible.

She had begun tearing at her clothes, shredding and ripping the gossamer lace that covered her matronly bosom. She was doing a mad dance of agony, far different from anything she had ever essayed on the stage. One minute she was standing there, screaming, writhing, and the next instant her torso seemed to disintegrate in a blinding, deafening crash.

The entire upper part of her body was literally blown to bits. The concussion of the explosion stunned the men who had been approaching her; the sight of her mangled body collapsing to the floor caused mass hysteria and fainting among the women.

Claire Farnsworth had had her brief hour of glory, had felt hundreds of eyes appraising her admiringly. None of those eyes appraised her admiringly now. Her figure was so horribly mutilated it made

even toughened policemen turn away to avoid nausea when they came surging into the ballroom a few minutes later.

CHAPTER TWO

"If I Want to Live—"

THE girl seated in front of Dan Holden's desk had inherited her mother's dark beauty, her finely modeled contour of face and form, and despite the grief that marked her tense features, she was stunningly attractive. What impressed Dan most, though, was the fine, patrician quality of breeding, that marked her as a young woman in ten thousand.

Patricia Farnsworth was rumpling a handkerchief in her lap, speaking urgently, rapidly, and for an instant she lowered her head, stared moodily at her hands.

Dan interrupted her gently. "I must ask you again, Miss Farnsworth, to keep your head up when you talk. I know this is all very painful to you, but after all"— he smiled ever so slightly— "you know the saying about a detective being able to gain as much knowledge from a person's eyes as from his speech."

"I'm sorry," the girl murmured, and she raised her eyes to meet his. It wasn't her eyes Dan wanted to see, though, it was her lips—although Dan couldn't tell her that.

He wouldn't tell her, he wouldn't tell anyone in the world his secret—that he was stone deaf.

It was just two years ago that Dan Holden, bored to distraction with the idle rich set to which he had been born in New York, had set himself up as a private investigator. Run-of-the-mill criminology held no interest for him—he left that strictly to the police. But in a brief year's time he had gained the profound respect of the law and law breakers by the unerring, relentless way in which he had hounded countless human parasites into the arms of the law—or into sudden, inexplicable death.

Dan Holden had no argument with ordinary gunmen. But for human leeches, blackmailers who preyed on helpless women and men, he had nothing but loathing.

It was just a year ago that he had shot it out with a confidence man who had bled the last penny from a crippled old antique dealer. The con man had died with a bullet in his lung, but one of his bullets had clipped Dan above the ear, cracking his skull and destroying his hearing. The surgeons had done a marvelous job—there wasn't even a trace of the incision they had made to insert the silver plate in his head.

For two months Dan had thought gloomily that his crime fighting career was over. A deaf detective would be worse than useless. Then, exacting a promise of secrecy from his doctors and nurses, he had set doggedly about the business of mastering lip reading. When he had returned to his office a week ago, June Lawrence, his secretary, didn't even suspect that he was deaf. He was reading Patricia Farnsworth's lips now.

"As you know," the girl was saying, "it's been a week now since mother was —since she died; and the police have done absolutely nothing. They don't even know what killed her. They claim she must have been carrying an explosive that went off accidentally—which is ridiculous."

Dan pushed a button on his desk and almost immediately a door at the far end of the room opened. A pretty, level-eyed girl stepped in and appraised Dan and Patricia Farnsworth impersonally. Dan could not hear her speak, but he could see her lips form the words: "Yes, Mr. Holden?"

"The clippings on the Farnsworth case please, Miss Lawrence." One reason for chosing June Lawrence as a secretary

was her newspaper training; she not only possessed the quick, incisive mind of a newswoman, she also knew how to take exact and expert care of Dan's "morgue," his clipping file in which he kept every item of crime news that appeared in New York papers.

THE bundle of clippings the girl laid before him was bulky, for the late Claire Farnsworth's career had been as spectacular as her death. Dan, scanning them quickly, saw one thing clearly: beyond the fact that the woman had been killed by an explosion of some kind, the police had discovered practically nothing as to the cause of her death.

The possibility of an infernal machine had been ruled out—such an instrument of death would have left some fragment of steel or other metal by which it could be identified, either imbedded in her body or splattered about the ballroom. There had been no trace of such an agent.

And, one article went on to point out, nothing had been discovered to account for Mrs. Farnsworth's obvious pain just before the explosion. The articles were full of far-fetched speculation and theory, and one, from the *Evening Globe*, made much of the discordant whining sound that had been heard before the woman had begun to twist and grimace with agony.

The whole thing was bizarre; it piqued Dan's interest, but he shook his head slowly as he looked up at the taut-faced girl. "I'm afraid, Miss Farnsworth," he said gently, "that investigation of your mother's death is strictly within the province of the police. It has what appear to be mysterious angles, of course, but I'm sure the police will be able to fathom——"

"But the police," she said bitterly, "are talking of suicide." She suddenly thrust her hand into her bag, drew out an envelope, held it out to him. "I found that just this afternoon, in one of her dresser drawers."

Dan glanced at the typewritten address: "Mrs. Thomas Farnsworth, 240 Park Ave., New York City," saw that it had been postmarked the day Claire Farnsworth had died. Inside was a slip of paper, bearing three cryptic words: "Death whines tonight!" The message was typewritten, and there was no signature.

Dan nodded grimly. "Indicating the possibility—I should say the probability—that your mother's death was premeditated. By all means, Miss Farnsworth, take this to the police immediately."

"Oh, the police—" the girl began bitterly. She rose, strode over to a window, stood peering out into the late afternoon dusk. Presently she turned, said, "Then you won't help me?"

Dan shrugged a little unhappily as he read her lips. "I'm sorry. I'm afraid it's not a case that is within my boundaries."

She left, disappointment and hurt showing in her face. There was a corresponding look of pained wonderment in Miss Lawrence's clear grey eyes when she entered a moment later to pick up the file.

"On the contrary," she said with asperity, "I would think the case is definitely within the boundaries of the Holden Investigating Company, if our past activities are any criterion. If there ever was a case of blackmail—"

"Blackmail?" Dan stared at her in mild surprise. "When did you hear talk of blackmail?"

"Why, from her. She said that she had overheard her mother talking on the phone, telling someone that she would not pay any more, that she had told her husband the whole story and was not afraid of anything that might happen."

"Ah," Dan said softly. "She said that?" It suddenly came to him that the girl had been talking while she stood there in the shadows beside the window, that Miss Lawrence had heard every word on the dictaphone she used in taking down conversations in his office. He reached for

his hat, was halfway to the door when she called to him:

"There are letters for you to sign before you go."

He did not look back at her, did not answer, but strode on out toward the elevators. June Lawrence, staring in surprise and exasperation at his disappearing back, shook her head gloomily.

"Sometimes I wonder," she said musingly, "if he didn't leave some part of him behind in the hospital."

DESPITE his haste, Dan Holden found no trace of Patricia Farnsworth when he descended to the street. Although it was near dinner time, and he realized he might be intruding on the strict routine incidental to a home of great wealth such as the Farnsworths, he hopped into a cab and gave their Park Avenue address.

Miss Farnsworth was not in, the butler informed him. Was Mr. Farnsworth in? The butler grudgingly took Dan's card, and after a lengthy interval came back to report that "the master" was in and would see him in the library.

Tom Farnsworth, a power in Wall Street, was still dominating in appearance, although greying and elderly. The man whose millions could buy anything, even a pretty young actress wife, showed that the past week had been a terrific strain on him. His greeting was polite but reserved. Dan didn't recognize the second man in the room, a distinguished Latin type. Farnsworth handled the introductions suavely.

"I've heard of you, Mr. Holden." He was guarded, suspicious. He nodded toward the foreigner. "Count Uprenzi, Mr. Holden. What can I do for you, sir?"

Dan's brief nod took in both men. He wasted no words. "I've decided, Mr. Farnsworth, to accept the commisssion to investigate your wife's death."

"Commission?" The man's steely eyes narrowed. "Ah yes, I see—Patricia's hysteria has caused her to go to you for help." His voice was suddenly cold, incisive. "You've no commission from me, Mr. Holden. The matter is entirely in the hands of the police. That is all I have to say to you." He nodded toward the door. "Judson will show you out."

Dan Holden smiled a trifle as he nodded to the two, turned and walked toward the hall. As the butler opened the front door for him he said tersely: "Tell Miss Farnsworth to call me at my office. Tell her my answer is yes." He was still smiling to himself, grimly, when he reached the sidewalk and started across the street. "Patricia's hysteria," he mused. "If there was ever anyone who had control of herself, it's that young lady . . . ."

CHAPTER THREE

The Cult of Death

THE dark little man in the purple turban—the rest of his garb was immaculately tailored Bond Street—entered the dim-lit room with sinuous, feline grace, strode to the center of the chamber and turned to face the six women seated in a semi-circle before him. He raised his right hand to forehead, palm out, in ritualistic salutation, and five of the women repeated the gesture after him. These five wore, loosely draped over their expensive street clothes, robes of shimmering purple silk; the sixth, twenty years younger than others, was dressed in ordinary clothing.

The five women in purple regarded the man with something between awe and adoration. The sixth, who was Patricia Farnsworth, showed no emotion whatsoever, but her black eyes peered in keen scrutiny at the deep-etched lines of his ascetic Oriental face, studied the intense, almost fanatic light in his deep-set eyes.

As the man who called himself Krishna Singh intoned a cabalistic liturgy in Hindu, the five women repeated it in monotone, as they would repeat words that had no meaning to them. A casual observer of this tableau in an obscure Greenwich Village flat would instantly take it to be a meeting of some mystic cult. The Cult of Life, Krishna Singh called his little coterie. Patricia Farnsworth, sitting there quietly, awaiting her initiation rites, was present because Dan Holden suspected it was, instead, a cult of death. It was nine days, now, since Patricia's mother had died.

Outside, in the dusk of Barrow Street, the man who could not hear slipped unobtrusively into an areaway beside the building. It was late afternoon in midwinter, and the early nightfall shrouded him as he made a little running jump and sprang upward to seize the lowest rung of a fire escape ladder. He pulled himself up with quick agility, went catlike up the ladder until he reached the third floor, where a crack of light glimmered from behind a drawn shade.

The window was closed, and only faint murmurs came from the candle-lit room, but that did not matter to Dan Holden. He could see the moving lips of Krishna Singh. The Hindu had come to the end of his chant, had raised his eyes to those of Patricia, was speaking to her.

"It is your wish," Dan saw his lips say, "to join our ranks, to fill the void left by the untimely passing of your mother?"

Dan saw Patricia's head incline slightly.

"These other seekers after the truth," Krishna Singh went on, "your mother's friends, say that you are likewise one who seeks the Profound Verities, one who is eager to probe the mystic, unsearched voids with us in search of the Higher Realms of Insight, of Unity, of Oneness with the immutable laws of the universe."

"Rubbish." Dan growled to himself as Patricia nodded again, and then the detective's eyes narrowed quickly, his hand went to the gun in his shoulder holster.

"We will test you," the Hindu had said, and he gestured toward the pallid tapers glowing in the niche behind him. Instantly the flames dimmed, faded to mere pinpoints, so that the room was thrown into almost complete darkness. Dan, gun in hand, was about to crash his way through the window when the lights went up again in the candles, and then he was held spellbound, momentarily paralyzed, by the sight they revealed.

Patricia Farnsworth was standing before Krishna Singh, her beautiful face a pale mask against her black hair, her eyes staring in fascinated terror straight ahead of her, her arms rigid at her sides. She stood that way, helplessly immobile, because her slender body was encircled in the coils of a monster python.

THE snake, its tail coiled about the girl's feet, had twined itself up and around her, had reared back its hideously fanged head a few inches from her face, poised as though ready to strike straight at her quivering white throat.

Dan checked himself just before he pulled the trigger. He knew he could send a bullet square into that gaping mouth— but he also realized that the death convulsions of the reptile would crush the life from the girl in a twinkling. Then Krishna Singh's lips were moving again in his coldly smiling face, and Dan read the words:

"The serpent, ancient symbol of evil. . . . If we fear its power, if we tremble before it, we are lost. Knowledge and wisdom give us strength. Do you have faith in my knowledge to save you from this omen of evil?"

Dan could see the girl's desperate effort to retain consciousness, her Spartan attempt to master nausea and fear. Then her lips formed the word "yes," and as the Hindu murmured something unintelligible the python quickly loosed its coils from her body, dropped to the floor

and slithered out of sight through a doorway behind Krishna Singh.

"You have proved yourself," the Oriental intoned. "You have shown yourself worthy of joining the Cult of Life." He seized the trembling girl by the arm to steady her, then crossed swiftly to the side-table, took from a drawer a small metal plaque hung on a slender silver cord. He slipped the cord over Patricia Farnworth's head, let the plaque slide down beneath her bodice.

"This talisman, which we all wear, makes you one of us, though still a novitiate. You will learn more as we meet from time to time, but remember this always: All life is vibration, all life is pulsation, all life is rhythm." The Hindu turned abruptly to the others. "We part, now, to meet again."

Dan Holden watched while the five middle aged, richly attired and fastidiously groomed women slipped off their purple robes, gave and received the mystic salutation to the Hindu, and departed. Patricia had been the first to depart, and Dan knew that she would obey his instructions and go straight to his office once she reached the street. He lingered on the fire escape until the last bejewelled dowager had departed, then he raised the window quietly dropped light footed to the floor, gun in hand.

Krishna Singh, who had been facing the door, turned about and stared idly at Dan.

"I was about to invite you in," he said diffidently. "I thought you might be getting cold out there on the fire escape."

Dan kept the gun trained on him as he strode to the table, pulled open the drawer and took out a handful of metal plaques similar to the one the Hindu had fastened about Patricia Farnsworth's neck.

"I suppose," Dan said, "you hang one of these on each of your victims." He fingered one of the plaques, a thin, solid piece of bronze, inscribed with Indian symbols.

He banged it against the table, twisted it in his fingers. It was a harmless piece of metal, nothing more.

"Victims?" The Oriental raised his brows questioningly, a little mockingly.

"You won't try to deny," Dan went on, "that there was one of these hanging from Claire Farnsworth's neck when she was killed."

"I don't like your tone," Krishna Singh said slowly, "or your imputation that I had anything to do with Mrs. Farnsworth's death. Nor do I like your intrusion here, whoever you are. I think I will call the police. . . ."

He paused, cocked his head toward the front windows, listened intently. Dan Holden heard nothing, but he followed the little Oriental as the latter skipped across the room, stared out the window into the street below.

"That whine," the Hindu muttered. "It sounds like—"

DAN heard no whine, but by the time his eyes had focussed on the dim thoroughfare, had picked out the oddly contorted figure of the woman on the sidewalk opposite, there was a queer, almost electric tingling at the base of his skull. He thought for a moment that a live wire had come in contact with his head and he ducked involuntarily, slapped at the back of his neck.

A twinge of pain reminded him of something he had tried to forget—the silver plate the surgeons had inserted beneath his scalp. He realized now that the tingling, the vibration that was setting his nerves on edge, came from the plate. For the first time in a year it seemed that he was hearing, and the sound that his numbed auditory nerves conveyed to his mind was a piercing, crescendoing whine.

But the figure down there on the sidewalk made him forget his own sensations, for the figure was doing a dance of death. He recognized her—Maidy Lehman, wife of Jules Lehman, the publisher. She had been one of the six in the room here, had been the last to leave. Her position showed that she had been about to enter a limousine at the curb.

Her head was thrown back, her painted mouth opened in a scream of mortal pain and terror. Her fleshy frame shuddered like a great mound of jelly as she struggled to raise palpitant arms to her chest. She was still standing upright, but her knees seemed to have caved in, her hat was hanging askew across her forehead like a drunken derelict's.

Somehow that open, agonized mouth was all the more terrible to Dan because he could hear no sound coming from it. She seemed like a woman in a nightmare who was trying to scream and couldn't. But she *was* screaming, horribly, piercingly. Men and women were running toward her from nearby houses. They would not reach her in time, Dan realized, nor was there anything he could do to help her—nothing he could do but stare and wait for it to happen.

It did happen, within a matter of seconds, and although Dan could not hear the explosion, he felt its concussion. While Dan watched, Maidy Lehman died as her friend, Claire Farnsworth, had died. She had been tearing and rending at the clothing about her chest and waist, had reduced it to shreds, when her torso seemed suddenly to puff out, like an exploding balloon, then to collapse into a mangled mass of flesh and blood and splintered bone.

It was not so much the sudden disintegration of the woman down there on the sidewalk as the almost simultaneous cessation of the throbbing within his own skull that snapped Dan Holden out of his trance. He spun about, toward the spot where Krishna Singh had been standing—then he swore tonelessly. Dan's deafness had betrayed him again; the Oriental was no longer in the room.

Dan did not waste precious time searching for him—he had a mission now that was much more important. Krishna Singh's words as he had placed the plaque about Patricia's neck: "This talisman, which we all wear—" had just flashed back to him. Claire Farnsworth, wearing such a talisman suspended from her neck, had been suddenly blasted into eternity by an explosion at her chest. Maidy Lehman, lying down there, still warm but dead from a shattered torso, had been wearing such a metal plaque. And now Patricia Farnsworth, because she trusted in Dan . . . .

CHAPTER FOUR

Panic on Park Avenue

DAN bolted toward the door through which he had seen the women leave, groped his way through an unlit hall till he found a stairs, hurried down it, out through the unlatched street door. He pushed his way through the gathering crowd, paused a brief instant to stare at the mutilated body of Maidy Lehman.

The explosion had stripped it bare of clothes from the waist up, and Dan noted with wonderment that it was the lower part of her torso rather than her chest that had suffered most. Dan had the ridiculous notion that her corset had exploded about her body.

He could not run for fear of attracting attention, but he walked rapidly the half block to Seventh Avenue, hailed a cab and barked the address of his office on West Forty-fourth Street to the driver.

The girl was there, all right, sitting in the inner office, placidly smoking a cigarette. Dan dashed through the outer room, went past the startled Miss Lawrence without a word, and lunged at Patricia Farnsworth. The raven-haired girl's eyes widened in astonishment as he reached for her throat, fumbled for the slender silver chain about her neck and jerked the bronze plaque from its place of concealment.

He flipped the chain over her head, backed away a step and hurled the plaque against a far wall. As it tingled harmlessly with a metallic clang to the floor, Dan colored a bit at the angry flash in the girl's eyes.

"Sorry to be so abrupt, but that thing —it might have been a matter of minutes. or seconds."

He went over, picked up the plaque, fingered it gingerly. "Tell me, did you ever see your mother wearing one of these?"

"Yes, I saw something like it several times, when she was undressing. She would never tell me what it was, though."

Dan nodded grimly. "I don't know how, or why, but the plaque she wore had something to do with her death—might have caused it. Just like Mrs. Lehman's plaque may have caused her—" He stopped, but the girl seemed to read his mind.

"Mrs. Lehman, too?" she whispered. "When?"

"Just now. She was the last to leave the Hindu's. It happened before she could get into her car." An unprofessional warmth came into his eyes. "I saw you in the room there. You were splendid—you were very brave."

She looked him straight in the eye. "I knew you would be there, somewhere, to guard me." A bitterness that seemed foreign to her, clouded her gaze. "I went through with it, as you asked me to, because I believe you can help me find and punish whoever killed my mother. Oh, I know she was just as silly and as flighty as those other women there this afternoon —her fellow cultists—but she was a good mother to me, good and kind and sweet. That's why, if it's the last thing I do, I'm going to see her avenged."

"Tell me," Dan said gently, "what you found out."

"Little that you hadn't guessed. These six women, including my mother, are—or were—members of this new-life cult. I did just as you told me to do—went to Maidy Lehman and told her I wanted to join the organization. At first she protested she didn't know what I was talking about, but when I told her that mother, before her death, had expressed a desire that I someday be admitted to the circle, she agreed to take me to the meeting this afternoon.

"Of course," the girl went on, "mother had never mentioned a word to me about belonging to such a sect, but when you asked me yesterday to try to remember anything unusual that had come into her life recently, it came back to me that she had been absent from home regularly on Thursday afternoons, without telling anyone where she was—and that quite often she returned home just before dinner in Maidy's car, or that Maidy would be in her car, so I guessed that it was some sort of club they attended together." She paused. "But how did you know where to find us?"

Dan shrugged. "When you phoned this noon, told me you were going to the Lehman place on what looked like a good lead, I stationed myself nearby, trailed you when you left. Of those other four women there today, I recognized only the wife of Robert Todd, the manufacturer. Who are the others?"

"Mrs. Wellman, Mrs. Forbes, and Countess Uprenzi."

"Uprenzi—the wife of the polo player, eh? He was at your home with your father when I went there night before last."

"Yes. They, like all the others, are all old friends of mother's."

Dan nodded toward the phone. "I've got to go now. Please call each of the women. Tell them, if they value their lives, to take off the plaques they are wearing around their necks. Tell them to come

here, with their husbands, immediately. You wait here. Don't under any circumstances, go out alone."

The girl reached for the phone. "I know. I'm in it up to my neck now." She smiled a little, the first time Dan had seen her smile. "But I'm not afraid—as long as you're on the case."

Miss Lawrence wondered, a moment later, why Dan was blushing as he paused at her desk on his way out to the elevator. He handed her a piece of paper with the names of six women written on it. "Get after this right away. Dig up everything you can on each one of these; everything good—and anything bad, if you can find it."

THE police had roped off the section of the street where Maidy Lehman had died when Dan got back to Greenwich Village. He ducked under the rope, started toward the spot. A heavy hand clamped on his shoulder, spun him around. A bluecoat was scowling at him.

"What's the matter, fellow, you deaf? I said you can't go over there."

"Sorry—I thought you were talking to someone else." Dan flipped out his identification papers.

"Okay—but the next time a cop challenges you, you'd better obey him." Dan nodded absently, strode on. The police, he saw, were going from house to house, questioning occupants. He followed them into the house where Krishna Singh had performed his strange initiation rites an hour before.

It was a dilapidated six-family apartment house, and apparently Krishna Singh had been its only occupant. Of the Oriental there was no trace, nor had he left behind anything that gave Dan a clue to his origin, or where to look for him, or anything about him. Apparently he used the place only as a ritualistic chamber.

Leaving the building Dan crossed the

street to where the body of Maidy Lehman still lay on the sidewalk, a sheet covering it. The police, completely baffled, were apparently determined not to move it until they had discovered some clue as to the means of her death.

"They'll probably wait a long time," Dan muttered to himself as he stooped down to lift a corner of the sheet for a final inspection. Again he had the ridiculous impression that the woman's corset had exploded about her. He dropped the sheet, stepped out into the street to avoid the circle of internes and police. The toe of his shoe scraped against a little piece of metal that had been lying in a muddy pool in the gutter. He leaned over, picked it up quickly and slipped it into his coat pocket.

It was a miniature bronze plaque, similar to the one he had removed from Patricia Farnsworth's neck, and the chain attached to it was broken. Did it belong to Maidy Lehman? Had she dropped it as she was crossing the street? If so, Dan couldn't be so sure that the plaques were connected with the deaths of the women cultists.

He wasn't, he told himself grimly, sure of anything.

As he reentered his office he looked a question at the efficient Miss Lawrence. She nodded toward his consultation room, and her lips formed the words: "They're in there, all of them." She permitted herself a sardonic smile. "Some came in tears, some with jeers, but all in velvet gowns. Here's what I could find on them, including the two that are dead."

Dan hurriedly scanned the sheaf of papers she handed him. All six members of the Cult of Life, he saw, were respectably married millionaire's wives, noted for their charities, their decorous lives. They all resided on Park Avenue, or near it.

And, Dan noted, each of the six had at one time been a showgirl.

AS MISS LAWRENCE had warned him, Dan faced an array of ermine, jewels and scowls when he entered the inner room. He nodded pleasantly to the group, walked over and stood behind his desk where he could face them all, see their lips.

Dan held up his hand for silence. "You're wondering why I had Miss Farnsworth get you here so urgently. I'll be brief. It's because it is my duty to warn you, each of you ladies, that you are in imminent danger of death, death such as overtook Mrs. Farnsworth and Mrs. Lehman."

"Maidy!" . . . "Mrs. Lehman!" . . . A little wave of consternation, of startled disbelief rippled over the throng.

"Mrs. Lehman died on Barrow Street just an hour ago, her torso was blasted as Mrs. Farnsworth's had been," Dan clipped out. He smiled grimly. "The so-called ethics of my calling forbid my soliciting you as clients—I have discharged my duty by warning you. However, I think you are exceedingly foolish if you do not tell me, or the police, about your secret society, so we can try to figure out why someone, perhaps the Hindu, Krishna Singh, is determined to, shall we say, liquidate the group."

The storm that broke in the room then made Dan momentarily thankful for his deafness. The four husbands were shouting angrily at once, demanding to know what he meant, demanding that the women tell about this man, Krishna Singh, and the four women were indignantly, tearfully, denying that they had ever heard of Krishna Singh, insisting that they hadn't the least idea what Dan was talking about.

Dan shrugged. "If your secret is worth more to you than your lives, there's little point in your wasting more time here." He waved indifferently toward the door. They had started out in a group when Elizabeth Todd, the broker's wife, suddenly stopped, gave a little gasp of terror.

"Listen! That sound! It's just like that terrible whining that started just before Claire was killed!"

The others stood tense, listening and waiting. Dan cursed his deafness and rang for Miss Lawrence.

"Tell me," he said quickly, "what do you hear?"

The imperturbable young woman stood in an attentive attitude a moment, then walked casually over to the washstand in the corner of the room. "I hear the plumbing whining because of this leaky tap," she said. She gave the faucet a twist, and the metallic drone stopped.

"Well, of all the nonsense!" Exasperation fought with shaky relief in Elizabeth Todd's voice as she flounced out. The others followed her, still wrangling, protesting, accusing and denying.

Dan turned to Patricia Farnsworth, who had remained behind. "Just about what I expected to happen. Those four women are frightened out of their wits, but an even stronger fear is sealing their lips."

The girl looked at him musingly. "But isn't there something you can do to help them, despite themselves?"

Dan snorted. "Don't worry, they'll be back—and they'll be yelling louder for protection when they come back than they were with indignation just now. For some reason they're afraid to go to the police. I have a hunch we'll be hearing from them before this time tomorrow. Now, young lady, I'm going to see you home."

Dan's hunch was right. When he reached the office the next morning the usually complacent Miss Lawrence was making a harassed attempt to talk on two telephones at once; Dan saw her lips form the words: "But I tell you he's not here now—" Then she saw him, and said imploringly, "Will you take these madmen off my hands? It's Mr. Todd and Mr. Forbes, and they're beside themselves

because of letters their wives have just received—"

"Tell them," Dan said simply, "to bring their wives and their letters here, immediately. I suppose," he went on when she had delivered the messages, "that Mr. Wellman and Count Uprenzi will also call. If they do, tell them—"

"They've already called. All of them said their wives had received typewritten letters with the threat: 'Death whines tonight'."

"Tell them also to come here." He looked solemnly at Miss Lawrence a moment. "It would seem that 'Death,' whoever or whatever he is, is getting impatient."

He turned toward his private office. "Get Miss Farnsworth on the phone, too. Tell her I'm sending my car for her right away. I promised her I'd let her in on any developments."

JITTERY fear and sullen anger were riding high in the countenances of the eight men and women who came streaming into Dan's office by twos a few minutes later. Dan's greeting was as affable as before, although a trifle sardonic, and he ignored their questions by the simple expedient of not looking at them until they were all there, including Patricia Farnsworth. Then, with the group seated in a semicircle in front of him, he said:

"My secretary has told me of the letters you received this morning. I can see by your acceptance of my invitation to return here that you take the warnings, or threats, seriously. Perhaps we can get some place now. First, are you ready to tell me about this Cult of Life, and the man Krishna Singh?"

The four matrons started talking at once, but Robert Todd, the broker, shouted them down. "I had the whole thing out with Elizabeth last night," he said, peering sideways at his red-faced wife. "This dirty little Hindu fakir approached her first, interested her in his occult balder-dash, and persuaded her to get her friends together for lessons in the tommyrot he preaches.

"A bunch of idle women, with time to waste, they were easy prey to his sugges-tion that they form a secret society. They met once a week, practiced their foolish rituals, imagined themselves apart from and above mere mortals, and—well, that seems to be all there is to it."

"It doesn't explain why," Dan said quietly, "two of the group have died recently, one of them outside the meeting place." He peered at Elizabeth Todd. "Is there any reason why you should fear this Krishna Singh?"

She flushed angrily. "Certainly not."

"Then why," Dan said slowly, "shouldn't we call in the police?"

The four women looked at each other in a flutter of uncertainty, and Mark Well-man, of the Wellman Manufacturing Company, said uncomfortably: "The thing is messy and foolish enough as it is, without more publicity."

"I say," the fidgeting Count Uprenzi interrupted him, "that we ought to get the women out of the city immediately, away from the immediate source of this danger, whatever it is. I'm taking Brenda out to our Westchester place right now. If the rest of you want to come—"

Dan snapped to his feet. "Sensible, very sensible. Get out there now, all of you. I'll detail one of my men to ride in each of your cars. You'll be compara-tively safe there until this evening—and I'll be out then."

"But what about this Singh fellow?" Uprenzi asked.

"Every policeman in New York is look-ing for him now," Dan replied. "Oh, I didn't give away any of your secrets—I merely tipped off headquarters that he had been with Mrs. Lehman just before she died." He threw Patricia Farnsworth a quick look. "Back home for you, young lady." He disregarded her quick frown of protest.

As he followed them out into the outer office Miss Lawrence pushed a type-written note across her desk at him. "That just came in, special delivery," she said.

Dan picked it up, read: "Death laughs at deaf men."

The secretary looked at him quizzically. "What does it mean?"

"It means," Dan said cryptically, "that I'd better keep my eyes open." And to himself he added, "It also means that our friend, Mr. Death, has managed to dis-cover my handicap, which makes the odds about a hundred to one—on him!"

CHAPTER FIVE

The Whine of Death

THE lights of Dan's roadster stabbed through the winter night of West-chester like angry lances, as if they were reflecting his own mood. His day had been fruitless so far as clews to Krishna Singh were concerned. Nor was his tem-per improved, when he swung off the Bronx River Parkway and into the grounds of the Uprenzi estate, by sight of the slight figure that darted out from the driveway shrubbery, almost into the path of his car.

He recognized her instantly in the glare of the headlights as he ground the car to a stop—the raven-haired girl he had distinctly told to stay safely at home to-night.

"Why in thunderation don't you do as you're told?" he growled as she opened the door of the car, slipped in beside him.

Her eyes glowed at him for an instant in the dim reflection of the headlights; he could not see if her lips were moving. Then she had a pad and pencil in her hands, and was scribbling a message by the light of the dash lamp.

"Had to be here," Dan read. "Drove my own car out, waited for you here."

Dan looked at her quickly. "Why do you write? Why don't you speak to me?"

Again she hesitated, looking into his eyes, and then she wrote: "I said something to you this morning that no man should disregard. You didn't even look at me. So knew what I suspected—that you were deaf, could only read lips."

"What did you say to me?" Dan asked her.

She pondered a moment, then shook her head. "Work up ahead—" she wrote. "Let's go!"

Dan meshed the gears with a crash and the car shot ahead. "Since you're here," he said bitterly, "there's nothing to do but take you in. Just try to remember, though, that I won't be much good to you or anyone else if my supposed secret becomes generally known."

The girl did not say anything. Her eyes were set, with taut purposefulness, on the lighted house ahead.

THE few hours that had elapsed since Dan had seen these people, now gathered in the great living room of the Uprenzi mansion had mounted up like so many harrying years onto their shoulders. These women of forty, who had once been the toast of the town, were haggard wrecks. Their husbands, men of power and wealth, were hardly commanding figures now. Of them all, Countess Uprenzi approached the closest to hysteria.

"We thought you'd never come," she clamored as Dan strode into the room, Patricia at his side. "It's been dark for two hours, and that terrible creature might strike at any moment—"

"I've had men stationed on all sides of the house ever since you arrived here," Dan said crisply. "You're as safe here as you could expect to be any place. It's just a question of sitting tight until the police round up your playmate, Krishna Singh—and it ought to be pretty difficult

for a man of his description to elude them long."

It was later, just before nine o'clock, that the first warning of trouble came. Dan was sitting with Patricia on the sun porch adjoining the living room. The girl had said: "I think I can understand why they let themselves get mixed up with a rascal like Krishna Singh. Women who have been beautiful and adored when they were young become panicky when they find themselves growing old. They'll grasp at anything that promises rejuvenation, even a fakir's rosy and silly promise of 'eternal youth through internal beauty'."

Dan wanted to tell her that he thought she would never grow old, but she suddenly held up a warning hand, sat tensely in her chair listening.

"The sound!" she whispered. "The whining—it's starting!"

"Tell me," Dan said quickly, "what is it like?"

"It sounds—it is far away, dim, muted . . . a low, growling whir I can scarcely hear. Yet I *can* hear it. Now it's rising, upward like someone playing a scale on the lower pipes of a huge organ!

"It's not loud—it just seems powerful, like it was filling the air completely. It's going up, and up, like a siren slowly starting. It's like a scream now, a woman's scream, though still far away, muted. It's whining its way upward and upward! Lord," she gasped, "it's hideous—it's an unearthly, shrill screech that—" she shook her head as if to free it of the mad stridency—"it hurts my eardrums . . . it's shriller now, piping like a witch's wail! It's—it's fading, fading up into nothingness. Now it's gone—I can't hear it any more. . . ."

"And now," Dan said grimly. "*I* can hear it!"

As on the night before, when Maidy Lehman had died, the silver plate in his skull was tingling, throbbing, vibrating like a taut fiddle string under a drawn low. Dan leaped to his feet, jerked out his automatic. The terrified herd out there in the living room were stampeding, running pell-mell toward the dim-lit music room beyond.

Dan saw what was attracting them, sprinted ahead to forestall them. It was blonde and buxom Elizabeth Todd, standing alone in the middle of the room, and her open, agonized mouth, her quivering, contorted limbs told the story. Her lips managed, just before Dan reached her, to form the words: "My head!" and then Dan was across the threshold, his gun slipped back in its holster, reaching out to seize her, to probe swiftly for any device concealed about her that might be causing her agony.

As Dan ran, the throbbing at the base of his skull mounted in intensity, became a thundering roar as he entered the room. Then, when he was still five feet from the struggling woman, it seemed as though a monster club had struck him on the head.

He spun backward, like a prize-fighter under the impact of a smashing blow, sprawled dizzily to the floor.

He forced himself to his feet, started toward her again—and again, when he was but a few feet from her, the tumult inside his skull sickened him. The closer he got to her, the more violent became the excruciating throbbing in his head. It was as though she were emanating a powerful, paralyzing aura of pain and violence that increased in intensity the nearer he approached her.

Dan staggered back, helpless. He could do nothing but stand there, with the others, and watch the swift and dreadful culmination of the woman's agony. She was tearing at her mouth now with clawed hands, digging, gouging until her chin ran red; her lips were froth-flecked and shredded.

Dan turned on the cowering, hysterical throng behind him. "Back!" he shouted.

"Get back! There's nothing we can do to help her! She's going to—"

IT HAPPENED while his back was turned, and the concussion blasted him suddenly forward, spun him half around so that he saw the horror that had been Elizabeth Todd before she collapsed, even while her face was still disintegrating. There was a gaping, six inch hole where her mouth had been; her lower jaw hung like a loose piece of red meat; her throat and cheeks were splattered like fine spray through the air.

With Elizabeth Todd's death came almost instant relief to Dan. As when he had watched Maidy Lehman die, the shivering pulsing within his head ceased a brief moment after the explosion. Of the other women in the room, Patricia Farnsworth alone had not fainted.

"Get them out of here," Dan commanded the men tersely. "That's no sight for them to see when they revive. Count—" He looked about swiftly. "Where's Count Uprenzi?"

"Here—here I am." The count, his eyes dilated, came pounding into the room. "I was upstairs seeing about the guest rooms when I heard the explosion. My God, what's happened?"

"It's rather obvious what's happened," Dan snapped. "You saw no one upstairs?"

The count was staring in fascinated disbelief at the mangled body on the floor. "No one but the servants."

"What's below here?"

"Below here?" The man seemed dazed. "Why, the basement—the furnace room, and the game room, and—"

"Show me the cellar stairs, quickly," Dan barked, and as the grey-faced nobleman led him at a loping trot toward the rear of the house his automatic was again in his hand.

"You'll be needed back there," Dan said when Uprenzi had shown him the cellar stairs and snapped on the light. As the door closed behind him, he hurried on down the stairs.

The basement of the huge house was a veritable labyrinth of rooms and passageways. Dan, going from room to room, snapping on lights as he went, kept aiming in the direction of the area below the music room above where Elizabeth Todd had just died. Ever since Dan had seen the initiation rites of Patricia Farnsworth when the Hindu had inducted her into the Cult of Life, he had been pondering the things his eyes had revealed to him there.

The spectacle of the python twining itself about the girl, he was ready to dismiss as a bit of suggestive phenomena. He, with the women inside the initiation room, had been the victim of mass hypnotism. But the words he had read on Krishna Singh's lips: "All life is vibration; all life is pulsation," had been humming deeper and deeper into his consciousness—just as the sound of death had hummed in his head upstairs.

The cylindrical column of pulsating, invisible death that had caught and encircled Elizabeth Todd, the wall of vibrating menace that had repulsed him when he tried to help her must have had its origin either above her or below her. Somewhere down here—

The suddenness with which the lights went out stunned him for a moment, the utter and complete blackness that swallowed him left him without even sense of balance. Ordinary men, thrown into darkness, can retain some sense of equilibrium by the recording of the inner ear. But Dan Holden, robbed of sight and hearing, swayed like a disembodied soul in a black vacuum.

He did the only thing he could do, let his legs collapse beneath him and dropped himself to the floor. That act saved his life—momentarily—for as he sprawled on hands and knees he felt the impact of a hurtling body strike him, trip over him. Dan felt his assailant go plunging past, felt the glancing steel of a knife thrust scrape across his back.

His gun had been knocked from his hand; his frantically searching fingers could not locate it. He waited then, crouching, tensed, knowing that even the sound of his breathing might locate him for his antagonist, whom he could not hear, could not see. Dan Holden was no coward, but the realization that any moment might bring a knife thrust into his vitals choked up his lungs with the effort to restrain his breathing.

Squatted on his haunches, he kept his hands waving slowly in front of him, and his groping, eager fingers suddenly touched cloth. He seized hold, grasped a man's arm, and flung himself backward with all his strength. Again he felt a body surging across his own, and beyond, and an instant later a streak of light stabbed through the darkness, zigzagged across the floor.

It was a flashlight, Dan realized, flung from the pocket of his attacker and snapped on by its fall to the cement. By its light Dan saw the wiry, spiderlike little Oriental, Krishna Singh, spring to his feet, whirl and face him with a snarl.

THE man was small, but he had a knife, a long, murderous looking dagger of glistening steel. He held it in his right hand, close against his chest, as he advanced with little mincing steps, bent forward, poising to spring in with the upward, disemboweling stroke of Asiatic knife fighters.

Dan, still on hands and knees, braced himself for a flying lunge, but he did not take it. The Hindu suddenly stopped in mid-stride, his eyes dilating. The knife slapped convulsively up against his chest as though snapped there by a magnet, his body began to tremble and quiver. Krishna Singh had suddenly and completely lost all interest in Dan Holden, and Dan knew why—the throbbing, tingling vibration at the base of his skull told him what was happening.

Krishna Singh was screaming, but before his screams became inarticulate Dan saw his lips form the words: "He betrayed me—the white dog betrayed me!" Then he was dancing the mad dance of death, trying futilely to release his grip on the dagger that seemed to be constricting his hand like a high voltage wire.

He got it out of his hand, but its point caught in the lapel of his coat, and it was there that it exploded, flashed with a roar into nothingness, blasting his ribs bare.

The lights in the room flashed on then, and Dan was aware of the figure that stood beside the light switch. The room looked like a laboratory.

"Neat, the way it works, isn't it?" The lips that formed the words were Uprenzi's, and for a moment Dan thought the man had lost his mind, for he was smiling complacently, regarding the crumpled form of Krishna Singh on the floor as a biologist would regard a guinea pig. Then Dan saw the gun in Uprenzi's hand, pointed unwaveringly at Dan's middle, and he knew.

The man's lips parted in a quiet little chuckle. "Sound-proofed here, of course. Nothing can be heard upstairs, except the whine—that can be heard anywhere within a certain range. They don't know the Hindu has gone—they won't know when you go."

Dan did not move, did not speak. He knew, now, that this man in front of him, the man who had so suddenly changed from cringing bewilderment to laconic matter-of-factness, was not mad; he was coldly, murderously sane.

"You're the only man of nominal intelligence here tonight," Uprenzi went on banteringly, "so it's a shame I can't spend more time with you. But"— he nodded toward the upper floors— "duty calls."

"The duty of blackmail and mutilation and death," Dan said challengingly.

Uprenzi laughed a little. "Why, certainly. I'm surprised at your vehemence. A man must live, you know."

"And weren't you living well enough?"

Uprenzi fingered his revolver impatiently. "Are you so naive as that? When did an impoverished foreign nobleman ever bring his title to this country except to sell it? One gets tired, eventually, of living on bluff. This estate? My home on Park Avenue? All bluff, and very poor bluff, as my creditors could tell you. Not being lucky enough to marry a woman of money, I married one I thought could get me money."

The count smiled condescendingly. "You're rather a young fellow, so you wouldn't remember, but twenty-five years ago there was a very juicy scandal in New York. A playboy of the time was found murdered in an expensive hotel suite. It was established that there had been a party in the suite, a large and not very proper party, but the identity of the guests was never learned, the mystery never solved.

"The countess, my wife, was a showgirl then. She was, in fact, one of a group of showgirls hired for the evening to entertain the party. When she foolishly boasted to me one night that she knew several Park Avenue matrons who would be much better pleased to forget their pasts, I saw in her a gold mine, and I married her without delay.

"Married to a nobleman, it was simple for her to reestablish contact with these women who had ascended the social scale, simple for me to start maneuvering them into a position where I could make them pay for silence."

"But Krishna Singh—"

"Ah, Singh, poor dupe, was merely a cog in the wheel, a more or less innocent cog. I paid him a good salary to use his knowledge and talents as a mysticist and fakir to organize the women into a clique

—his main purpose was to get them to wear the metal talismans, but he was also to serve as the sacrificial lamb when the police began closing in. I had him spirited out here when things got too hot for him in New York. He apparently lost his head when he saw you a moment ago.

"THAT murder the women had watched years ago gave me an idea —to have them actually participate in a murder, or make them think they had done so. That was simple for Singh. He recruited a homeless derelict from the streets, hypnotized the man, and used him as a subject at one of the seances in the meeting place on Barrow Street.

"He told the silly women that they were to join with him in demonstrating the power of mind over matter. The dissipated derelict represented evil, he said. To the accompaniment of ritualistic hocus-pocus, they all concentrated their mental energies on exorcising the evil that resided in the subject. The strain was too much for the derelict's heart—he died before their eyes —or so they thought, with the aid of Krishna Singh's hypnotism.

"Singh swore them to secrecy—told them they were in it as much as he. That's why they didn't suspect him when they began getting extortion notes.

"I arranged a system of collection that concealed my identity. Things were going along nicely—they were demanding more and more jewels from their husbands, turning them over to my agent, when Mrs. Farnsworth unfortunately chose to rebel. I made an example of her, but the others did not get my point. When Mrs. Lehman died in the same manner, the remaining three became hysterical, tried to run away, with your help.

"I saw to it that they ran straight here, where I could work on them directly. Mrs. Todd, just now, overheard me talking to my wife about my plans, so she, unfortunately, also had to go. The remaining two, though, are the choice morsels of the lot. They both have joint bank accounts with their husbands."

"But how," Dan was fighting desperately for time, "how did you kill these women?"

The sallow faced man smiled proudly. "They once said that I, Carlo Uprenzi, was Marconi's ablest pupil. The fools didn't know that I was a hundred years ahead of him, that I was the greatest student of sonics the world has known. I killed them with sound."

He waved his hand like a lecturing professor. "Sound is vibration. Vibration is life—but it is also destruction. Soldiers marching over a bridge in unison will wreck the bridge by vibration. Strike a tuning fork near a glass tumbler and the tumbler will shiver into fragments. All metal objects such as plates and rods have their vibration pitch. Find that vibration rate, set it up automatically, and the object will begin to pulse and throb. Intensify the stimulus and the vibration becomes more intense. Magnify the impulse a million times, and the vibration within the object becomes so terrific it disintegrates, in an explosion."

He pointed proudly to a mechanism resting in a large open suitcase on a work bench. "My masterpiece—a portable sonic projector that can vibrate metals into sudden disintegration.. The beam it sends out is so intense—you know what it did to the plaque on Claire Farnsworth's chest when I focussed it on her from the balcony of the Perrault ballroom after plugging it in on a light socket. You saw what it did to the metal corset stays of Maidy Lehman when I focussed it on her from the vacant house beside which she was about to enter her car on Barrow Street. You saw what it did to Elizabeth Todd when I focussed it up through the ceiling here at the spot on the floor above where I had told her to stand."

He was standing beside the machine

now, and the smile on his lips turned suddenly feral. "When you unwisely started to interfere with my plans I spent a little well placed money in investigations of my own. I learned from hospital records of the silver plate in your head. We'll see now, just what kind of a tune it dances." He sighted his gun at Dan's chest. *"Don't move!"*

Dan could not have moved if he had tried. The whirring, throbbing vibrations he had experienced in his head before were as nothing to the paralyzing surge of mutating violence that struck and held him now that he was in the direct range of the sonic projector. It was as though a million sledge hammers beat upon his brain simultaneously, and it was through misted, staring eyes that he saw the door behind Uprenzi's gloating face open swiftly, saw the slender, dark haired figure slip through, creep up behind the man manipulating the projector.

In one brief flash Dan saw Patricia Farnsworth's lips form the words: "I heard what you said about my mother!" He saw her fling herself like an avenging tigress upon Uprenzi's back, saw the two of them fall forward against the table, sprawl in a floundering heap on the floor, dragging a mass of apparatus with them.

Something seemed to snap inside Dan's head then, but before he collapsed he had a vision of Patricia fighting free of the wreckage, of Uprenzi, lying flat on his back, clawing at a bronze laboratory plate pressed against his face and shoulders, a bronze plate on which rested the whining sonic machine. Dan saw the blinding flash that blasted plate and machine and man, and then he saw nothing more.

* * *

Dan knew, definitely, that he was in heaven, because he could hear an angel's voice, and his head was pillowed in clouds. He thought, vaguely, that angels must be very much like humans, because this one was saying exactly what he would have liked to have heard from a girl on earth before he died.

"Oh, darling, if you could only hear me if you had only heard me this morning—"

"What did you say this morning?" he murmured.

"I said—" He was suddenly aware that it wasn't clouds but a woman's lap that was pillowing his head, was conscious of an excited trembling in the arms that held him. "You heard me! You knew I was talking without seeing my lips!" There was eager gladness in the voice.

Dan opened his eyes, looked up into the girl's. "Uprenzi seems to have brought me two wonderful things—and the least of the two is my hearing."

THE END

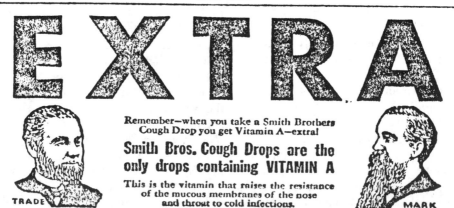

The type for the Introductory Essay
Was set by Ray B. Browne
On Addressograph-Multigraph 3500
At Bowling Green, Ohio
In Baskerville typeface